STRESS, COPING, AND HEALTH IN FAMILIES

RESILIENCY IN FAMILIES SERIES

Hamilton I. McCubbin, *Series Editor*

Volumes in This Series

Dedication

This book is dedicated to Ruth Dickie, a special colleague and friend of the School of Human Ecology and the Center for Excellence in Family Studies. Ruth Dickie received her B.S. in 1934 and M.S. in 1947 in Foods and Nutrition and then taught in the University of Wisconsin Medical School. A campus leader in the support of women in science and a strong believer in the important role of the family in society, she felt the field of Home Economics played a prominent role in the nation's health and well-being. A long-time supporter of the School and the Center, she stepped forward to fund the lecture and publication series, Resiliency in Families.

STRESS, COPING, AND HEALTH IN FAMILIES

Sense of Coherence and Resiliency

EDITORS

HAMILTON I. McCUBBIN

ELIZABETH A. THOMPSON

ANNE I. THOMPSON

JULIE E. FROMER

RESILIENCY IN FAMILIES SERIES

SAGE Publications
International Educational and Professional Publisher
Thousand Oaks   London   New Delhi

Originally published by the Board of Regents of the University of Wisconsin System and t Center for Excellence in Family Studies, 1994, under the title of *Sense of Coherence an Resiliency: Stress, Coping and Health*.

For information:

SAGE Publications, Inc.
2455 Teller Road
Thousand Oaks, California 91320
E-mail: order@sagepub.com

SAGE Publications Ltd.
6 Bonhill Street
London EC2A 4PU
United Kingdom

SAGE Publications India Pvt. Ltd.
M-32 Market
Greater Kailash I
New Delhi 110 048 India

Printed in the United States of America

Library of Congress Cataloging-in-Publication Data

Stress, coping, and health in families : Sense of coherence and
resiliency / edited by Hamilton I. McCubbin ... [et al.].
    p. cm. -- (Resiliency in families series ; v. 1)
  Includes bibliographical references.
  ISBN 0-7619-1396-3 (cloth : acid-free paper)
  ISBN 0-7619-1397-1 (pbk. : acid-free paper)
  1. Family--Mental health. 2. Family--Health and hygiene. 3.
Stress (Psychology) 4. Adjustment (Psychology) 5. Resilience
(Personality trait) 6. Life cycle, Human. I. McCubbin, Hamilton I.
II. Series.
  RC455.4.F3 S79 1998
  155.9'24--ddc21
                                98-9082

This book is printed on acid-free paper.

98 99 00 01 02 03 04 10 9 8 7 6 5 4 3 2 1

Contents

I. Overview and Theory

II. Coherence and Families at Risk

Contributors

Kathryn Hoehn Anderson
School of Nursing
University of Wisconsin–Eau Claire
Eau Claire, WI

Aaron Antonovsky
Jerusalem
ISRAEL

Lois K. Baker
Cedarville College
Cedarville, OH

Franz Baro
Faculty of Medicine
Katholieke Universiteit Leuven
Leuven
BELGIUM

Jeffrey D. Brooks
Department of Social Behavioral Sciences
Fayetteville State University
Fayetteville, NC

Thomas C. Cesario
Department of Medicine
University of California, Irvine
Irvine, CA

Rodney M. Coe
Department of Community and
   Family Medicine
Saint Louis University
St. Louis, MO

Benjamin N. Colby
Department of Anthropology
School of Social Sciences
University of California, Irvine
Irvine, CA

Kelly M. Elver
School of Human Ecology
University of Wisconsin–Madison
Madison, WI

Lisa M. Fiorentino
Department of Nursing
University of Pittsburgh at Bradford
Bradford, PA

Louise H. Flick
School of Nursing
St. Louis University Medical Center
St. Louis, MO

Julie E. Fromer
School of Human Ecology
University of Wisconsin–Madison
Madison, WI

Timothy J. Gallagher
Institute for Social Research
University of Michigan
Ann Arbor, MI

Ann W. Garwick
School of Public Health
University of Minnesota
Minneapolis, MN

Alison Gottlieb
The Shriver Center
Waltham, MA

Kristien Haepers
School of Health and Social Sciences
Coventry University
Coventry
UNITED KINGDOM

Maria M. Hall
School of Public Health
Saint Louis University
St. Louis, MO

Sharon M. Homan
School of Public Health
Saint Louis University
St. Louis, MO

Sayuri Kennedy
Well-Being Project School
  of Social Sciences
University of California, Irvine
Irvine, CA

Jeanne C. King
Department of Management
California State University
San Bernadino, CA

Hamilton I. McCubbin
School of Human Ecology
University of Wisconsin–Madison
Madison, WI

Marilyn A. McCubbin
School of Nursing
University of Wisconsin–Madison
Madison, WI

Louis C. Milanesi
Department of Psychology
University of Wisconsin–Stout
Menomonie, WI

Shiraz I. Mishra
Program in Social Ecology
University of California, Irvine
Irvine, CA

Joan M. Patterson
School of Public Health
University of Minnesota
Minneapolis, MN

Richard J. Pomazal
Department of Marketing
Wheeling Jesuit College
Wheeling, WV

Janice Post-White
School of Nursing
University of Minnesota
Minneapolis, MN

James C. Romeis
School of Public Health
Saint Louis University
St. Louis, MO

Elisabeth K. Ryland
Department of Management
California State University
San Bernadino, CA

Shifra Sagy
Department of the Sociology
  of Health
Faculty of Health Sciences
Ben-Gurion University of
  the Negev
Beersheba
ISRAEL

Linda F. Tegarden
Department of Management
California State University
San Bernadino, CA

Anne I. Thompson
School of Human Ecology
University of Wisconsin–Madison
Madison, WI

Elizabeth A. Thompson
School of Human Ecology
University of Wisconsin–Madison
Madison, WI

Morton O. Wagenfeld
Department of Sociology
Western Michigan University
Kalamazoo, MI

Shookooh Yousefi
Department of Medicine
University of California, Irvine
Irvine, CA

Series Preface

Families at Their Best

The scholarly work of Aaron Antonovsky on *salutogenesis* brings our current emphasis in Resiliency in Families into sharper focus by underscoring the importance of the *sense of coherence* as a vital dispositional world view that expresses the individual's and the family's shared dynamic feeling of confidence that the world is comprehensible, manageable, and meaningful. The construct of sense of coherence fits within the broader rubric of *resiliency*, the positive behavioral patterns and functional competence individuals and families demonstrate under stressful or adverse circumstances.

It was more than coincidence that the Center for Excellence in Family Studies at the University of Wisconsin–Madison would launch its initial lecture and publication series, Resiliency in Families, by inviting Professor Antonovsky to present and discuss his current work and efforts with colleagues who have studied and examined his theories, propositions, and hypotheses. At the core of salutogenesis and the sense of coherence is the fundamental belief that individuals and families have dispositional qualities that serve to promote their health and well-being. The search for knowledge about these central concepts, incorporating a cross-cultural perspective, will shed light on why some families manage life events with relative ease and recover from adversity with renewed strength, harmony, and purpose. The invitational conference laid the foundation for this special publication entitled *Stress, Coping, and Health in Families: Sense of Coherence and Resiliency,* the first publication in the Resiliency in Families Series.

The Center for Excellence in Family Studies, approved and established by the Board of Regents of the University of Wisconsin System, has also created for itself a research focus and agenda that would best be stated in this inaugural publication. The theme of Resiliency in Families places the creation, integration, application, and dissemination of knowledge about the *power of families* of all forms, structures, ethnic groups, and cultures to recover from adversity as the highest priority in the Center's agenda. In its efforts to advance research on resiliency in families, the Center will draw from and foster the advancement of research that:

- searches for family resources (e.g., financial well-being, management skills) that will buffer the family from the disabling effects of stressors, promote the family's recovery in the face of adversity, and promote adaptation.

- searches for family member strengths and capabilities (e.g., the sense of coherence, personality) that will buffer the family from the disabling effects of stressors, promote the family's recovery in the face of adversity, and promote adaptation.

- searches for established patterns of family functioning (e.g., family traditions and routines) that will buffer the family from the disabling effects of stressors, promote the family's recovery in the face of adversity, and promote adaptation.

- searches for new and instituted patterns of functioning (e.g., effective utilization of health care and mental health services) that families create to facilitate the family's recovery from adversity and that promote adaptation.

- searches for family dispositional traits and competencies (e.g., the sense of coherence, hardiness) that families develop over time that will buffer the family from the disabling effects of stressors, promote the family's recovery in the face of adversity, and promote adaptation.

- searches for family processes of appraisal (e.g., schema, paradigms) that will buffer the family from the disabling effects of stressors, promote the family's recovery in the face of adversity, and promote adaptation.

- searches for family patterns of unproductive coping and adaptations (e.g., avoidance, denial), which have the short-term value of promoting adaptation but which, if adopted as an established pattern, have adverse maladaptative outcomes.

- searches for family patterns of productive coping and adaptations (e.g., problem-solving behavior, social support), which have both short- and long-term positive adaptive outcomes.

- searches for family-oriented intervention programs and public policies that have the value of promoting the resistance resources in families under stress and fostering the resiliency in families faced with crises and adversity.

- searches for dysfunctional patterns in families that increase the family's vulnerability to stressors and that curtail the family's recovery from adversity.

Out of the ten strategic agendas of resiliency in families research, only one focuses upon the study of dysfunctional families. Consistent with the salutogenic framework, research on the resiliency in families underscores the importance of understanding the natural resistance resources in families and the capabilities and patterns of functioning that families call upon to manage the ebb and flow of life and all its hardships. From this salutogenic and resiliency orientation, the well-being of families can be best understood by studying the natural capabilities of families to endure, survive, and even thrive in the face of crises. While helpful, the theories and methodologies flowing from the study of dysfunctional families may limit and skew our search for the productive responses and capabilities of families. The resiliency in families may have the greatest potential of coming to light through theories and research that focus on why families succeed and endure in spite of adversities and crises. With this perspective in mind this publication, *Stress, Coping, and Health in Families: Sense of Coherence and Resiliency,* is offered as the first in the series of publications devoted to search for knowledge about families at their best.

HAMILTON I. McCUBBIN
Editor, Resiliency in Families Series

Preface

Stress, Coping, and Health in Families: Sense of Coherence and Resiliency presents a unique collection of studies. Basing their work on the firm foundation of Aaron Antonovsky's salutogenic theory and the concept of the sense of coherence, the authors have pushed back the boundaries of existing research and launched studies and theories in new directions.

Thinking salutogenically involves reevaluating one's perspective and looking for the salutary factors, the resources that help one to stay healthy. Departing from the prevailing illness-based models, Antonovsky's sense of coherence recognizes the inherent abilities of the human system that counteract the tendency toward stress and disease. Three aspects intertwine to form the sense of coherence: (1) comprehensibility, the ability to understand and comprehend the situations of life; (2) manageability, the ability to manage demands; and (3) meaningfulness, the ability to derive meaning from the situations and demands that one confronts.

Although the sense of coherence was originally developed as an individual concept, describing the generation of situationally appropriate coping responses in one individual, this book places salutogenic theory in the context of the family system. Some authors have continued to study the sense of comprehensibility, manageability, and meaningfulness of individual family members, while other authors have applied the concept to the collective family unit and expanded the definition of a system to fit various family configurations.

This book is divided into four parts. Part I: *Overview and Theory* is centered on the work of Aaron Antonovsky and provides a general overview of salutogenic theory and its intellectual origins, definitions of the sense of coherence and key related concepts, and detailed discussions of the structure and reliability of the Orientation to Life Questionnaire. This part also broadens salutogenic theory and research, creating links to resiliency and family systems by focusing on ethnicity and culture and their role in the study of coherence.

Part II: *Coherence and Families at Risk* focuses on the sense of coherence in families dealing with the stressors of serious illness, single parenthood, homelessness, or living in an unfamiliar culture. Families faced with stressors and strains react in different ways and rely on the various resources that are available to them. The authors of this part explore the influence of culture and family on the creation and maintenance of the sense of coherence as well as the prediction possibilities for health care intervention and psychological support programs.

Part III: *Coherence and Aging* examines a specific segment of the population—the elderly and the family groups to which they belong. The authors hypothesize that the health risks caused by the stressful events that accompany aging, such as the retirement transition or the need to provide care for elderly family members, can be predicted or buffered by the sense of coherence.

The final part of the book, Part IV: *Coherence and Immunology*, attempts to link the appraisal processes of coherence to physiological changes. The authors present their studies of immunological responses and sense of coherence scores as they confront the issues of cancer outcomes, quality of life, and the universality of the sense of coherence scale.

This publication attempts to make important linkages between the sense of coherence and health, the sense of coherence and families, and the sense of coherence and the management of stress and change. By focusing on the valuable and exemplary work of Aaron Antonovsky and his emphasis on salutogenesis, we expect to advance the study of resiliency in individuals and families.

HAMILTON I. MCCUBBIN
ELIZABETH A. THOMPSON
ANNE I. THOMPSON
JULIE E. FROMER
Editors

Acknowledgments

There are a number of people who deserve thanks for their direct and indirect contributions to this project. We turn our attention to our colleagues who kept the project moving with their special efforts and discipline: Wade Masshardt for his superior graphics and wizardry with computer technology and Kelly Elver for her steadfast organization and leadership in guiding and juggling our research projects. We thank our staff, Christine Davenport, George Fisher, Diane Sosa, and Gloria McCord, whose time and efforts on other ever-competing demands and projects created those essential moments for us to keep this publication foremost in our planning and priorities. We also thank the University of Wisconsin Foundation for their exceptional efforts to enrich the academic programs in the School and its Centers through special gifts from alumni and friends of the University. The Resiliency in Families Series emerged as a collaborative venture with the University of Wisconsin Foundation, in whom Ruth Dickie had the greatest trust. We are grateful for the efforts of Andrew "Sandy" Wilcox, Timothy Reilley, Marion Brown, Martha Taylor, John Feldt, and Nancy Gibson of the University of Wisconsin Foundation.

In particular, we want to acknowledge our debt to the person to whom this book is dedicated. Professor Emeritus Ruth Dickie was a dedicated scholar and humanitarian. Through her personal efforts she touched the lives of students, colleagues, and untold numbers of people who benefited from her wisdom. She was demanding as a colleague, finding some way for us all to see what was good about what we did and what our profession has contributed. In her eyes we were forever on the verge of being better at what we were doing. It is not surprising that her investment in the future, one of the legacies she left behind, would be focused on resiliency in families, the discovery of positive patterns and functions in the face of adversity. Through her gift to the creation of a lecture and publication series, resiliency in families, her presence will always be felt and appreciated. In preparing this publication, the proceeds from which will be returned to nurture this endeavor, we feel privileged to have this opportunity to fulfill her wishes.

I. Overview and Theory

Chapter 1

The Sense of Coherence

An Historical and Future Perspective

Aaron Antonovsky

On the several occasions in the past year or so when I have faced the challenge (not the burden, to use code words for those who are into sense of coherence research) of making a state of the art statement, I faced a dilemma. The audience has frequently been made up of persons on a continuum with a bimodal distribution, both peaks being toward extremes. On the one hand, there are those who have vaguely heard about Antonovsky, salutogenesis, and/or the sense of coherence (SOC) and were somewhat intrigued. On the other hand, there are those engaged in SOC research—particularly the peri-doctorates—who know what I have written better than I do. Shall I engage the latter and try to say new things, knowing how well they know the old? Or shall I turn to the newcomers, patiently trying to clarify, from the start, the basic ideas of what I call the salutogenic model?

What I have chosen to do here is to divide what I will say into three more or less equal parts. First, addressing myself primarily to newcomers to the SOC model, and looking back, I will briefly clarify what I regard as the core of the salutogenic question and the sense of coherence answer. Second, I will discuss two current issues pertinent, I hope, to all—empirical studies of the SOC, and its cross-cultural character. Finally, I will, largely for those who are well grounded in the salutogenic model, look to the future, proposing three major issues on the research agenda: structural sources of the SOC; its developmental dynamics; and the SOC at the collective level. Seeking to provide nourishment for all will probably lead to frustration. But then again, perhaps I will be fortunate. Sometimes rehearing or rereading (no less than restating) the old leads to a deeper understanding. Sometimes a glimpse of the future kindles a desire to learn more about the past of an idea.

Looking Back

Asking a New Question

Exactly 15 years ago, during my first sabbatical at the University of California, Berkeley, I was asked to give a talk at my host institution, the School of Public Health. The sabbatical had come after more than four years of very intense involvement in setting up a community-oriented medical school in Beersheba, Israel, a period which offered little time for research. But evidently this had been a time of gestation, for the hints and ideas and threads of this talk, reworked and elaborated in a graduate seminar, turned into the first presentation of the salutogenic model in *Health, Stress, and Coping* (Antonovsky, 1979).

I later wrote about this work: "... completing the book left me not only with a sense of exhilaration but also with a sense of relative isolation. In posing the question of salutogenesis, I had detached myself from my own work as well as from the work of just about everyone else ... [who] focused on the need to explain pathology. Further, the sense of coherence answer to the salutogenic question intensified the feeling of isolation" (Antonovsky, 1987, p. 33). Let me try to explain why coining a neologism (and a Graeco-Latin one at that) and writing about what seems to be just another generalized resistance resource led to a strong sense of isolation.

In the first quarter century (roughly 1950–75) of formal medical sociology research, the subdiscipline with which I identify, those of us who focus on sociology *in* medicine, had made contributions of which we could be proud. In essence, we had provided both the theoretical and empirical basis for the biopsychosocial model for which George Engel (1977) would later receive credit. Whatever the problem studied—social class and mental illness, cultural incongruity and heart disease, or delay in early detection of cancer—we added to the understanding of the factors that contribute to disease. We were critical of our medical colleagues for neglecting the psychosocial, and of our psychological colleagues for neglecting the social. But at the same time, we accepted other elements of the medical paradigm. Above all, in the spirit of Talcott Parsons (1951), we perceived disease as deviance, as the departure from the norm and the normal, as that which has to be explained.

Surprisingly, even those of us who were conflict sociologists made this assumption. If in other areas of life we tended to see conflict, deviance, and heterostasis as immanent and even modal, when it came to disease we assumed, as did the biological scientists, that people remain healthy unless some special bug or combination of bugs "is caught." We too, then, aspired to become experts in this or that disease, in defenses against it, and in cures. In a word, we adopted a pathogenic orientation. We worked with a dichotomy; people either did or did not have the particular disease in which we had expertise. Those of us with an interest in preventive health behavior were no different. We thought in terms of preventing disease X, studying the social risk factors that presumably led to it. We had no interest in communicating with the experts in disease Y. Psychosocial bugs—we called them stressors—we knew, were bad for the health. We tried to understand the sick role and why people went to the doctor.

Though I had taken a first step to depart from this mode of thinking by declaring my interest in dis-ease (Antonovsky, 1972) and had, at the first international conference on stressor life events, proposed focusing on resistance resources (Antonovsky, 1974), I did not really depart from the mainstream until I coined the term salutogenesis in 1978. It was then that my sense of isolation emerged. It did not help that my work was greeted with enthusiasm by the various proponents of holistic health, preventive health, and alternative medicine. They were and are no less pathogenically oriented than others. They want to kill the bugs earlier, while the more traditional focus is on repairing damage after it has been inflicted. But what they both fail to understand is that, as I wrote in 1979 in the pre-AIDS, pre-TB-resurgence, pre-new-flu-epidemic era, "the bugs are smarter."

Salutogenesis makes a fundamentally different philosophical assertion about the world than does pathogenesis. It directs us to study the mystery of health in the face of a microbiological and psychosocial entropic reality, a world in which risk factors, stressors, or "bugs" are endemic and highly sophisticated. Anyone who has ever raised a child knows, at a gut level, just what I was talking about. Putting it at a higher level of intellectual sophistication, I posited that open systems, no less than closed systems, were characterized by immanent forces of entropy ... *except that the former were open to negentropic forces as well.*

Thus, in posing what I regarded as a fundamentally new question, some of whose implications I have hinted at above—seeing health ease/dis-ease as a continuum, regarding stressors as ubiquitous and open-ended in their consequences, emphasizing the crucial importance of what I called salutary factors—I parted company from my own past and from my colleagues. Hence the sense of isolation. Fortunately, this was not long-lasting. Evidently, salutogenesis was a concept whose time had come. It offers a fresh, rich, and exciting way of looking at the matters that concern all in the health field and increasing numbers of researchers and practitioners are finding it useful. By the time a fuller development of the model appeared (Antonovsky, 1987), I no longer felt isolated.

I have no illusions. A salutogenic orientation is not likely to take over. Pathogenesis is too deeply entrenched in our thinking. It is indeed comforting to think that some nonexistent state we call health is the norm. We take comfort from the repeated results of studies showing that some 75% of the population feel in excellent or good health. No matter that the data that go below the surface show a dramatically different picture.[1] And, in truth, one might add that those who suffer from disease X have justified first claim on our compassion, so that top priority might reasonably be assigned to searching for the magic bullet that will help them. Nonetheless, I submit that adopting a salutogenic orientation—the core of which is the study of persons, wherever they are on the health ease/dis-ease continuum, moving toward the healthy end, and the clinical application of the results of such study—can make a substantial difference in one's work.

The Answer to the Question

Once one changes the question, no longer asking what causes or what prevents this or that disease, or even what leads to dis-ease, but rather what underlies the movement toward health, no matter how it is defined,[2] one finds that both ideas and data are very scarce, as is to be expected when the question has not yet been posed. As I look back, I believe that the answer to the salutogenic question that emerged is linked to my having conceived of the question in terms of entropy in open systems. I came to be aware that the emerging fundamental question in all of the natural sciences, no less than in history and the social sciences, can be formulated as that of **order out of chaos**.

Think, then, of health as the state of that system we call the human organism, which manifests a given level of order. We know a great deal about the disorder or entropy-promoting "bugs." What interested me were the negentropic forces that operated through the central nervous system. This was the case because it is the brain that coordinates the entire system, much as a conductor directs an orchestra. There are, of course, negentropic forces, from genes through nutrition to drugs, which operate directly to promote order in this or that subsystem of the organism. The sleepiness of the cellist and the fight the clarinetist had with her spouse may affect the music which emerges, but the conductor is paramount.

Thinking in these terms led to the sense of coherence construct quite naturally. To the extent that the person (or, if one wills, the brain, the conductor) saw the world as ordered, believed that the myriad of stimuli bombarding the organism made sense or could be structured to make sense, she or he could mobilize the resources that seemed to be appropriate to cope with whatever bugs were current. I did not wish to call this construct "a sense of control" or even "under control," for this would be to promote a paranoid "you can't trust anyone else" world view as the key to health. *Coherence* seemed to be just the right word.

It took me some time to realize that in the initial clarification of the SOC I had given undue emphasis to the cognitive aspect of the construct, to what I came to call *comprehensibility,* the extent of the belief that the problem (from the world as a whole to a given current issue) is clear. Somehow, writing with the brain in mind and with order as a key refrain centers attention on the intellect. Bandura (1977), by contrast, had, in developing his construct of "self-efficacy," stressed the instrumental aspect of coping, the belief that one can engage successfully in appropriate coping behavior. I came to formulate this dimension as the component of *manageability,* the extent of the belief that not only did one understand the problem, but that the requisite resources to cope with the problem successfully were at one's disposal.

Looking back now, I see that I should also have learned more from the commitment of Kobasa's "hardiness" construct (1979). Though what I now call the *meaningfulness* component of the SOC is not quite the same as commitment (and quite different from Kobasa's original measure of that component), what the two share is the stress on the motivational dimension—the extent of the belief that coping "makes sense" emotionally, that one wishes to cope.

In sum, the underlying achievement in my work in the past 15 years has been to formulate what I regard as a radically new question and to propose an answer. I put it that—if I am to be allowed a slight touch of megalomania—all of science would be richer if it focused on studying the mystery of the even temporary, contingent emergence of systemic order or, in my particular area of competence, if we sought to explain movement toward health rather than toward disease. And, replying to this salutogenic question, I submitted the theoretical proposal that the strength of the sense of coherence is at least *a*, if not *the*, decisive factor in shaping order out of chaos in the human organism. All that remained now was to test the theory.

But before turning to the present, one further point should be emphasized. Much as salutogenesis is a very broad construct, seeking to understand health rather than any given diagnostic category of disease, so the SOC is, in two senses, broader than the coping resources that have been studied. First, it is most emphatically not a coping style or a substantive resource. The crucial idea is that, since people confront such a wide variety of bugs, no specific style or resource is ever appropriate all the time. The person with a strong SOC, believing that she or he understands the problem and sees it as a challenge, will select what is believed to be the most appropriate tool for the task at hand. Second, the SOC distills the core of specific coping or resistance resources (money, social support, mastery, a confidant, a belief in God, and so on), and expresses what they have in common: they enhance one's sense of comprehensibility, manageability, and meaningfulness. In this way, the SOC offers an *explanation* of how these resources may contribute to health.[3]

The Contemporary Scene

Studies Involving the Sense of Coherence

The theoretical groundwork, then, had been laid—initially in 1979, with the publication of *Health, Stress, and Coping,* and more richly in 1987, when *Unraveling the Mystery of Health* appeared. The major step in the interim period had been to operationalize the sense of coherence construct. My own experience had largely been in survey research, which led me to prepare a closed questionnaire. I have repeatedly said and written that not only is there no one "good" way of doing research, but that it is essential that other techniques, such as clinical assessments of the SOC, be used. Unfortunately, to date almost no such efforts have been made.

The original and still current measure of the SOC is a 29-item, 7-point semantic differential scale called the Orientation to

Life Questionnaire. Included as an appendix in *Unraveling the Mystery of Health*, a 13-item short form was also suggested. As far as I know, it is unique in the repertoire of similar scales in that its construction was guided by the principles of the late Louis Guttman's facet theory (see Antonovsky, 1987, pp. 75–79). The scale was first used in 1983, in its Hebrew version, and in English and Hebrew in a few subsequent studies. But it was not until the publication of *Unraveling the Mystery of Health* that its use began to spread.

Though publication of the scale in the book placed it, as far as I was concerned, in the public domain, evidently courtesy still obtains. Many researchers wrote asking permission to use the scale, to clarify issues, or to let me know how things were coming. This correspondence led, in early 1991, to the creation of an informal "SOC network," linked by a newsletter sent to those actively engaged in research which in some way involves the sense of coherence. As of November, 1993, eight issues have appeared. In this way, for example, prior to any publication, A. C. in Toronto, R. C. in St. Louis, E. H. in Bern, L. F. in Aurora, CO, J. P. in Minneapolis, M. S. in Perth, and C. T. in Stockholm learned that all are working in cancer research and using the sense of coherence.

But in the present context, what is important is that the network has enabled newsletter reporting of an up-to-date record of publication, including frequently unknown theses and dissertations, and maintaining an ongoing repository of both technical and substantive data. This, in turn, has allowed me to prepare a chapter, "The Structure and Properties of the Sense of Coherence Scale" (Antonovsky, see Chapter 2), which I trust will be useful to all those interested in empirical work. Let me bring to your attention the essentials of this chapter.

To my knowledge, the SOC questionnaire has been completed by almost 10,000 persons (plus over 4,000 who have completed SOC-13). Of greater import than the sheer numbers are the facts that it has been used in 14 languages in 20 countries and that relatively few of the respondents have been members of that traditional captive audience: Psych 101 students. More than half are women; all social classes are represented (from homeless drug addicts to executives in multinational corporations and university professors); and age ranges from early adolescence to the advanced elderly.

Given this experience, can it be said that the questionnaire "works"? I would start with a point often unmentioned in methodological manuals, because the data are not hard. I have repeatedly had reports from interviewers and colleagues that respondents find the SOC scale items interesting and challenging, but not easy. They provoke thought. One would, then, hope that the data are serious.

The instrument clearly has internal consistency. The lowest Cronbach's Alphas in some 50 studies have been .82 for SOC-29 and .74 for SOC-13. The relatively few studies having test-retest data show correlations ranging from .54 after two years (an elderly sample) to .97 after five weeks (Afrikaner farmers and businessmen), suggesting the validity of the assertion that a person's SOC is stabilized in adulthood.

Evidence supporting consensual validity of the scale lies in its acceptance, by and large, by colleagues in different disciplines, working in different areas and with different populations. There have only been a few cases in which the wording of items or the number of alternatives have been modified. Construct validity is suggested by the correlations of the SOC with analogous constructs: .50 with Kobasa's Hardiness Scale; −.56 with Sheridan's Global Inventory of Stressors; .75 with Colby's Adaptive Potential Scale. Finally, there are data from a wide variety of studies linking the SOC to generalized perceptions of self and environment, perceived stressors, measures of health and well-being, and attitudes and behaviors. The overall picture, though far from conclusive and with enough nonsignificant results to make things exciting, for the most part points to the respectable level of criterion validity—another way of saying that the underlying hypothesis is not to be rejected. This conclusion is supported by use of the "known groups" technique; groups that reasonably should be expected to differ scored accordingly on the SOC scale.

Finally, the various factor analyses that have been conducted all conclude that the facet-theoretical design of the measure indeed succeeded in producing an item inventory with one global factor. This has been frustrating to those who wish to use separate measures of the three components of the SOC. Constructing such measures is a job still to be done.

In sum, less than four years after the appearance of *Unraveling the Mystery of Health*, there is considerable evidence that from a methodological point of view, the SOC scale is a robust tool, and from a substantive point of view, the underlying hypothesis of the salutogenic model has something to it. The time has come, now that some 65 journal papers, dissertations, and theses have appeared with empirical data, to confront the task of a tentative assessment of just what has been learned, what are the weak and strong points of the model, and which questions arouse one's curiosity.

As one who has seen more of the data than anyone else, though I have not done any systematic comparisons, I might give a few examples of such questions (and answers based on impressions). Are there consistent social class gradients in the strength of the SOC? (Theory suggests a strong positive answer; so do the data.) Are there gender differences? (Theory is double-edged; the data seem to show that males may have somewhat higher scores, but there are no gender differences in some special populations.) Is the SOC a buffer variable, more important for some populations than others, or does it make direct and roughly equal contributions to health among all persons? (Theory affirms the latter; the data seem to be equivocal. See Sagy & Antonovsky, 1990.) Perhaps the most fundamental question of all is: Does formulating the research problem in salutogenic rather than pathogenic terms make any difference? My unequivocal answer is yes. But then again, I am hardly the objective outsider.

The Cross-Cultural Character
of the Sense of Coherence

My original training had a strong anthropological component. I have lived and worked in different cultures. I have also experienced considerable intergenerational class mobility, and have been a member of both a minority and a majority subculture. I should like to think that there have been two consequences of these life experiences: a heightened awareness of the crucial impact of the sociocultural context on the character and meaning of stressors and the nature of coping; and some capacity for empathy, for understanding how someone in different shoes sees the world.

Given this background, a central concern in developing SOC theory and the scale was to work with a construct and its operational translation *that would make sense to everyone.* (Was it Clyde Kluckhohn's aphorism that read: "All men have some things in common with all other men ..."? Sorry, in those days one spoke of "men.") One had to, then, work with these "things in common." This mode of thought was, on the methodological level, identical to the idea noted above that the SOC was a construct that referred to the core, to the commonalities, of the various resistance resources that had been studied. Money and knowing someone, social support and organizational membership, fight and flight, active and passive, confronting and denying, internalizing and externalizing—these were all resources or behavioral strategies that might or might not be useful in confronting a given stressor, which were or were not normative in different cultural contexts. Blinded by cultural blinkers, many researchers had come to think that one or another was an appropriate tool for all persons in all situations.

By contrast, the SOC was a construct intended to be universally meaningful and applicable. My argument was that *seeing the world as comprehensible, manageable, and meaningful would facilitate the selection of culturally appropriate and situationally efficacious resources and behaviors.* I posited that the three questions—Does one think that one understands? Does one think that one can manage? Does one wish to manage?—were cross-culturally meaningful. Moreover, the referents or the stimuli (that which one feels more or less coherent about) also had to be universally meaningful.

The empirical data suggest that this is indeed the case. As noted above, the questionnaire has been used with a wide variety of persons in 20 countries. The number of non-responses to any given item is very small. The Cronbach's Alphas are similar from one study to the next. It would seem that not only the researchers—who, after all, tend to have shared modes of thought and language—but also the respondents, whose language is Hebrew or Finnish, Flemish or Serbo-Croatian, Swedish or English, Afrikaans or Russian, feel that it is meaningful to be asked about not being understood by people around them, life being full of interest, being treated unfairly, having mixed-up feelings, always having people who can be counted on, or feeling like losers.

At this point, however, there is one major caveat. To the best of my knowledge, all of the SOC studies to date have been carried out among samples in cultures of European origin, with one exception. In a brief note, I have learned that, when translated into Tswana (a language spoken by over four million people in Botswana and South Africa), the questionnaire simply did not work. Clearly, there are fascinating things to be learned from careful analysis of the hypothesis that the SOC construct and its operationalization are cross-culturally valid.

Agenda for the Future

I turn, finally, to that which is the most exciting and gratifying thing that can happen to a researcher—a rich agenda for the future that her or his work has opened up. I shall, given the limitations of space, discuss three issues which most interest me. This is not to underestimate the importance of other issues, particularly the potential of SOC ideas for clinical application. The issues I will consider are: first, the structural sources of the SOC; second, its developmental dynamics; and third, the SOC at the collective level.

Where Does the Sense of Coherence Come From?

Though far from unhappy that my work has been taken up by people from many disciplines, I have felt some unease that this is less true of my own. As far as can be calculated, no more than 20% of those engaged in SOC research are sociologists. The reasons for this are, I believe, that it is an *individual* who is more or less healthy; the sense of coherence is an *individual* dispositional orientation (though see below). Work in the past 15 years has appropriately been focused on the SOC as the "independent" variable and health as the "dependent" variable. The concern of sociology is social structure. Now, however, that there are enough data to at least tentatively support the hypothesis that the SOC is a significant factor in promoting movement toward health, the question that increasingly fascinates me is that of the sources of the SOC. This question opens the way for a return to more traditional sociological concerns. My initial efforts in this direction are found in two recent publications (Antonovsky, 1991, 1993) and in a study for which data are now being collected.

In the 1991 publication I attempted to analyze, within a systems theory information-processing framework, how social structures shape both the nature of the conflicts (stressors, problems) immanent in human existence and the strength of the SOC. A number of points should be stressed. First, to disregard the power of history, the generational experiences of the macrocosmic events of war and depression, population shifts and revolutions, is to disregard the context within which the strength of the SOC of each of us is molded. Second, there is no doubt that early socialization experiences in the family are crucial. But these experiences are shaped by the family structure, which in turn is shaped by the broader context.[4] To write of childhood experiences without locating these in the class structure, without reference to parental occupation or to race, is to doom us to a lack of understanding. (For a model of a study that links social stratification, class, work, values, and family in a cross-cultural study, see Kohn & Slomczynski, 1990.)

The third point to be made, and perhaps the most important one because it is most unpalatable and hence tends to be disregarded, can be summed up simply: *There are many roads to a strong SOC.* A social structure that provides a *canon* or a set of fundamental principles, facilitates behaviors to be performed that are within its framework, and rewards and reinforces such behavior, will in all likelihood foster a strong SOC. The *content* of the canon is irrelevant. Any clear ideology will do, ranging from Nazism, the white man's burden, Bolshevism, patriarchy, and fundamentalism through Calvinism, Mormonism, and orthodox Judaism to Gemeinschaft and civility. The horror some of these roads arouse in us is unhappily irrelevant to their effectiveness in promoting a strong SOC. It is, however, crucial to see that, except for the type of social organization which is characterized by civility (Walzer, 1991; Coser, 1991), all the other roads are based on particularism ("we" are the elite) and lead to a strong SOC *for those who have power.* The SOC of those with little power is concomitantly weakened.

I should, further, clarify that a canon is not a set of rules that dictates detailed behavior in all situations. So rigid a canon would be doomed to failure, for in freezing details it would destroy the flexibility essential to confronting the infinite and frequently unforeseen kaleidoscope of human existence. What is required is the freedom to select concrete behaviors by justifying them in the framework of the principles of the canon.

These, then, are some of the general considerations of which we must be aware in studying the origins of the SOC. But they do not spell out systematically the pathways through which the SOC is shaped. In a study that has just gone into the field, we have sought to pinpoint these pathways without sacrificing richness and complexity. High and low SOC scorers in a completed longitudinal study of Israeli retirees are being interviewed using a life history, depth interview technique. The interview schedule, however, is not free associative, but rather planned to explore the experiences hypothesized to foster the three components of the SOC.

The Developmental Dynamics
of the Sense of Coherence

I have often committed myself, orally and in writing, to the hypothesis that the strength of a person's SOC is more or less stabilized by roughly the age of 30, that is, when one has been in the "normal" work and family situation of one's culture and subculture for a number of years. Most people in the world do not, thereafter, go through radical and lasting changes in their life situations. (Even in the U.S., a substantial majority of persons married by age 30 stay married.) Hence for most, there are no major changes in the quality of the experiences that affect the strength of the SOC.

The person who has reached adulthood and is in a "good," that is, SOC-reinforcing, family and work situation will maintain her or his level. This does not mean that life is static. There will be the continuing, immanent, normative entropic stressors of life, such as the death of one's parents. There will be harsh, unanticipated, uncontrollable experiences, such as one's child being hit by a car. Whatever pain such experiences bring, they will be coped with successfully, allowing the maintenance of a dynamic balance. And there will be macrosocial changes, such as the closing of one's plant, or a war, or developmental transformations such as retirement or divorce, which indeed change one's life situation. But again, the person with a strong SOC will be able to find negentropic resources in the new situation to maintain this strength.

I have proposed, however, focusing on an adult whose earlier experiences were more in the direction of chaos than of order, that the chances of a major strengthening of a weak SOC are few. There are, of course, minor fluctuations in response to a particular experience. Even a sad sack sometimes hits it lucky for a while before the self-fulfilling prophecy messes her or him up again. And very occasionally, immigration, serious therapy, or even a chance encounter, if they initiate radical and lasting behavioral and experiential change, may overcome the powerful handicap of the first three decades or so. By and large, however, the person with a weak SOC in adulthood will manifest a cyclical pattern of deteriorating health and a weakening SOC.

Having made my position clear, two points must be added. First, my position is a hypothesis, based on theoretical considerations, and is not based on empirical evidence. I may very well prove to be wrong. Only longitudinal, prospective studies can tell.

Second, one must clarify what is meant by a "major strengthening" of the SOC, and differentiate it from a "statistically significant" difference. The two are in different though related realms of discourse. The former is an individual, clinical concept. Very few, I proposed, will move, in adulthood, from an SOC score of 124 to 162 (or the reverse), the latter being a high average score in most samples. If, however, a substantial number of people, in a sample of persons experiencing a given mode of therapy, increase their SOC score by five points on the average, this will be a statistically significant change.[5] If one thinks in the latter terms, that is, small-scale, incremental change in the lives of people that will lead to small-scale but significant (in the substantive sense) and meaningful change in their SOC, it may well be that the conservative hypothesis, even if supported, is not that pessimistic. Thus, for example, a team of factory workers that acquires responsibility for a complex set of tasks with the commensurate authority to decide upon the pace of work, the division of labor, and so on, is not undergoing a major transformation of life circumstances. But, I would suggest, such changes might lead to an average five-point improvement. And, I submit, this is not to be sneezed at.

One further comment for clarification. One must differentiate between the *substance* of a world view and a strong SOC (perceiving stimuli as very comprehensible, manageable, and meaningful). The issue comes to the fore in Patterson and Garwick's fine chapter in this volume (see Chapter 4). They discuss how a "world view"—"a set of beliefs or meanings about existential issues such as the purpose and meaning of life"—is forged, modified by normative life cycle transitions and by major non-normative life events. Thus they give the example of how a diagnosis of chronic illness in a family member may change the substance of one's world view. A person who formerly found life highly meaningful because of her or his work now finds caring for the ill child or spouse a full and adequate replacement. Or, to give a far less palatable yet conceptually identical example: A high Nazi German official becomes, in 1945, a high East German Communist apparatchik and, in 1990, a high-level member of the business community of reunified Germany. The substance of the world view has changed radically; the strength of the SOC, hardly at all. People with a strong SOC, confronted with a radical change in life circumstances, will find a new meaning content appropriate to the change. The problem is: What of those with little meaning in their earlier world view?

Reference to the Patterson-Garwick chapter, whose major concern is a *family*-shared explanatory system, leads us naturally to the final section of this chapter.

The Sense of Coherence at the Collective Level

I close with a discussion of the third major issue that I see as a hallmark of work on the agenda of SOC research: the sense of coherence at the collective level. Even though reference to the SOC as a collective property has been made in my work (Antonovsky, 1979, p. 136; 1987, pp. 170–179), both I and almost all others who have worked with the SOC have treated it as a characteristic of an individual. Of course all of us are aware of the influences of collectives on a person's sense of coherence. But this is very different from asking whether it makes any sense to speak of a collective as perceiving the world as coherent. At the philosophical level, the question is: "Does a collective—a family, a work group, a kibbutz, a social class, a nation—have a mind that perceives?" This question has hardly been addressed, perhaps because it is fraught with theoretical and methodological difficulties.

In Antonovsky and Sourani (1988), a related but distinct issue was studied: the extent to which individual spouses perceive that part of the world that we call the family as coherent. That is, we narrowed the focus, and we obtained the perceptions of two individuals. Only a minimal attempt was made, in that article, to somehow integrate these perceptions into what reasonably could be called the "family" perception. In the same way, there is a difference, for example, between the life situation common to members of a given social class and the perceptions of that situation by individual members of that class.

The range of those who study collectives is considerable. Yet few, to the best of my knowledge—from Marxists, who have spoken of class consciousness for well over a century, to family social scientists—have ever attempted to grapple with, much less have succeeded in resolving, the profound theoretical and methodological problems involved. The issue is not only fascinating—it is of crucial importance in studying the stress process for a reason of which few of us, surely including myself, have been adequately aware: many of the serious stressors in life are collective stressors. This notion has two elements. On the one hand, a given stressor—the threat of unemployment, retirement of a family member, the breakdown of a political system, the birth of a child who has a serious disability—poses a threat (or challenge) to a definable collective. On the other hand, the stressor can only be coped with successfully by a collective.

My own attention was brought to this issue forcefully by my colleague Shifra Sagy, whose doctoral dissertation on our retirement project represents one of the first serious attempts to wrestle with the problem (Sagy & Antonovsky, see Chapter 11). She started from the tenet: "it is the family who retires." Accepting the premise that the SOC is a major variable in determining the health of the individual who "technically" is the retiree, her task was to obtain data on the family SOC, that is, to get inside the group mind, much as when we interview, we presume that, if we are good, we can get into the mind of the individual. (Use of the "group mind" justifies the "who" in "the family who retires.") Her contention was that the use by the social scientist of the phrase "the individual sees the world as coherent" is as much an abstraction from whatever "objective reality" may be as is the phrase "the family sees the world as coherent."

Many have argued that this notion is nonsense. Conceivably one might conclude, for example, that a group has a strong SOC on the basis of data showing that most of its members, or those who have the most power, have a strong SOC; or on the basis of assessment of behavior by an outside observer; or using consensual individual reports of shared views or the analysis of "cultural" productions of a group. All these methods, however, involve the putting together of the perceptions, behaviors and productions of individuals. To say that "the collective thinks, feels, perceives" is, I believe most problematic. What is clear to me is that it merits very hard work.

Summary

As stated at the outset, I have sought to provide some sustenance for those who are newcomers to the salutogenic model, first and foremost by proposing that to think salutogenically will have major, productive consequences for one's work. There was also an attempt to show that this model, and the sense of coherence construct, is squarely linked to the central problem on the frontiers of science: order out of chaos. Moving from the past to the present, the significance of the cross-cultural character of the model was stressed, and reference made to the key methodological issues in measuring the SOC. Finally, addressed primarily to those who are colleagues in SOC research, I have pointed to the three issues that I would place high on the agenda for future research: How does a strong, stable SOC come into being, particularly in the context of history and social structure? Am I wrong in contending that major change in the SOC after early adulthood is most unlikely? And finally, do only you and she and I have an SOC, or can one speak of and study "their" SOC?

Clearly, and delightedly, there is much more to be done.

Notes

1. Chapter 1 of *Health, Stress, and Coping* is devoted to a presentation of data that document this claim. There is nothing in the data today, 15 years later, that would lead me to change my mind.

2. I am fully aware of the extensive literature, theoretical and operational, which deals with the definitions of health and disease. To consider it here would be an impossible task.

3. This does not, of course, describe the pathways through which the SOC works to affect health. For this discussion, see Antonovsky (1987, chap. 6), in which the SOC is linked to behavioral, emotional, and intra-system endocrinological-immunological functioning.

4. I can recall no more powerful and satisfying model linking history, economics, culture, social and family structure, socialization patterns, and personality formation than is found in the work of Abram Kardiner (1945), despite the inadequacies of the psychoanalytic framework within which it was formed. I have sought to keep this model in mind in working on the SOC.

5. This is not an imaginary example. It has been reported by Dr. Jon Kabat-Zinn of the University of Massachusetts Medical Center in Worcester, but study results have not yet been published.

References

Antonovsky, A. (1972). Breakdown: A needed fourth step in the conceptual armamentarium of modern medicine. *Social Science & Medicine, 6,* 537–544.

Antonovsky, A. (1974). Conceptual and methodological problems in the study of resistance resources and stressful life events. In B. Dohrenwend & B. Dohrenwend (Eds.), *Life events: Their nature and effects* (pp. 245–258). New York: Wiley.

Antonovsky, A. (1979). *Health, stress, and coping.* San Francisco: Jossey-Bass.

Antonovsky, A. (1987). *Unraveling the mystery of health.* San Francisco: Jossey-Bass.

Antonovsky, A. (1991). The structural sources of salutogenic strengths. In C. L. Cooper & R. Payne (Eds.), *Individual differences: Personality and stress* (pp. 67–104). New York: Wiley.

Antonovsky, A. (See Chapter 2). *The structure and properties of the sense of coherence scale.*

Antonovsky, A. (1993). Complexity, conflict, chaos, coherence, coercion, and civility. *Social Science & Medicine, 37,* 969–974.

Antonovsky, A., & Sourani, T. (1988). Family sense of coherence and family adaptation. *Journal of Marriage and the Family, 50,* 79–92.

Bandura, A. (1977). Self-efficacy: Toward a unifying theory of behavioral change. *Psychological Review, 84,* 191–215.

Coser, R. L. (1991). *In defense of modernity: Role complexity and individual autonomy.* Stanford, CA: Stanford University Press.

Engel, G. L. (1977). The need for a new medical model: A challenge for biomedicine. *Science, 196,* 129–136.

Kardiner, A. (1945). *The psychological frontiers of society.* New York: Columbia University Press.

Kobasa, S. C. (1979). Stressful life events, personality and health. *Journal of Personality and Social Psychology, 37*, 1–11.

Kohn, M. L., & Slomczynski, K. M. (1990). *Social structure and self-direction: A comparative analysis of the United States and Poland.* Cambridge, MA: Basil Blackwell.

Parsons, T. (1951). *The social system* (pp. 428–479). Glencoe, IL: The Free Press.

Patterson, J. M., & Garwick, A. W. (See Chapter 4). *Theoretical linkages: Family meanings and sense of coherence.*

Sagy, S., & Antonovsky, A. (1990). Coping with retirement: Does the sense of coherence matter less in the kibbutz? *International Journal of Health Sciences, 1*, 233–242.

Sagy, S., & Antonovsky, A. (See Chapter 11). *The family sense of coherence and the retirement transition.*

Walzer, M. (1991). The idea of civil society. *Dissent, 38*, 293–304.

Chapter 2

The Structure and Properties of the Sense of Coherence Scale[1]

Aaron Antonovsky

The major purpose of this chapter is straightforward: to present the available evidence bearing upon the utility of the sense of coherence scale. (In its operational format it is called the Orientation to Life Questionnaire.) Given the widespread interest in the scale, it seems appropriate to do so.

In 1979 I published a volume (Antonovsky, 1979) which presented a theoretical model designed to advance understanding of the relations among stressors, coping, and health. It was more thoroughly and systematically developed in a book which appeared in 1987 (Antonovsky, 1987), whose Appendix contained the scale. This model purported to be radically different, in three central respects, from previous research in the stress process. First, its point of departure was to highlight the inadequacy of the *pathogenic* orientation, which dominated all biomedical as well as social science disease research: the search for factors which led to heart disease, cancer, mental illness, etc., or, at its broadest, to "breakdown," as I had put it in an earlier paper (Antonovsky, 1972). This orientation, at best, gave attention to coping mechanisms as buffers or moderators. Stressors, however, were so ubiquitous in human existence, I came to see, that the miracle and the mystery were that organisms ever survived for any length of time. A *salutogenic* orientation was proposed. I have, in *Unraveling the Mystery of Health* (Antonovsky, 1987, chap. 1) and elsewhere, discussed in detail the implications of this orientation.

The core implication of salutogenesis led to the second radical departure from assumed wisdom. If adaptive coping is indeed the secret of movement toward the healthy end of the health ease/dis-ease continuum, then primary attention must be paid to what I had earlier called "generalized resistance resources" (Antonovsky, 1974). What came to concern me more and more, however, was a theoretical understanding of *why* such resources—wealth, ego strength, cultural stability, social support—promoted health. Or, to put it in other words, what did they have in common? I came to call the answer to this question the *sense of coherence* (henceforth, SOC). Resources were seen as leading to life experiences which promoted the development of a strong SOC, a way of seeing the world which facilitated successful coping with the innumerable, complex stressors confronting us in the course of living. The SOC is defined as follows:

> a global orientation that expresses the extent to which one has a pervasive, enduring though dynamic feeling of confidence that (1) the stimuli deriving from one's internal and external environments in the course of living are structured, predictable, and explicable; (2) the resources are available to one to meet the demands posed by these stimuli; and (3) these demands are challenges, worthy of investment and engagement (Antonovsky, 1987, p. 19).

These three components are called comprehensibility, manageability, and meaningfulness.

The third important difference is found in the cross-cultural and cross-situational character of the SOC construct. Close consideration of the definition will show that the SOC contrasts to such concepts as self-efficacy, internal locus of control, problem-oriented coping, the challenge component of hardiness, and mastery. These are strategies hallowed in particular cultures or subcultures, and may well be appropriate to particulate stressors. The SOC is, hopefully, a construct (and the items which constitute its operationalization) which is universally meaningful, one which cuts across lines of gender, social class, region, and culture. It does not refer to a specific type of coping strategy, but to factors which, in all cultures, are always the basis for successful coping with stressors. This, of course, does not mean that different groups will have an equally strong average SOC.

Constructing the Sense of Coherence Scale

The next step, then, was to test the power of the theoretical model empirically. The reader interested in the many complex issues and arguments of the model would do well to refer to Antonovsky, 1987, as well as to later publications (Antonovsky, 1990, 1991). The details of construction of the SOC scale are given in Antonovsky (1987, chap. 4). For present purposes, it is important to note that I was strongly influenced in this task by the facet theory of my friend and colleague, the late Louis Guttman (Shye, 1978).

In constructing the SOC scale, I made the conscious, theoretically guided choice to have each scale item include four facets which describe a stimulus, and a fifth, the SOC facet, which expresses one of the three components (comprehensibility, manageability, or meaningfulness) of the construct. Since the SOC is seen as a generalized orientation, I wanted as wide a variety of stimuli as possible to be represented in the questionnaire. The mapping sentence (the technical procedure which provides the systematic basis for item selection) finally arrived at allows 243 different profiles (combinations of elements of each of the five facets). No two items of the final 29-item scale have an identical facet structure.

After the usual procedures of consulting with colleagues, pretesting, and revising, an SOC scale was ready for field testing. The results of the field test with a national sample of Israeli Jewish adults, using, alternatively, multiple choice and semantic differential formats (the latter turned out to be superior), proved promising and were published in 1983 in a local journal (Antonovsky, 1983).

Having what seemed to me to be a sound theory and a good instrument, my own next step was to embark on a large-scale empirical study. This was a longitudinal study of the health consequences of retirement. For present purposes, however, it is far more important to say that the SOC scale appeared as an Appendix in my 1987 book (Antonovsky, 1987). Gratifyingly, it has attracted the attention of a fair number of colleagues engaged in empirical research. To my knowledge, at present count, there are 113 persons or teams in 20 countries who have used or are using the SOC scale as a more or less central concept in their research. The present report is based on the published work of these colleagues and is the first published discussion of the methodological issues with which any scale intended for repeated use must contend. Indicated references (*) include the 38 publications which have appeared to date with empirical data relating to the SOC construct, though not all have data relating to the concerns of this chapter. Reference will be made to the 23 doctoral dissertations and master's theses which have been completed and to unpublished data which colleagues have made available to me only when appropriate.

In sum, on the basis of a comprehensive theoretical model, a systematic closed questionnaire was developed, usable both for interview and self-completion. The SOC scale consists of 29 five-facet items; respondents are asked to select a response on a seven-point semantic differential scale with two anchoring phrases. There are 11 comprehensibility, 10 manageability, and 8 meaningfulness items. Thirteen of the items are formulated "negatively" and have to be reversed in scoring, so that a high score always expresses a strong SOC. The published scale allows for the possibility of using a short form of 13 of the 29 items. Unless "SOC-13" is noted, reference is always to SOC-29.

Though the core of this report will deal with questions of reliability and validity, there are other issues to which I would call attention which are of significance to the researcher and not often mentioned in methodological reports.

Feasibility

I would start with a point on which I have no hard data, but which is nonetheless of significance. Interviewers on my own studies and colleagues in Israel and elsewhere have reported that respondents find the SOC scale items interesting and challenging. They provoke thought. This is both a moral issue—we owe a debt to respondents who take the time to cooperate in our research—and a practical issue, if we assume that thought is likely to contribute to lowering random response error.

On the other hand, items which require thought may take up valuable time and lead to non-response. Yet from all reports, completion of SOC-29, whether in interview or self-completion, has taken less than 15–20 minutes; SOC-13 saves some 5 minutes, since it takes time to get the hang of the format. The scale has been used at least once in a telephone interview with no apparent difficulty. As to non-response, in our study of retirement, out of 805 retirees and 260 respondents in the kibbutz control group, at most 25 persons failed to answer any given item. (Interestingly, the "poorest" items in this sense among this group of elderly persons were those which asked about "in the next ten years.") When failure to answer more than 4 of the 29 items was used as the mark of a respondent who could not be scored on the SOC, 1.1% of the retirees and 1.5% of the kibbutz members were so classified.

One particular problem which merits further investigation has been noted by several researchers: some respondents tend to give only extreme (1 or 7) responses. If indeed this is a problem, it could be handled by clear instructions, a trial example, or insertion of a middle anchoring phrase.

To date, the SOC scale has been used in 14 languages: Afrikaans, Czech, Dutch (Flemish), English, Finnish, German, Hebrew, Norwegian, Rumanian, Russian, Serbian, Spanish, Swedish, and Tswana. A total of almost 10,000 persons have completed SOC-29 and over 4,000 SOC-13 (3,568 and 1,684, respectively, in published studies). These totals do not include respondents interviewed in longitudinal studies. More than half of these respondents are women. All social classes are represented. Unlike the experience with many scales, used primarily with the captive audience of college students, respondents have been adults of all ages, though a few studies have been of adolescents and children as young as ten.[2]

Reliability

Internal Consistency

The Cronbach's Alpha measure of internal consistency has been reported to me for 26 studies using SOC-29. The average Cronbach's Alpha, unweighted for sample size, in the 8 published studies is .91 (range, .86–.95); in the 3 theses/dissertations, .85 (range, .82–.86); in the 15 unpublished studies, .88 (range, .83–.93). The Cronbach's Alphas in those studies which have used SOC-13 are somewhat lower, as expected with fewer items, but still acceptable. The average Cronbach's Alpha, unweighted for sample size, in the 5 unpublished studies is .82 (range, .74–.91); in the 4 theses/dissertations, .81 (range, .78–.84); in the 7 unpublished studies, .78 (range, .74–.84). Kalimo and Vuori (1990), using a method developed by Tarkkonen, reported a reliability coefficient of .93 in their Finnish national study of 706 adults aged 31–44.

An instrument can be said to be reliable only with respect to a given population. The fact that consistently high internal consistency has been found in a considerable variety of populations, in different languages and cultures—though all Western—is of significance. It should also be noted that the fact that the scale includes the three SOC components does not lower internal consistency, an issue dealt with below in the section on factor analysis.

Test-Retest

The theoretical model of the SOC construct postulates that a person's SOC is stabilized by the end of young adulthood, thereafter showing only minor fluctuations, barring major changes in patterns of life experiences. This important theoretical commitment has yet to be tested. There have been relatively few test-retest reports. In our own study of Israeli retirees and a kibbutz control group (Sagy & Antonovsky, 1990), SOC-29 correlations were, respectively, .52 and .56 between the first and second interview scores (n's = 639 and 228), conducted after one year, and .54 and .55 after two years (n's = 587 and 213). The six-month test-retest correlations in Coe's study of 189 U.S. male patients at veterans' medical center clinics aged 55 and over were .80 for SOC-29 and .77 for SOC-13 (Coe, Romeis, Tang, & Wolinsky, 1990). A study of entering Israeli medical students (Carmel & Bernstein, 1990) reported correlations of .76 after one year and .41 after two years (n = 33). Fiorentino (1986) reported a one-year test-retest correlation of .78 among 71 U.S. factory workers, most of whom were women. In Radmacher and Sheridan's (1989) study of 307 U.S. college students, 68% of whom were women, the two-week test-retest correlation was .91. Unpublished data on 53 Serbian teacher training students show a one-year test-retest correlation of .86; among 98 Dutch psychology students, retested after six weeks, r = .80; and among Afrikaner farmers and businessmen, after five weeks, r = .97.

Validity

There is, of course, no "gold standard" measure of the SOC construct. Having consulted some half-dozen texts and not a few methodological papers, I must confess to being confused about the varying definitions of different types of validity which abound in the sociological and psychological literature. The core question is whether the SOC scale measures what it purports to measure. I can, then, only organize the discussion as I understand the types of validity and leave it to the reader to judge the evidence.

Content, Face, and Consensual Validity

Given the facet approach to construction of the scale, I would submit that it indeed constitutes a reasonable representative sample of the theoretical aspects of the SOC construct. An item was only included after three colleagues, familiar with the theory, had independently concurred that it indeed referred cleanly to one and only one of the three SOC components. Each item, as noted above, also was constructed to express one and only one element of each of the four stimulus facets. Finally, each item was intentionally chosen to represent a distinct profile. Thus, deductively, the construction of the scale promoted content validity. Inductively, *post hoc* examination of the scale suggested face validity in that it was adequately representative of the theoretical construct.

Consensual validity, estimated by the reaction of colleagues to the published scale, seems high. To the best of my knowledge, there have been only a few cases in which SOC items have been modified. Thus, for example, Nyamathi (1991), in her study of homeless, minority women, found it appropriate to use SOC-13, to simplify some of the wording, and to use five rather than seven alternatives. Strumpfer (unpublished) took the same approach in his study of South African colored farm workers. I should also note that a few colleagues have taken issue, in correspondence, with two items (numbers 10 and 17), both of which refer to changes in life. They were troubled, on theoretical grounds, by the fact that the less one reported changes, the higher one scored. Given the considerable variety of populations studied and the numbers of researchers engaged in using the published scale, it seems reasonable to conclude that the scale as it stands has content validity. This does not, of course, mean that there will be no eventual modifications of the scale.

Construct (Convergent and Discriminant) Validity

Prior to my publication of the SOC scale, two independent attempts were made to build scales designed to measure the construct, based on its presentation in my earlier book (Antonovsky, 1979). The researchers, being North Americans, were, I believe, influenced by a cultural emphasis on control and mastery. Rumbaut and his colleagues at the University of California, San Diego, developed a 22-item scale. In unpublished data, they reported a correlation of .64 between their scale and SOC-29 in a study of 336 under-graduates. Dana found a correlation of .72 between the two measures among 179 undergraduates (Dana, Hoffman, Armstrong, & Wilson, 1985). Dana's study also reported a significant though much lower correlation of .39 with the 40-item scale developed by Payne (1982).

In this context, one further study should be mentioned. Colby, an anthropologist at the University of California, Irvine, and his colleagues have developed the construct of "Adaptive Potential," consisting of three components: adaptivity in the ecological world, altruism in the social world, and creativity in the interpretive world. The construct is measured by a 104-item scale. In an unpublished paper, Colby carefully discussed the conceptual congruence and difference between adaptive potential and the SOC. In a study of 488 undergraduates, he found a correlation between the two measures of .75 (using five item-response alternatives on both measures).

I should also note that I have explicitly emphasized that a closed questionnaire is only one legitimate method of measuring the SOC (Antonovsky, 1987, pp. 63–64). I noted that I would welcome structured interviews, ethnomethodological descriptions, or projective tests to measure the SOC. Nonetheless, to date only one such attempt, using a sentence-completion approach, is being made, in Germany.

To the best of my knowledge, no data are available which bear on the question of discriminant validity, which would test whether the SOC is unrelated to constructs with which it has no theoretical affinity. Hart, however, commenting on the lack of a relationship between the SOC and interpersonal support measures, wrote that this "may be interpreted as evidence to support the discriminant validity of the SOC scale;" that is, the SOC "functions independently of socially based stress resistance resources" (Hart, Hittner, & Paras, 1991, p. 144).

Criterion Validity

As noted, there is no "gold standard" for the SOC. The crucial question is whether the SOC scale does correlate (preferably predictably) with phenomena, external to the SOC, with which the theory argues it should be correlated. Table 1 presents information from *published* studies which bear on the question of relation between the SOC and other measures with which there are theoretical grounds to expect that they would be correlated. In order not to drown the reader in data, I have given only the essential details about each study. Thus, for example, details about the measures used are omitted; levels of significance are not presented, except for nonsignificance. Nor do I present data where statistical techniques other than zero-order correlations, such as multiple regressions, are used to report the relations between the SOC and other variables.

Readers are urged to consult the original publications for precise information (and, of course, to learn about the studies, few of which were conducted in order to study the criterion validity of the SOC).

As is well known, editors have an unfortunate bias against publishing papers with negative results. This should be kept in mind. Nonetheless, reviewing the data from theses, dissertations, and correspondence about as yet unpublished studies which have reached me, my sense is that the picture presented by the published data is not misleading.

Table 1
Correlations of the Sense of Coherence (SOC) with
Measures serving as Tests of Criterion Validity
(from published studies)

Part A. Generalized Perceptions of Self and Environment

First author	Sample	N	Variable	r
Dahlin (1990)	Swedish hi-risk childhood adults	148	Internal Locus of Control	.44
Nyamathi (1991) (SOC-13)[a]	U.S. minority homeless women	581	Self-esteem	.63
Petrie (1990)[b]	New Zealand pain patients	107	Self-esteem	.49
Williams (1990)	U.S. nurses	162	Hardiness	.50
Antonovsky (1986)[c]	Israeli adolescents	418	Anxiety: trait	−.61
			state (routine)	NS
			state (exam)	−.31
Carmel (1990)	Israeli medical students	93	Anxiety: trait	−.69
Hart (1991) (SOC-13)	U.S. undergraduates	59	Anxiety: trait	−.75
Radmacher (1989)	U.S. undergraduates	307	Anxiety (MAACL-R)	−.47
Margalit (1990) (SOC-13)	12-16 year old Israelis	742	Eysenck personality:	
			neuroticism	−.36
			psychoticism	−.17
			extraversion	.23
Margalit (1990) (SOC-13)	12-16 year old Israelis	742	Fam. Env. Scale:	
			relationship	.26
			personal growth	.22
			system maint.	.20
Margalit (1988b)	Kibbutz mothers, fathers of disabled, control group	127	Fam. Env. Scale:	
			relationship	.32
			personal growth	.11–.51
			system maint.	NS–.24

[a] Used a language simplified, 5-point version of SOC-13.
[b] Used 5-point version of SOC-29.
[c] Used an early 17-item version of the SOC.

Table 1 is organized in four parts, though it was not always clear that a given datum should be placed in one or the other. Part A refers to those measures which express a global orientation to oneself and one's environment, as does the SOC. Of the 19 correlations between these measures and the SOC, only two are not statistically significant: those with the state anxiety and the family environment system maintenance scales. The consistently high correlations with trait anxiety are striking, as is the correlation of .50 with hardiness, the construct which perhaps has greatest affinity with the SOC.

Table 1
Part B. Perceived Stressors

First author	Sample	N	Variable	r
Carmel (1990)	Israeli medical students		Stressor perception:	
		93	at entry	−.32
		68	end of 2nd year	NS
Carmel (1991) (SOC-13)	Kibbutz members	230	Recent life events	−.22
			Using the SOC scale	−.17
Larsson (1990)[d]	Swedish factory supervisors	217	Work load	−.33
			Work control	.28
Radmacher (1989)	U.S. undergraduates	307	Perceived stressors:	
			life events	−.24
			Global Inventory	−.67
Ryland (1990) (SOC-13)	U.S. faculty	284	Perceived stressors:	
			life stress	−.24
			work stress	−.40
Williams (1990)	U.S. nurses	162	Perceived stressors:	
			life events	−.27
			Global Inventory	−.56

[d] Used a 19-item version of the SOC.

Part B refers to perceived stressors. All but one (medical school stressors at the end of the second year of studies) of the 11 correlations are significant. Of particular note are the high correlations with Sheridan's Global Inventory of Stress. As Williams (1990, p. 183) pointed out, the GIS and SOC "encompass many of the same things ... [the GIS] may also be picking up the antithesis of those qualities or characteristics found in people with personality characteristics which mediate between stress and illness ... these two instruments appear to be measuring similar phenomena in a 'mirror image.' "

Table 1
Part C. Health and Well-being

First author	Sample	N	Variable	r
Coe (1990)	U.S. male patients, 55+	240	6 months predict to: perceived health	.47
Dahlin (1990)	Swedish hi-risk childhood adults	148	Global health eval.	.46
Fiorentino (1986)	U.S. prod. workers	118	Health status	.19
Ryland (1990) (SOC-13)	U.S. faculty	284	General well-being	.62
Sagy (1990a)	Older Israelis:			
	retirees	805	Global health index	.42
	kibbutz control	260	Global health index	.32
Carmel (1991) (SOC-13)	Kibbutz members	230	Physical well-being	.21
Carmel (1991) (SOC-13)	Kibbutz members	230	Functional ability	.12
Coe (1990)	U.S. male patients, 55+	240	6 months predict to:	
			disability days	−.35
			bed days	−.31
			doctor visits	−.22
			hosp., ER contact	NS
Larsson (1990)[b]	Swedish factory supervisors	217	Physical symptoms	−.26
			Syst. blood pressure	−.31
			Diast. blood pressure	−.17
			Cholest., triglyc., and glucose	NS
Williams (1990)	U.S. nurses	162	Serious. of illness	−.39
Carmel (1991) (SOC-13)	Kibbutz members	230	Psychol. well-being	.23
			Using the SOC scale	−.18
Coe (1990)	U.S. male patients, 55+	240	6 months predict to: morale (mental health)	.71
Dahlin (1990)	Swedish hi-risk childhood adults	148	Psychosom. (SCL-90)	−.70
Larsson (1990)[b]	Swedish factory supervisors	217	Psych. symptoms	−.59
			Subj. well-being	.40
			Subj. health status	.25
Nyamathi (1991) (SOC-13)[c]	U.S. minority, homeless women	581	Health measures:	
			emot. distress	−.63
			somatic cond.	−.46
Petrie (1990)[d]	New Zealand pain patients	107	Millon Inventory:	
			well-being	.64
			distress	−.50
Dahlin (1990)	Swedish hi-risk childhood adults	148	Quality of life	.76
Sagy (1990b)	Israeli retirees	805	Life satisfaction	.54

[b] Used 5-point version of SOC-29.
[d] Used a 19-item version of the SOC.
[c] Used an early 17-item version of the SOC.

The SOC construct, as noted, emerged out of a salutogenic orientation. It was designed to predict and explain movement toward the health end of the health ease/dis-ease continuum. Part C of Table 1 includes all published data which bear upon the correlation between the SOC and some measure of health, illness, and well-being. Of the 32 correlations, only those for emergency room contacts and hospitalization in one study, and for levels of cholesterol, triglycerides, and glucose in another are not significant. The large majority of measures are based on self-report, which raises the question of possible contamination, an issue of great importance but which cannot be discussed here. It should also be noted that though the salutogenic model assigns a primary *causal* role to the SOC (though it rejects a simplistic linear mode of thought and considers feedback), the present chapter excludes consideration of the issue of causality.

Finally, Part D presents data from five studies relating to attitudes and behavior. It is of interest that the two correlations with a social support measure are very low. It would take us too far afield to discuss the theoretical issue raised, but one brief point may be in place. In our discussion of the strong negative relationship between the SOC and perceiving losses in retirement, we noted that a person with a strong SOC adopts attitudes and behaviors which are functional for coping (Antonovsky, Adler, Sagy, & Visel, 1990). She or he *activates* those resources which are seen as appropriate when the need arises. We may also note the correlations with problem- (positive) and emotion- (negative) focused coping, which surely needs exploring.

Table 1
Part D. Attitudes and Behaviors

First author	Sample	N	Variable	r
Hart (1991) (SOC-13)	U.S. undergraduates	59	Interpers. support	NS
Margalit (1990) (SOC-13)	12-16 year old Israelis	742	Social skills	.27
Nyamathi (1991) (SOC-13)[c]	U.S. minority homeless women	581	Social support avail.	.14
Antonovsky (1990b)	Israeli retirees	805	Attit. to ret. losses	−.39
			Attit. to ret. gains	NS
Larsson (1990)[b]	Swedish factory supervisors	217	Prob. focus coping	.29
			Emot. focus coping	−.53
Nyamathi (1991) (SOC-13)[c]	U.S. minority, homeless women	581	Hi-risk behaviors	−.24
Sagy (1990b)	Israeli retirees	805	Activity level	.26

[b] Used 5-point version of SOC-29.
[c] Used an early 17-item version of the SOC.

Table 2
Normative Data from Published Studies Using the SOC-29

Sample	N	Mean	SD	CVA[a]	First author
Swedish hi-risk childhood, 41–56	148	152.6	22.0	.144	Dahlin (1990)
Kibbutz fathers (controls)	67	152.5	14.5	.095	Margalit (1988b)
Israeli retirees: men, age 65	428	152.2	22.8	.187	Sagy (1990a)
Kibbutz men, age 65	130	152.2	22.8	.150	Sagy (1990a)
Kibbutz mothers (controls)	67	151.0	15.3	.101	Margalit (1988b)
Israeli medical students at entry	93	150.2	16.5	.110	Carmel (1990)
Finnish grped. adult sample, men	340	150.2	21.9	.146	Kalimo (1991)
Kibbutz fathers, disabled children	67	146.3	19.4	.133	Margalit (1988b)
Finnish grped. adult sample, women	329	146.1	22.7	.155	Kalimo (1991)
Kibbutz women, age 60	130	145.7	20.2	.139	Sagy (1990a)
Israeli retirees: women, age 60	368	145.0	23.4	.161	Sagy (1990a)
Czech controls in cancer study	153	145.0	—	—	Krivolahvy (1990)
Kibbutz mothers, disabled children	67	140.1	22.6	.161	Margalit (1988a)
U.S. male pts. at VA clinics, 55+	240	139.6	36.4	.260	Coe (1990)
Finnish univ. students, 52% women	117	138.6	23.1	.167	Salmela-Aro (1989)
New Zeal chronic pain, 78% women	107	138.6[b]	14.9	—	Petrie (1990)
Israeli Jewish national sample	297	136.5	19.8	.145	Antonovsky (1987)
U.S. production workers, 76% women	111	133.0	26.5	.199	Fiorentino (1986)
Israeli cerebral palsy, 18–33	34	131.1[c]	0.8	—	Margalit (1990)
U.S. undergraduates, 68% women	307	129.5	24.5	.189	Radmacher (1989)
Czech cancer patients	17	117.0	—	—	Krivolahvy (1990)

[a] CVA: coefficient of variation (standard deviation/mean), a measure of heterogeneity of responses in a sample (Blablock, 1972, p. 88).
[b] Used 5 alternatives. Here multiplied by 7/5.
[c] Item mean and SD given in original. Here former multiplied by 29.

Known Groups

The primary purpose of Tables 2 and 3 is to provide readers with normative data. They present the SOC means and standard deviations of a variety of samples which have appeared in published studies. But the data also allow us to refer briefly to the idea that a valid scale should produce differences on mean scores among samples that would be expected, on theoretical grounds, to differ.

It is striking that a large sample of minority homeless women, many of whom are also addicted to drugs, have the lowest SOC-13 scores. [An unpublished thesis on a similar population (Knowlton, 1991) reports an even lower SOC.] At or near the bottom of the SOC-29 scores are Czech cancer patients, Israeli young adults with cerebral palsy, New Zealand chronic pain patients, and older American patients in Department of Veterans Affairs (VA) clinics. At the other extreme, scoring high, we find kibbutz members, American university faculty, and Israelis who have reached on-time retirement age. Undergraduates, it might be noted, tend to score on the low side.

While the picture presented by these data must be considered preliminary, it does, I believe, tend to support the validity of the scale.

Table 3
Normative Data from Published Studies Using the SOC-13

Sample	N	Mean	SD	CVA[a]	First author
Kibbutz (religious), mean age 46	105	68.7	10.0	.146	Carmel (1991)
U.S. university faculty, men	145	66.7	9.8	.147	Ryland (1990)
U.S. university faculty, women	157	66.4	10.6	.160	Ryland (1990)
Kibbutz (secular), mean age 43	125	66.4	9.9	.149	Carmel (1991)
U.S. male pts. at VA clinics, 55+	240	61.9	17.8	.288	Coe (1990)
Israeli adolescent girls	371	59.2	11.0	.186	Margalit (1990)
Israeli adolescent boys	371	58.6	10.4	.177	Margalit (1990)
U.S. undergraduates	59	58.5	12.1	.207	Hart (1991)
U.S. minority homeless women	581	55.0[b]	0.7	—	Nyamathi (1991)

[a] CVA: coefficient of variation (standard deviation/mean), a measure of heterogeneity of responses in a sample (Blablock, 1972, p. 88).

[b] Used wording simplification and 5-point scale. Item mean and SD given in original. Here former multiplied by 13 and by 7/5 to be comparable to other means.

Factor Structure of the
Sense of Coherence Scale

In the detailed discussion of the construction of the SOC scale, I wrote, "The reader is duly warned, then, that the present version of the SOC scale is not wisely used to study component inter-relations"

(Antonovsky, 1987, p. 87). In light of the facet-theoretical design of the measure, there is no basis for deriving distinguishable scores for comprehensibility, manageability, and meaningfulness. This point was noted above in the discussion of internal consistency. To check this contention, I had conducted a smallest space analysis (Shye, 1978) and a factor analysis on the original Israeli national sample data. Both demonstrated that no separate meaningful factors could be identified using the present version of the scales.

None of the published studies report a factor analysis of the SOC scale. Given the significance of the issue, mention will be made of several unpublished data sets. Coe reported the result of a factor analysis on the responses of 189 U.S. veterans (Coe, Romeis, Tang, & Wolinsky, 1990). On the original baseline survey data, a principle components analysis produced one true factor (eigenvalue 12.45, 42.9% of variance). All 29 items loaded on this factor at 0.40 or above. "An oblique (oblimax) rotation produced somewhat different results (but the same interpretation) ... We conclude that content of items can be sorted into separate factors, but the MA, ME, and C dimensions are present in each of them" (Coe, personal communication).

Pottie's (1990) methodological thesis was devoted to the SOC scale, and particularly to its factor analysis. She used a Flemish sample of 297 adult education students, 84% women. The English summary by K. Haepers noted that "inspection of the principle factor solution showed that all the SOC items—except two (items 10 and 17)—are loading high on the first factor. The eigenvalue of this factor is ... 7.06." The report concluded that "the Flemish SOC questionnaire is an internal consistent instrument to measure the SOC as a global construct in which certain 'accents' can be highlighted."

In a paper based on a study of 488 American undergraduates submitted for publication, Colby et al. wrote, "Principle component factor analysis also did not help identify the latent factors of these two scales" (the SOC and another scale). In a publication which has just come to my attention, Flannery and Flannery (1990, p. 418) factor analyzed the data from 95 adult education students. The analysis "suggests that a single factor solution may be the most parsimonious explanation." Frenz, Carey, and Jorgensen factor analyzed the data from a heterogeneous population ($N = 373$). "The initial analysis," they wrote, "identified five factors which were highly correlated with each other. Subsequent analysis of the factor scores suggested the scale has one core factor ... [and] appears to be a unidimensional instrument measuring SOC." Holm et al., using data from 545 American undergraduates, wrote, "Although it is possible to separate the SOC inventory into two highly correlated factors, it appears that the best solution consists of one global factor."

Conclusion

The sense of coherence construct, the core of a complex theoretical model, refers to a global orientation to one's inner and outer environments which is hypothesized to be a significant determinant of location and movement on the health ease/dis-ease continuum. The SOC scale was developed, using a facet-theoretical design, to operationalize this construct and provide one way of testing this hypothesis. Its use to date in scores of studies in many cultures and with reference to a great variety of problems in the area of health and well-being is, of course, gratifying to me. It expresses the sense of colleagues that the tool is a useful one. But, of more importance, this use has provided a substantial set of data which bears upon the feasibility, reliability, and validity of the scale.

It has been the purpose of this chapter to share with the reader the evidence to date which, I believe, leads to the reasonable conclusion that the scale is indeed one that can and should be used. Provided, of course, that the researcher is persuaded that the construct is *theoretically* appropriate to studying the problem of concern.

Having said this, four concluding remarks are in place. First, there is no doubt in my mind that in five years or so, sufficient evidence will have accumulated to provide the basis for a second generation SOC scale. For the time being, however, I would strongly urge researchers to use the scale as it stands, to allow comparability, rather than for individuals to make this or that change to "improve" the questionnaire.

Second, as I have noted above, a closed questionnaire is only one legitimate tool. Much as advances have been made in the Type A Behavior Pattern construct by using a standard interview and a closed questionnaire, it would be useful to have alternative techniques to study the SOC.

Third, the SOC scale was developed to measure the construct as a global orientation and explicitly not to measure the components of comprehensibility, manageability, and meaningfulness. Some researchers, attracted on theoretical grounds by one or another of these components, have calculated scores on technical grounds. It would indeed be a contribution were separate measures of the components to be developed, with relatively low intercorrelations. (For a theoretical discussion of the dynamics of component interrelations, see Antonovsky, 1987, pp. 19–22.)

Finally, interested readers might wish to know that an SOC international network has been established which includes colleagues actively engaged in empirical research using the SOC. These contacts have been the source for the data presented in this chapter. A periodic newsletter is issued, designed to share data and ideas, establish subnetworks of colleagues working in the same area, and call attention to publication.

Notes

1. Reprinted from *Social Science and Medicine, 36*(6), Aaron Antonovsky, "The Structure and Properties of the Sense of Coherence Scale," pp. 725–733. © 1993, with permission from Pergamon Press Ltd., Headington Hill Hall, Oxford OX3 OBW, UK.

2. There is now under way an international effort, coordinated by Malka Margalit of the School of Education, Tel Aviv University, to develop a version of the SOC for children.

References

Antonovsky, A. (1972). Breakdown: A needed fourth step in the conceptual armamentarium of modern medicine. *Social Science and Medicine, 6,* 537–544.

Antonovsky, A. (1974). Conceptual and methodological problems in the study of resistance resources and stressful life events. In B. Dohrenwend & B. Dohrenwend (Eds.), *Stressful life events: Their nature and effects.* New York: Wiley.

Antonovsky, A. (1979). *Health, stress, and coping.* San Francisco: Jossey-Bass.

Antonovsky, A. (1983).* The sense of coherence: Development of a research instrument. *Newsletter and Research Report,* W. S. Schwartz Research Center for Behavioral Medicine, Tel Aviv University, *1,* 1–11.

Antonovsky, A. (1987). *Unraveling the mystery of health.* San Francisco: Jossey-Bass.

Antonovsky, A. (1990a). A somewhat personal odyssey in studying the stress process. *Stress Medicine, 6,* 71–80.

Antonovsky, A. (1991). The structural sources of salutogenic strengths. In C. L. Cooper & R. Payne (Eds.), *Personality and stress: Individual differences in the stress process.* New York: Wiley.

Antonovsky, A., Adler, I., Sagy, S., & Visel, R. (1990b).* Attitudes toward retirement in an Israeli cohort. *International Journal on Aging and Human Development, 31,* 57–77.

Antonovsky, A., & Sagy, S. (1986).* The development of a sense of coherence and its impact on responses to stress situations. *Journal of Social Psychology, 126,* 213–225.

Antonovsky, A., & Sourani, T. (1988).* Family sense of coherence and family adaptation. *Journal of Marriage and the Family, 50,* 79–92.

Antonovsky, H., Hankin, Y., & Stone, D. (1987).* Patterns of drinking in a small development town in Israel. *British Journal of Addiction, 82,* 293–303.

Bernstein, J., & Carmel, S. (1987).* Trait anxiety and the sense of coherence. *Psychological Reports, 60,* 1000.

Bernstein, J., & Carmel, S. (1991).* Gender differences over time in medical school stressors, anxiety, and the sense of coherence. *Sex Roles, 24,* 335–345.

Blablock, H. M. (1972). *Social statistics* (2nd ed.). New York: McGraw-Hill.

Bowen, G. L. (1989).* *Family adaptation to relocation: An empirical analysis of family stressors, adaptive resources, and sense of coherence.* Technical Report 856, Alexandria, VA: U.S. Army Research Institute for the Behavioral and Social Sciences.

Carmel, S., Anson, O., Levenson, A., Bonneh, D. Y., & Maoz, B. (1991).* Life events, sense of coherence, and health: Gender differences on the kibbutz. *Social Science and Medicine, 32,* 1089–1096.

Carmel, S., & Bernstein, J. (1989).* Trait anxiety and sense of coherence: A longitudinal study. *Psychological Reports, 65,* 221–222.

Carmel, S., & Bernstein, J. (1990).* Trait anxiety, sense of coherence, and medical school stressors: Observations at three stages. *Anxiety Research, 3,* 51–60.

Coe, R. M., Romeis, J. C., Tang, B., & Wolinsky, F. D. (1990).* Correlates of a measure of coping in older veterans: A preliminary report. *Journal of Community Health, 15,* 287–296.

Dahlin, L., Cederblad, M., Antonovsky, A., & Hagnell, O. (1990).* Childhood vulnerability and adult invincibility. *Acta Psychiatrica Scandinavica, 82,* 228–232.

Dana, R. H., Hoffman, T., Armstrong, B., & Wilson, J. (1985, April). *Sense of coherence: Examination of the construct.* Poster presented at the Southwestern Psychological Association meeting, Austin, TX.

Fiorentino, L. M. (1986).* Stress: The high cost to industry. *Occupational Health Nursing, 34,* 217–220.

Flannery, R. B., & Flannery, G. J. (1990). Sense of coherence, life stress, and psychological distress: A prospective methodological inquiry. *Journal of Clinical Psychology, 46,* 415–420.

Hart, K. E., Hittner, J. B., & Paras, K. C. (1991).* Sense of coherence trait anxiety and the perceived availability of social support. *Journal of Research in Personality, 25,* 137–145.

Kalimo, R., & Vuori, J. (1990).* Work and sense of coherence: Resources for competence and life satisfaction. *Behavioral Medicine, 16,* 76-89.

Kalimo, R., & Vuori, J. (1991).* Work factors and health: The predictive role of pre-employment experiences. *Journal of Occupational Psychology, 64,* 97–115.

Knowlton, V. (1991). *Sense of coherence and self-perceived health status in homeless women.* Unpublished master's thesis, Department of Nursing, University of Lowell, Lowell, MA.

Krivolahvy, J. (1990).* I. Sense of coherence: Methods and first results. II. Sense of coherence and cancer. *Ceskoslovenska Psychologie (Czech)*, *34*, 511-517.

Larsson, G., & Setterlind, S. (1990).* Work load/work control and health: Moderating effects of heredity, self-image, coping, and health behavior. *International Journal of Health Sciences, 1,* 79-88.

Lavee, Y., & Olson, D. H. (1991).* Family types and responses to stress. *Journal of Marriage and the Family, 53,* 786-798.

Margalit, M. (1983).* Learned helplessness and the sense of coherence among learning disabled children. *Studies in Education (Hebrew), 20,* 153-158.

Margalit, M. (1985).* Perception of parents' behavior, familial satisfaction, and sense of coherence in hyperactive children. *Journal of School Psychology, 23,* 355-364.

Margalit M., & Cassel-Seidenman, R. (1987).* Life satisfaction and sense of coherence among young adults with cerebral palsy. *Career Development of Exceptional Individuals, 10,* 42-50.

Margalit, M., & Eysenck, S. (1990).* Prediction of coherence in adolescence: Gender differences in social skills, personality and family climate. *Journal of Research Personality, 24,* 510-521.

Margalit, M., Leyser, Y., & Avraham, Y. (1988a).* Subtypes of family climate among kibbutz mothers of disabled children. *International Journal of Special Education, 3,* 101-115.

Margalit, M., Leyser, Y., & Avraham, Y. (1989).* Classification and validation of family climate subtypes in kibbutz fathers of disabled and nondisabled children. *Journal of Abnormal Child Psychology, 17,* 91-107.

Margalit, M., Leyser, Y., Avraham, Y., & Lewy-Osin, M. (1988b).* Social-environment characteristics (family climate) and sense of coherence in kibbutz families with disabled and nondisabled children. *European Journal of Special Needs Education, B3,* 87-98.

Nyamathi, A. M. (1991).* Relationship of resources to emotional distress, somatic complaints, and high risk behaviors in drug recovery and homeless minority women. *Research in Nursing and Health, 14,* 269-278.

Orthner, D. K., Zimmerman, L. I., Bowen, G. L., Gaddy, G., & Bell, D. B. (1991).* *Development of a measure of family adaptation to the army.* Technical Report, Alexandria, VA: U.S. Army Research Institute for the Behavioral Sciences.

Payne, L. (1982). *Sense of coherence: A measure of health status.* Unpublished master's thesis, School of Nursing, University of Alberta, Alberta, Canada.

Petrie, K., & Azariah, R. (1990).* Health-promoting variables as predictors of response to a brief pain management program. *Clinical Journal of Pain, 6,* 43-46.

Pottie, C. M. H. (1990). *Antonovsky's "sense of coherence" and the operationalization of this concept in a Flemish version questionnaire.* Unpublished master's thesis, Faculteit der Psychologie en Pedagogische Wetenschappen, Katholieke University Leuven, Belgium.

Radmacher, S. A., & Sheridan, C. L. (1989).* The global inventory of stress: A comprehensive approach to stress assessment. *Medical Psychotherapy, 2,* 183-188.

Ryland, E. K., & Greenfeld, S. (1990).* An investigation of gender differences in occupational stress and general well-being. *Journal of Applied Business Research, 6,* 35–43.

Ryland, E. K., & Greenfeld, S. (1991).* Work stress and well-being: An investigation of Antonovsky's sense of coherence model. *Journal of Social Behavior and Personality, 6,* 39–54.

Sagy, S., & Antonovsky, A. (1990a).* Coping with retirement: Does the sense of coherence matter less in the kibbutz? *International Journal of Health Sciences, 1,* 233–242.

Sagy, S., Antonovsky, A., & Adler, I. (1990b).* Explaining life satisfaction in later life: The sense of coherence and activity theory. *Behavior, Health, and Aging, 1,* 11–25.

Salmela-Aro, K. (1989).* Mental health and goal system. *Psykologia (Finnish), 24,* 354–361.

Shye, S. (Ed.). (1978). *Theory construction and data analysis in the behavioral sciences.* San Francisco: Jossey-Bass.

Viikari-Juntura, E., Vuori, J., Silverstein, B. A., Kalimo, R., Kuosma, E., & Videman, T. (1991).* A life-long prospective study on the role of psychosocial factors in neck-shoulder and low-back pain. *Spine, 16,* 1056–1061.

Williams, S. J. (1990).* The relationship among stress, hardiness, sense of coherence, and illness in critical care nurses. *Medical Psychotherapy, 3,* 171–186.

*Publications with empirical data relating to the SOC construct.

Chapter 3

Ethnicity, Schema, and Coherence

Appraisal Processes for Families in Crisis

Hamilton I. McCubbin, Anne I. Thompson, Elizabeth A. Thompson, Kelly M. Elver, and Marilyn A. McCubbin

There is a dearth of research linking the appraisal processes incorporating cultural and ethnic factors to the ways in which families respond to and cope with family stress and crises. In the context of theory building and research on the sense of coherence, the family appraisal processes that integrate culture and ethnicity as independent or contributing factors in the shaping of coherence are not speculated upon nor studied in any systematic fashion. The interaction of culture, ethnicity or ethnic orientation, and the sense of coherence, one could argue, is important to the understanding of the developmental and mediating influence of coherence in the management of change and stress. This chapter attempts to advance this line of scientific inquiry in two ways: first, by identifying and defining the family processes of appraisal, focusing on the concept of family schema, inclusive of culture and ethnicity; and second, by studying family schema in aboriginal Native Hawaiian families, including their culturally related values, beliefs, and world views, and the relationship of family schema to the sense of coherence and family dysfunction. A serious commitment to the study of the sense of coherence mandates the study of the role of ethnicity and culture as an integral and contributing factor to the family's resiliency in response to stress.

Ethnicity, Culture, and Family Schema

The influence of culture on family life has been documented in the family literature. A comprehensive review by Tseng and Hsu (1991) reveals that, over time, culture has influenced family functioning in a great variety of ways: marriage forms, choice of mates, post-marital residence, the family kinship system and descent groups, household and family structures, the primary axis of family obligations, family-community dynamics, and alternative family formations (Nanda, 1980; Tseng & Tsu, 1986; Li, 1968; Berkner, 1972; Pelzel, 1970; Ishisaka, 1992; Mokuau, 1992; Miller, 1969). Historically, the family has been the conduit for cultural transmission, providing a natural atmosphere for traditions to be passed from generation to generation, and it has evolved throughout the ages to keep culture and ethnic heritage alive. In turn, the traditions themselves have given families a sense of stability and support from which they draw comfort, guidance, and a means of coping with the problems of daily life.

Both ethnicity and culture, used synonymously in this chapter, are defined as the customary beliefs, integrated patterns of human behavior (such as thought, speech, and action), social forms, and traits of a racial group. They are nurtured, cultivated, and transferred across generations and among family members through traditions and celebrations, as well as through family problem-solving efforts (McGoldrich, 1989). In solving problems and managing family life, the family's culture fundamentally influences two critical levels of family appraisal involved in the process of adaptation: the family's schema, and family paradigms (McCubbin & McCubbin, 1993; H. I. McCubbin, McCubbin, & Thompson, 1992; McCubbin, Thompson, Thompson, McCubbin, & Kasten, 1993). These processes of family life are the ways in which families give meaning to stressful life events and family struggles, and they appear to play a fundamental role in shaping the family's responses and strategies.

The concept of family schema, integral to the process of appraisal, may be traced to the general literature on the psychology of stigma that underscores the critical importance of ethnicity and culture (Taylor & Crocker, 1981; Fong & Markus, 1982; Bem, 1981). A family's schema may be defined as a structure of fundamental convictions and values. Shaped and adopted by the family system over time, the family's schema creates the family's *unique character* and serves as an overriding shared informational framework against and through which family experiences are processed and evaluated. A family schema, expressed through the family's "world view," includes cultural and ethnic beliefs and values and evolves into an encapsulation of experience that serves as a framework for evaluating incoming stimuli and experiences (Martin & Halverson, 1981; Segal, 1988; McCubbin, Thompson, Thompson, McCubbin, & Kasten, 1993). Highly resistant to change, a family schema could include values such as respecting and maintaining one's ethnic heritage, and honoring and respecting one's elders. It might include convictions such as caring for the land, valuing the meaning of dance and music, and valuing a native language. Not only does a family's schema give some order and stability to family life, it plays an influential role in shaping and legitimizing the family's established patterns of functioning, rules, and boundaries, as well as the family's problem-solving behaviors.

Hierarchical Ordering of the Family Appraisal Processes in Resiliency and Adaptation

The meaningful relationship between the family schema, paradigms, the sense of coherence, and family adaptation is integral to the family's appraisal processes as assessed by the Resiliency Model of Family Adjustment and Adaptation (see Figure 1). It is challenging to depict a dynamic family appraisal process which spans a period of time and involves the family unit with its identity and values, the community, and the members acting as individuals. It is vital, however, for behavioral scientists in general, and family scientists in particular, to tease apart the process in order to grasp the elements and processes of appraisal. As diagrammed in Figure 1, the family appraisal processes in family crisis situations involve five fundamental levels: schema (5), coherence (4), paradigms (3), situational appraisal (2), and stressor appraisal (1). Stressor appraisal is not depicted in Figure 1 because the current emphasis on family adaptation places the family's initial definition of a stressor aside and focuses upon family schema, coherence, paradigms, and situational appraisal.

> *Level 5. Family schema:* A generalized structure of shared values, beliefs, goals, expectations, and priorities, shaped and adopted by the family unit, thus formulating a generalized informational structure against and through which information and experiences are compared, sifted, and processed. A family schema evolves over time and serves as a dispositional world

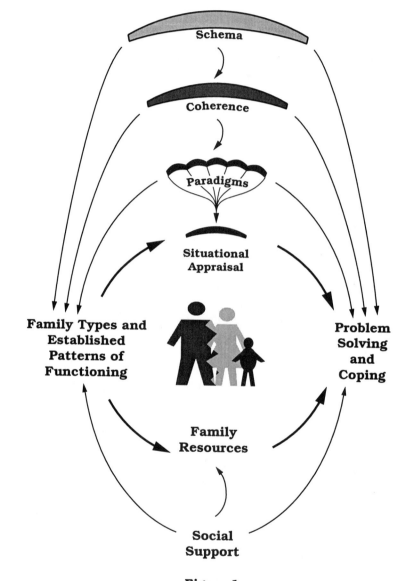

Figure 1
Focus on Appraisal Processes in the
Resiliency Model of Family Adjustment and Adaptation

view and framework to evaluate crisis situations and legitimate adherence to and change in the family's established patterns of functioning. While fostering family problem solving and coping, the family schema has as one of its central functions the development of family meanings. This aspect of family appraisal involves the creation of family "stories" or "understandings" shared by family members for the purpose of facilitating the family's adaptation to the crisis situation. The meanings are often described in cryptic phrases or special words such as "God's will" or the Hawaiian *malama,* used to encourage acceptance of adversity. These meanings transcend the immediate stressor and the situation and place the crisis in a larger context of experiences. From this perspective, the family schema facilitates the development of meaning through the processes of: classification (framing the situation in terms of shared values and expectations), spiritualization (framing the situation in context of the family's shared beliefs), temporalization (framing the situation in terms of the long view and long-term consequences as well as the positive aspects of the present), and contextualization (framing the situation in terms of nature and its order of things as well as the community and personal relationships and the interpersonal order of things) (McCubbin & McCubbin, 1993; McCubbin, Thompson, Thompson, McCubbin, & Kasten, 1993).

Level 4. Family coherence: A construct that explains the motivational and cognitive bases for transforming the family's potential resources into actual resources, thereby facilitating coping and promoting the health of family members and the well-being of the family unit. This is a dispositional world view that expresses the family's dynamic feeling of confidence that the world is comprehensible (internal and external environments are structured predictable and explicable), manageable (resources are available to meet demands), and meaningful (life demands are challenges worthy of investment) (Antonovsky, 1979, 1987; Antonovsky & Sourani, 1988).

Level 3. Family paradigms: A model of shared beliefs and expectations shaped and adopted by the family unit to guide the family's development of *specific* patterns of functioning around *specific* domains or dimensions of family life (e.g., work and family, communication, spiritual/religious orientation, child rearing, etc.). Once a paradigm is shaped and adopted and used to interpret phenomena and to guide family behaviors, family functioning in the absence of any paradigm cannot occur (Reiss, 1981; McCubbin, Thompson, Thompson, & McCubbin, 1992).

Level 2. Situational appraisal: The family's shared assessment of the stressor, the hardships created by the stressor, the demands upon the family system to change some of its established patterns of functioning. The appraisal occurs in relation to the family's capability for managing the crisis situation.

Level 1. Stressor appraisal: The family's definition of the stressor and its severity is the initial level of family assessment. Consistent with the classic work of Reuben Hill (1949), the family's response to a stressor will be shaped by the definition that the family attributes to the situation. In the context of a crisis situation, which places a demand on the family unit to change, this initial level (1) of appraisal becomes secondary to the adaptation process. This shift occurs due to the fact that families faced with changes in functioning are called upon to manage a host of stressors and demands, well beyond the impact of the initial crisis producing event.

The Appraisal Process:
A Brief Description

In the case of a stressful situation calling for predictable and straightforward responses, as in the case of a family member with a treatable injury (such as a broken arm), the family's appraisal process is activated with relatively little involvement of the family's schema (dispositional world view of beliefs, values, goals, and meanings) nor the family's sense of coherence (dispositional world view of confidence, comprehensibility, and manageability). This stressful situation involves the family's paradigms (specific beliefs and expectations that guide the family's *established patterns of functioning* in such areas as marital relationships, child rearing, health care, and intergenerational relationships), the family's appraisal of the stressor (the injury and its severity), and the related hardships that arise (availability of health care, insurance, quality of health care, emotional stability of the family unit and its members). All of these factors, particularly the family's paradigms, stressor appraisal, and situational appraisal, play central roles in the family's appraisal process and help to shape family behavior and responses.

In contrast, in the face of adversity, such as the birth of a child with a physical disability, the established patterns of family functioning are not adequate to manage the situation (the stressor and related short- and long-term hardships). This situation requires changes in the functioning of the family unit and the fifth (schema), fourth (sense of coherence), third (paradigms), and second (situation) levels of family appraisal are often called into action to guide the family's response to the situation (see Figure 2). Working backward from the initial stressor, family situational appraisals are first called into action by the demands of the crisis situation, challenging the way the family will function. Family routines will likely be altered; family roles related to providing physical care will need to be reexamined; family paradigms, which have served as the family framework to guide, affirm, and reinforce the established patterns of family functioning, will be challenged and called into question; and newly instituted patterns and accompanying roles and expectations will emerge. New paradigms will also emerge to reinforce and legitimate the new patterns of functioning—a necessary process to provide family stability and predictability. The family's sense of coherence, always available as a dispositional resource to facilitate adaptation, will be of greater importance in fostering the family's world view in the face of this adversity or challenge. The family's sense of coherence allows the family to maintain their confidence that the world is comprehensible, manageable, and meaningful. Thus the family's level of coherence shapes the degree to which the family transforms its extant or potential resources into actual resources and thereby facilitates the creation of new patterns of functioning, promotes harmony and congruency, and fosters coping and adaptation.

Because the family's established patterns of functioning are threatened, the family's schema, the hub of the family's appraisal process, is also involved. As already noted in the definition of family schema, culture and ethnicity may play a critical role in helping the family derive *meaning* by placing the family's situation into a broader set of values. This new *meaning* may result in the family framing the crisis situation as less threatening when viewed over time, when viewed in the context of the cultural acceptance of all children in the community, when viewed as a spiritual challenge, and when viewed as part of the natural ebb and flow of nature. This family world view may foster the adoption of new patterns of functioning and coping. When combined with the three other central processes of appraisal (coherence, paradigms, and situational appraisal), the family's schema serves the family unit by fostering the creation of the family's unique identity and enhancing the development of the family's sense of coherence (H. I. McCubbin, McCubbin, & Thompson, 1992).

Additionally, the family schema indirectly facilitates the family's shifting of paradigms and thus supports the necessary changes in the way the family functions. These paradigm shifts may be necessary for coping with the long-term needs of the family in managing a disability within the family context. Family meanings play a vital role in the transitional process of adopting new patterns of functioning, releasing old patterns, and achieving congruency and harmony between a family's paradigms, schema, and behaviors. Ultimately, culture and ethnicity shape family functioning, particularly in response to the crisis situations in which the family's stability and continuity may be threatened. To further this reasoning, the description of the integration of ethnicity into the family schema, coherence, meanings, and paradigms will draw from research on Aboriginal Native Hawaiian families.

As noted in Figure 2, which outlines the phases of family adaptation, the family appraisal processes play a critical set of roles in fostering family adaptations. In Adaptation Phase I, the appraisal process of schema, coherence, and paradigms fosters the demand for changes in the family's established patterns of functioning. The family may have temporary changes and appear to adapt (pseudo-adaptation) but may find itself in need of future changes, thus creating another process of crisis, appraisal, and change. In Adaptation Phase II, newly instituted patterns of family functioning (created by trial and error) may find acceptance and be legitimated and reinforced by emerging and accepted family paradigms, the family's dispositional sense of coherence, the family's schema. Family bonadaptation, characterized by an internal sense of family harmony, stability, and congruity (between schema, coherence, paradigms, and patterns of functioning), is presented as the desirable outcome of the appraisal and change process (McCubbin & McCubbin, 1993).

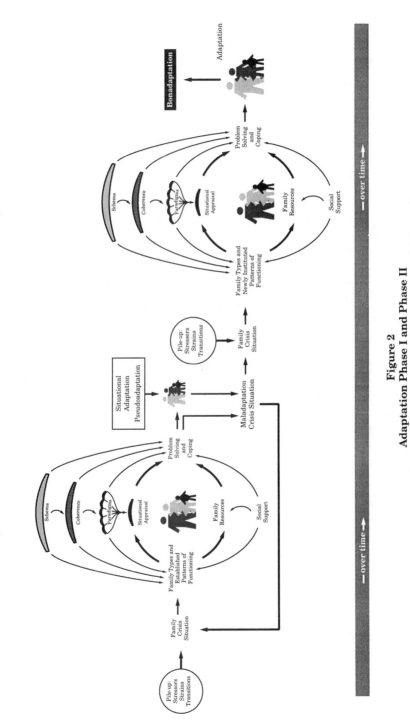

Figure 2
Adaptation Phase I and Phase II
of the Resiliency Model of Family Adjustment and Adaptation

Ethnicity, Culture, and Family Schema:
The Case of Aboriginal Native Hawaiians

To illustrate the role of ethnicity and culture in shaping a family's schema, the five components of the Native Hawaiians' family schema will be described (Frankl, 1984; Kanahele, 1986). The family's schema includes shared values and convictions regarding family *structure, self or group concept, spiritual beliefs, nature and the land, and time orientation.* Specifically, the Native Hawaiians emphasize the extended family, or tribal, structure. They have a common concern for the social and economic well-being of all individuals, and they have a family support network that encompasses both immediate and extended family. Predictably, the Native Hawaiians have developed a "we" group orientation where the needs of the whole rise above the needs of the individual (Herring, 1989). In the case of Native Hawaiians, the concept of *malama,* or caring, is the dominant theme that places the family group as a whole above the individual.

Spiritual-religious underpinnings also play an important role in shaping the family's response to the challenge of internal conflicts and family hardships. Native Hawaiians view the world in terms of a "Great Spirit"; spirituality is part of the entire world. From the Native Hawaiian perspective, spirits appear in many forms, and the individual strives for unity with the cosmos as the way to achieve spirituality. Native Hawaiians see spirituality as a natural outgrowth of *all* aspects of life. This spiritual orientation to life facilitates Native Hawaiians' ability to create a family paradigm that cultivates the belief that a "disabled" child or deviant member is "normal" and a valued member of the community, despite any physical, developmental, or psychological handicaps.

The two additional components of family schema that shape family behavior are nature and land, and time orientation. Native Hawaiians view the environment as living. Land cannot be owned and should be respected and preserved. From their point of view, what we do to the land we do to ourselves. The Native Hawaiian "world view" is that land is the basis for life. *Aloha aina* or *aloha malama* reflects their belief in loving and caring for the land. Resources must be nurtured and preserved for future generations. The Native Hawaiian extends the philosophy of harmony with the land to other aspects of life, with emphasis on achieving balance, a sense of wholeness, and harmony with nature.

From the Native Hawaiian perspective, time is relative and life is cyclical. Native Hawaiians, as well as Native American Indians, think of time in the present; families thrive if they take advantage of the positive aspects and the strengths of the moment. Clearly, the family's world view is shaped to some degree by the family's "roots" or ethnic and cultural orientation. Therefore, in the case of Native Hawaiians, the following causal ordering of variables in the family appraisal process may be advanced and presented as a hypothesis for further study and empirical testing.

It is proposed that the level of family dysfunction will be mediated by the family appraisal process involving the family schema, the family sense of coherence, and the family's resources of family hardiness, social support, and family problem-solving communication. All of these factors are critical variables presented in the Resiliency Model of Family Adjustment and Adaptation (McCubbin & McCubbin, 1993), which was used to guide the theory-building and empirical aspects of this investigation.

A Path Analysis of the Family Appraisal Process: The Case of Native Hawaiian Families

The opportunity to examine the relationship between family ethnic orientation, coherence, and family functioning is rare. In 1993, at the invitation of two agencies involved in providing educational and social (prevention-oriented) services to Native Hawaiian families, particularly to families with preschool-age children, social and behavioral scientists from the Center for Excellence in Family Studies were challenged to develop ethnically relevant and culturally sensitive measures of family functioning that could be used in future studies of families of Native Hawaiian families.

The importance of studying Aboriginal Native Hawaiians has already been established by virtue of their "at risk" status among minority populations in the United States (Blaisdell, 1989; Mokuau, 1992). The health risks for Native Hawaiians are astounding. Native Hawaiians have the worst health profile in the United States. More than 65% of Native Hawaiians are obese, and their mortality rates from cancer, heart disease, and diabetes are the highest in the nation. The mortality rates for Native Hawaiians, when compared to the average mortality rates for all races in the United States (adjusted for age/sex per 100,000), are striking: 26.4 from infectious diseases (versus 13 for all races); 29 from diabetes (versus 9.8 for all races); 46.1 from strokes (versus 35.1 for all races); 183.9 from cancer (versus 132 for all races); and 273 from heart disease (versus 189 for all races).

In this investigation, one hundred and fifty-five families ($N = 155$) of preschool-age children were invited to participate in a study designed to record: (a) the family's "pile-up" of normative and non-normative life events and changes and their assessment of the severity of each of the changes they experienced; (b) the family's level of support from the community in which they lived; (c) the family's world view or schema, emphasizing their involvement in and valuing of their cultural heritage and the meaning they attached to cultural values; (d) the family's problem-solving communication style and the degree to which they were affirming and less inflammatory in their approach to issues and problems; and (e) the criterion for the study, the family's level of dysfunction including having members abusing substances, member(s) having emotional difficulties, and interpersonal abuse.

Methodology

Procedures

Families were notified by the director of each of the agencies and asked to participate. Families were chosen at random by the agencies from their list of eligible families who met a single criterion: Each family had to have one or more child members of preschool age. Given the brief time (one month) in which this investigation was to be conducted, the target sample was limited to 150. This target was exceeded, and the resulting sample was 155. It should be noted, however, because of missing data on several of the measures, the total number of usable responses to the questionnaires dropped to 101 families. Despite the small sample size, the uniqueness of the sample and the data encouraged the research team to examine the data and to share the results, recognizing the limitations of the sample and thus limiting the generalizability of the findings.

Subjects

The agencies did not provide the total list of potential families, nor did they systematically record the number of families who refused to participate. However, the agencies indicated that a low percentage of contacted families refused to participate (less than 10 families). When the desired number of families ($N = 150$) was achieved, the selection process ended. The majority of respondents were parents (96.8%), 1.3% were grandparents, and .6% were significant others. The average age of the family members [of which the majority (92.3%) were women] who responded to the questionnaires on behalf of the family was 29 years (range 12 years to 57 years). On average, the respondents had 3 children (range 1–9 children). Family income ranged from less than $5,000 (9.7%) to over $50,000 (5.2%). The majority of families were in the income range of $10,000 to $34,999 (60%). A notable percentage (41.6%) were on General Assistance or AFDC (welfare) support. It is interesting to note that slightly over half (52.3%) of the families were two-adult households while the remaining families (47.7%) were single-parent households.

Measures

The Family Dysfunction Index (McCubbin, Thompson, & Elver, 1993) is an eight-item self-report instrument with a four-point scale ranging from Not a Problem to Large Problem. The instrument measures the degree to which the family unit is faced with hardships that may be viewed as symptomatic of family dysfunction. This scale consists of items such as: A member appears to have emotional problems; A family member is using or abusing substances; and A family member is abusing another member. The overall reliability (Cronbach's Alpha) for the Family Dysfunction Index is .87.

The Family (Ethnicity) Schema Index (McCubbin, Thompson, Elver, & Carpenter, 1992) is a 39-item self-report instrument with a four-point scale of False, Mostly False, Mostly True, and True. The instrument measures the degree to which a family has cultivated a sense of cultural and ethnic values that are an important part of family life. Some items included in the Family Schema Index are: We believe that the land we live on is an important part of who we are; and Using our Native language helps us appreciate and value our ethnic/cultural roots. The overall reliability (Cronbach's Alpha) for the Family (Ethnicity) Schema Index is .87.

The Family Problem Solving Communication Index (M. A. McCubbin, McCubbin, & Thompson, 1992, 1994) is a 10-item instrument with a four-point scale (False, Mostly False, Mostly True, and True). The instrument consists of two subscales, Incendiary Communication and Affirming Communication. Incendiary communication is defined as that type of communication that is inflammatory in nature and tends to exacerbate a stressful situation, while affirming communication conveys support and caring and exerts a calming influence. Incendiary communication is measured by five items such as: When we have conflicts, we yell and scream at each other. Affirming communication is measured by five items such as: When we have conflicts, we are respectful of each other's feelings. The overall reliability (Cronbach's Alpha) for the instrument is .89.

The Family Hardiness Index (McCubbin, McCubbin, & Thompson, 1987) is a 20-item instrument with a four-point scale (False, Mostly False, Mostly True, and True). The instrument was developed to measure the characteristic of hardiness as a stress-resistant and adaptive resource in families. Hardiness functions as a mediating factor or buffer, mitigating the effects of stressors and demands and facilitating family adjustment and adaptation over time. Family hardiness specifically refers to the internal strengths and durability of the family unit. Hardiness is characterized by a sense of control over the outcomes of life events and hardships, a view of change as beneficial and growth producing, and an active rather than passive orientation in adjusting to and managing stressful situations. The Family Hardiness Index consists of four subscales. The Co-oriented Commitment subscale measures the family's sense of internal strengths, dependability, and ability to work together. The Confidence subscale measures the family's sense of being able to plan ahead, being appreciated for efforts, and being able to endure hardships and experience life with interest and meaningfulness. The Challenge subscale measures the family's efforts to be innovative, active, and to experience and learn new things. The Control subscale measures the family's sense of being in control of family life rather than being shaped by outside events and circumstances. Some items included in the instrument are: We have a sense of being strong even when we face big problems; We listen to each others' problems, hurts, and fears; and We tend to do the same things over and over ... it's boring. The Family Hardiness Index has an overall reliability (Cronbach's Alpha) of .82 and validity coefficients ranging from .15 to .23 with criterion indices of cohesiveness, flexibility, and stability.

The Family Coherence Index (McCubbin, Larsen, & Olson, 1982) is a four-item measure which uses a five-point scale ranging from Strongly Disagree to Strongly Agree. This scale is designed to measure the degree to which families call upon their appraisal skills to manage stressful life events, strains, and changes. It includes these items: Accepting stressful events as a fact of life; Accepting that difficulties occur unexpectedly; Defining the family problem in a more positive way so we don't get discouraged; and Having faith in God. The overall reliability (Cronbach's Alpha) for the instrument is .71.

The Community Support Index (McCubbin, Patterson, & Glynn, 1982), also referred to as the Social Support Index, consists of 22 items and uses a five-point scale ranging from Strongly Disagree to Strongly Agree. The scale was selected to measure the degree to which families are integrated into the community, view the community as a source of support and feel that the community can provide emotional, esteem, and network support. Some of the items included are: People can depend on each other in this community; and If I had an emergency, even people I do not know in this community would be willing to help. The psychometric properties of the Community Support Index include a reliability (internal reliability) index of .82 and a validity coefficient (correlation with the criterion of family well-being) of .40.

Results

A stepwise regression analysis was conducted to explain the variability in family dysfunction. Two independent variables emerged as being of paramount importance: family problem-solving communication and family hardiness. At first glance, the importance of coherence and family (ethnic) schema did not emerge and the evidence presented did not confirm their importance. On the other hand, the Resiliency Model of Family Adjustment and Adaptation places schema and coherence (see Figures 1 and 2) as having indirect influence upon any index of adaptation. Only through path-analytic techniques would the relative importance of family schema and family coherence be examined and possibly confirmed.

The respondents' age, income, number of children, and marital status were controlled for in all analyses because they were significantly correlated with some of the variables in the model. The validity of results derived from the path analysis is dependent on satisfying several assumptions. These include linear relationships among independent and dependent variables, no measurement error, one-way causality, the absence of multicollinearity, and uncorrelated residuals across equations (Pedhazur, 1982). Multicollinearity was not a problem in the data (all correlations were less than .80) (Lewis-Beck, 1980), and no relationships significantly deviated from linearity. Also, the residuals were not significantly correlated. Although it is impossible to assure complete freedom from the measurement error, the internal consistencies of all variables were satisfactory.

Even though we specified a priori hypotheses to predict the relationships among the variables, we adopted a theory-trimming approach. Path coefficients first were computed for the just-identified model in which each variable was assumed to be directly affected by all variables preceding it in the model. A series of hierarchical regression equations were used to derive standardized beta weights to estimate path coefficients. In each question, age, income, number of children, and marital status were entered first, followed by all other variables exerting an effect on the variable of interest. The variables whose paths to the dependent variable were under consideration were entered last, after the other variables were statistically controlled.

A trimmed model was then obtained by deleting all insignificant paths ($p \leq .05$) in the just-identified model, and the standardized beta weights of the remaining paths were recalculated. The resulting path diagram and the new standardized betas are presented in Figure 3. An analysis of the resulting trimmed model (Figure 3) reveals that many of the predicted paths were supported.

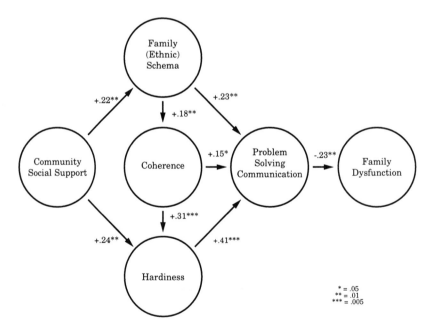

Figure 3
Trimmed Model for Family Schema
and Coherence for Native Hawaiian Families

Trimmed Model of
Native Hawaiian Families

In the trimmed model (Figure 3), family problem-solving communication (–.23) emerges as the critical explanatory variable for family dysfunction. The appraisal processes of family (ethnic) schema (+.23) and coherence (+.15), combined with family hardiness (+.41), explain the variability in family problem-solving communication. Additionally, as outlined in the Resiliency Model, another pathway emerges: Family (ethnic) schema is causally related (+.18) to coherence, which is causally linked (+.31) to family hardiness, which, as already established, is causally linked to family problem-solving communication. Surprisingly, community social support contributes to both family (ethnic) schema (+.22) and to family hardiness (+.24) in the final step in the causal pathways outlined in Figure 3. As expected, family (ethnic) schema is indirectly related to family dysfunction, primarily through coherence, hardiness, and family problem-solving communication. The unique, independent, but noteworthy contributions of both family (ethnic) schema and family coherence to family dysfunction are affirmed in this investigation.

Trimmed Model for Single-Parent
Native Hawaiian Families

If we carry this analysis another step and focus upon the identification of trimmed path models for single-parent families and two-parent/adult family units, separately, the relative importance of the appraisal processes involving family (ethnic) schema and family coherence can be tested further in the case of Aboriginal Native Hawaiian Families.

In the trimmed model for Native Hawaiian single-parent families (Figure 4), family hardiness (–.41) emerges as the critical explanatory variable for family dysfunction. Two variables, family problem-solving communication (+.36) and community social support (+.28), emerge as the key explanatory variables for family hardiness. In addition, as outlined in the Resiliency Model, another pathway emerges: Family (ethnic) schema is causally related (+.39) to coherence, which is causally linked (+.44) to family problem-solving communication, which, as already established, is causally linked to family hardiness. As expected, family (ethnic) schema is indirectly related to family dysfunction, primarily through coherence, family problem solving communication and hardiness. The unique and noteworthy contributions of both family (ethnic) schema

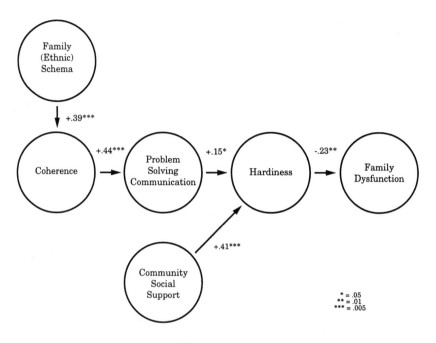

Figure 4
Trimmed Model for Family Schema and Coherence
in Single-Parent Native Hawaiian Families

and family coherence to family dysfunction are also affirmed in this analysis.

Trimmed Model for Two-Parent/Adult Native Hawaiian Families

In the trimmed model for two-parent/adult Native Hawaiian family units (Figure 5), family problem solving communication (–.43) emerges as the critical explanatory variable for family dysfunction. In this path analysis, family (ethnic) schema does not emerge as being either directly or indirectly related to family dysfunction. Rather, the family appraisal process involving coherence (+.25) emerges as causally linked to family hardiness, which in turn is causally related to family problem solving communication (+.41). In this case, the expectation of a causal role for family (ethnic) schema is not confirmed.

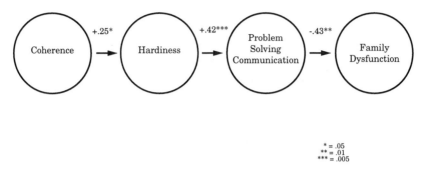

* = .05
** = .01
*** = .005

Figure 5
Trimmed Model for Family Schema and Coherence
in Two-Parent/Adult Native Hawaiian Families

Discussion

This investigation attempts to respond to the challenge that research on coherence be inclusive of other important variables; to better understand how families remain healthy and recover when confronted with stressful life events, the effects of two or more variables must be considered concurrently, such as hardiness and coherence or coherence and family schema. This effort to combine variables is clearly reflected in the literature: Kobasa, Maddi, and Puccetti (1982) examined hardiness and exercise, and Holahan and Moos (1986) explored personality characteristics and coping strategies, to note a few of the salient studies. The benefit of multivariate investigations, particularly when employing path-analytic techniques, is the examination and discovery of the possible causal ordering of variables that would go unnoticed by the more parsimony-seeking efforts to isolate the best set of predictors to explain family dysfunction. As noted, the emergence of family problem-solving communication and family hardiness as the two resistance resources and critical predictors of family dysfunction left the investigators with an unclear picture of the role and relative importance of the family appraisal processes involving family schema and family coherence. Of central importance to this investigation, had the analysis been limited to the traditional paradigm of isolating the "best set of predictors," the central value of coherence and the relative salience of family schema, inclusive of ethnic and cultural values, would have remained relatively obscure.

Coherence emerges as being of paramount importance to explaining, at least indirectly, the variability in family dysfunction. In all three path models, coherence appeared to have a relatively prominent role in the causal ordering of variables. In the case of all Native Hawaiian families, the family's sense of coherence, influenced by family schema, has an indirect relationship to family dysfunction through two pathways: one pathway through family hardiness and family problem-solving communication and another pathway directly through family problem-solving communication.

In the case of single-parent families, family coherence, also influenced by family schema, has an indirect relationship to family dysfunction, primarily through the single pathway of family problem-solving communication and family hardiness. Finally, in the case of two-parent/adult families, family coherence has an indirect relationship to family dysfunction through the single pathway of family problem-solving communication.

These findings support three general observations. The path models support Antonovsky's (1987) thesis that one's sense of coherence as a dispositional world view expressing the dynamic feeling of confidence, comprehensibility, manageability, and meaningfulness plays an important role in facilitating adaptation. Second, the findings suggest that the sense of coherence attenuates the severity of family dysfunction or pathology. Third, the findings suggest that the sense of coherence plays a catalytic role in family resiliency by combining with and fostering the family's resistance resources, such as family hardiness (the family's dispositional resource of having a sense of commitment, control, confidence, and challenge) and family problem-solving communication (affirming style of communication) (Antonovsky, Chapter 1 in this volume). The expectation that the family's sense of coherence would be ubiquitous and have powerful direct effects on family functioning was not supported.

Family schema, an important focus of this investigation, is introduced as a dispositional factor in family appraisal, contributing to family adaptation by fostering coherence and other family resources. Family appraisal, in turn, promotes family adaptation and functioning. This generally stated hypothesis was confirmed. For Native Hawaiian families, family schema with its emphasis on an ethnic world view has three pathways through which it influences family dysfunction. In the most direct pathway, family (ethnic) schema works through or in combination with family problem solving communication. In the second pathway, family (ethnic) schema works through the family's sense of coherence and family problem solving communication. In the third and final pathway, family (ethnic) schema works through the family's sense of coherence, family hardiness and family problem-solving communication.

In the case of single-parent Native Hawaiian families, family (ethnic) schema has a single, but important, pathway to family dysfunction. Specifically, family (ethnic) schema works through the family's sense of coherence, through family problem-solving communication and through family hardiness. Interestingly, in the case of two-parent/adult Native Hawaiian families, family (ethnic) schema did not emerge as being an important variable in explaining family dysfunction.

These findings on family (ethnic) schema support three general observations. The path models support the thesis (McCubbin & McCubbin, 1993) that the family's schema, as a dispositional world view expressing the family's values, beliefs, and expectations, plays an important role in facilitating adaptation by helping to shape and foster the development of other family resistance resources so important to adaptation. Specifically, the path models for all Native Hawaiian families and for single-parent Native Hawaiian families point to the importance of family (ethnic) schema to the family's sense of coherence, family problem-solving communication, and to family hardiness.

Second, as hypothesized, the findings suggest that the family (ethnic) schema attenuates the severity of family dysfunction or pathology. Third, the findings suggest that the family (ethnic) schema plays a catalytic role in family resiliency by combining with and fostering the family's resistance resources, such as family coherence (dispositional world view of confidence, comprehensibility, manageability, and meaningfulness), family hardiness (the family's dispositional resource of having a sense of commitment, control, confidence, and challenge), and family problem-solving communication (affirming style of communication) (Antonovsky, Chapter 1). The expectation that the family's schema would be ubiquitous and having powerful direct effects on family functioning was also not supported.

The emergence of the family's schema and the family's sense of coherence as important, although indirect, predictors of family adaptation or maladaptation raises several important issues worthy of note. While family scientists have argued for the independent and unique contributions of both family schema with its ethnic emphasis and coherence, and these same scholars have hypothesized that schema would be causally linked to coherence, no empirical data have been found to support these assumptions and hypotheses. Thus the trimmed path models may be viewed as offering initial evidence for both the value and the unique contributions of these two independent elements in the family's appraisal processes. Family schema as a dispositional family factor appears to contribute to the cultivation and maintenance of the family's sense of coherence. Both of these factors, schema and coherence, appear to play indirect roles in facilitating family adaptation by contributing to internal family capabilities and patterns of functioning (family hardiness) and to family behavioral responses to the crisis situation (family problem-solving communication).

It would be instructive to restate and organize the elements and foci of these two prominent levels of appraisal, family schema and coherence (see Table 1). This clarification would foster further investigations attempting to measure and evaluate the efficacy of these processes of appraisal at the family level, as in the case of the exemplary research conducted on the sense of coherence (Antonovsky, 1987; Antonovsky & Sourani, 1988) at the individual level.

The finding that family (ethnic) schema was not among the predictors for two-parent/adult families may be viewed as surprising. One could point to the obvious limitations of the study, referencing the limitations imposed by the sample, and in so doing offer appropriate caution to any effort to generalize beyond this study to all Native Hawaiian families or to ethnic groups in general. On the other hand, the findings may be viewed as an accurate portrayal of the nature of family schema. As discussed earlier (McCubbin, Thompson, Thompson, & McCubbin, 1992) a family's schema evolves over time and is shaped, in part, by the schema and world views of its members, particularly its adult members. Given the interracial and thus multi-ethnic nature of Native Hawaiian families, the family's schema may, in part, be multicultural and not singular in its focus, even if the families identify themselves as Native Hawaiians. The values and beliefs of the Japanese, Chinese, Filipinos, and Samoans, for example, may well be integral and valued elements of a family's schema, resulting in a blended schema—a mixing that is also likely to be apparent in the children in the family unit. The two adult voices may have jointly shaped the family's schema, creating a mixed multicultural world view to guide the family's patterns of functioning. For single-parent households, the self-identification process of being labeled Native Hawaiians may be reflective of the single adult voice forceful in shaping the clear Native Hawaiian family world view. Such is the dynamic of family schema and their dispositional quality. Therefore, the family's (ethnic) schema may

Table 1
Family Schema and Coherence
Comparative Functions of Family World View

	Family Schema	Family Coherence
References (Basic)	McCubbin & McCubbin, 1993	Antonovsky & Sourani, 1988
	McCubbin, Thompson, Thompson, McCubbin, & Kasten, 1993	Antonovsky, 1994
Appraisal Functions	**Classification** process of framing the family crisis situation in terms of shared values and expectations of the extended family and the tribal structure	**Confidence**
	Spiritualization process of framing the family crisis situation in terms of shared beliefs and the goal of unity with the cosmos as a way to achieve harmony	**Meaningfulness**
	Temporalization process of framing the family crisis situation in terms of the long view and long-term consequences but also take advantage of the positive nature of the present	**Manageability**
	Contextualization (nature) process of framing the family crisis situation in terms of nature and the order of living things; harmony with nature and the land is pursued with all aspects of life	**Comprehensibility**
	Contextualization (relationships) process of framing the family crisis situation in terms of human relationships, a "we" group orientation whereby the needs of the whole rise above the needs of the individual	

not have been assessed with sufficient clarity, particularly if the measures were designed to focus on Native Hawaiian families and their values.

The differences between single-parent and two-parent/adult households were also apparent when attention focuses on the central predictive variable directly related to the criterion of family dysfunction. While problem-solving communication and hardiness are important to both family structures, they vary as to their central importance. Family hardiness emerged as the central predictor for single-parent households while family problem-solving communication was central for two-parent/adult households. In some respects the findings were predictable, although not from the outset. Single-parent households emphasize the importance of having a sense of control, commitment, confidence, and challenge over and above that of positive problem-solving communication. This situation may well be a function of the number of adult members in the household and the realistic nature of singe-parent households called upon to be self-sufficient. In contrast, having at least two parents/adult members appears to underscore the importance of family problem-solving communication over and above that of family hardiness. The findings may not be viewed as surprising even though the results run contrary to expectation.

In working to understand the relationship between family schema and family coherence, one comes face to face with the importance of culture and ethnicity, an issue this study examines both theoretically and empirically. While the obvious limitations of the study and its design set parameters around the generalizability of the findings, it is reasonable to conclude that the exploration sheds light on an important set of issues—ethnicity, schema, and coherence. While the results affirm the importance of this line of inquiry, future research must be cautious and planful. Clearly, the need for measures of family schema, ones which are sensitive to ethnic groups and cultures, cannot be overstated. Of greatest importance is the need to advance the understanding of the complex interplay between the family's schema, inclusive of culture and ethnicity, in combination with the family's sense of coherence, aiming for a greater depth of knowledge of why some families are more resilient than others in the face of adversity.

References

Antonovsky, A. (1979). *Health, stress, and coping.* San Francisco, CA: Jossey-Bass.

Antonovsky, A. (1987). *Unraveling the mystery of health.* San Francisco, CA: Jossey-Bass.

Antonovsky, A. (See Chapter 1). *The sense of coherence: An historical and future perspective.*

Antonovsky, A., & Sourani, T. (1988). Family sense of coherence and family adaptation. *Journal of Marriage and the Family, 50,* 79-92.

Bem, S. L. (1981). Gender schema theory: A cognitive account of sex typing. *Psychological Review, 88*(4), 354–364.

Blaisdell, K. (1989). Historical and cultural aspects of Native Hawaiian health. *Social Process in Hawaii, 32*(1), 1–21.

Fong, G. T., & Markus, H. (1982). Self schemata and judgments about others. *Social Cognition, 2,* 191–204.

Frankl, V. E. (1984). *Man's search for meaning: An introduction to logotherapy* (3rd ed.). New York, NY: Simon & Schuster.

Herring, R. (1989). The American native family: Dissolution by coercion. *Journal of Multicultural Counseling and Development, 17,* 4–13.

Hill, R. (1949). *Families under stress.* New York: Harper & Row.

Holahan, C., & Moos, R. (1986). Personality, coping, and family resources in stress resistance: A longitudinal analysis. *Journal of Personality and Social Psychology, 51,* 389–395.

Ishisaka, H. A. (1992). Significant differences between Pacific-Asian and Western cultures. In J. Fischer (Ed.), *East-West directions: Social work practice, tradition, and change.* Honolulu, HI: School of Social Work, University of Hawaii.

Kanahele, G. H. S. (1986). *Ku kanaka: Stand tall. A search for Hawaiian values.* Honolulu, HI: University of Hawaii Press.

Kobasa, S., Maddi, S., & Puccetti, M. (1982). Personality and exercise as buffers in the stress-illness relationship. *Journal of Behavioral Medicine, 5,* 391–404.

Lewis-Beck, M. (1980). *Applied regression.* Beverly Hills, CA: Sage.

Li, Y. Y. (1968). Ghost marriage, shamanism, and kinship behavior in rural Taiwan. In *Folk religion and the world view in the Southwestern Pacific.* Tokyo: The Keio Institute of Cultural and Linguistic Studies, Keio University.

Martin, C. L., & Halverson, C. F. (1981). A schematic processing model of sex typing and stereotyping in children. *Child Development, 52,* 1119–1134.

McCubbin, H. I., Larsen, A., & Olson, D. (1982). The family coherence index. In H. McCubbin & A. Thompson (Eds.), *Family assessment inventories for research and practice.* Madison, WI: University of Wisconsin, Family Stress, Coping, & Health Project.

McCubbin, H. I., McCubbin, M. A., & Thompson, A. I. (1992). Resiliency in families: The role of family schema and appraisal in family adaptation to crises. In T. Brubaker (Ed.), *Families in transition.* Beverly Hills, CA: Sage.

McCubbin, H. I., Patterson, J., & Glynn, T. (1982). *The social support index.* Madison, WI: University of Wisconsin, Family Stress, Coping & Health Project.

McCubbin, H. I., Thompson, A. I., Elver, K. E., & Carpenter, K. (1992). *The family (ethnicity) schema index.* Madison, WI: University of Wisconsin, Family Stress, Coping, & Health Project.

McCubbin, H. I., Thompson, E. A., & Elver, K. E. (1993). *The family dysfunction index.* Madison, WI: University of Wisconsin, Family Stress, Coping, & Health Project.

McCubbin, H. I., Thompson, E. A., Thompson, A. I., & McCubbin, M. A. (1992). Family schema, paradigms, and paradigm shifts: Components and processes of appraisal in family adaptation to crises. In A. P. Turnbull, J. M. Patterson, S. K. Bahr, D. L. Murphy, J. Marquis, & M. Blue-Banning (Eds.), *Cognitive coping research in developmental disabilities*. Baltimore, MD: Paul H. Brookes.

McCubbin, H. I., Thompson, E. A., Thompson, A. I., McCubbin, M. A., & Kasten, A. (1993). Culture, ethnicity and the family: Critical factors in childhood chronic illness and disabilities. *Journal of Pediatrics, 91*(5), 1063–1070.

McCubbin, M. A., & McCubbin, H. I. (1993). Family coping with health crises: The resiliency model of family stress, adjustment and adaptation. In C. Danielson, B. Hamel-Bissell, & P. Winstead-Fry (Eds.), *Families, health, and illness*. New York, NY: Mosby.

McCubbin, M. A., McCubbin, H. I., & Thompson, A. I. (1987). The family hardiness index. In H. McCubbin & A. Thompson (Eds.), *Family assessment inventories for research and practice*. Madison, WI: University of Wisconsin, Family Stress, Coping, & Health Project.

McCubbin, M. A., McCubbin, H. I., & Thompson, A. I. (1992). The family problem solving communication index. In H. McCubbin, A. Thompson, H. Kretzschmar, F. Smith, P. Snow, M. McEwen, K. Elver, & M. McCubbin, Family system and work environment predictors of employee health risk: A discriminant function analysis. *The American Journal of Family Therapy, 20*(2),123–144.

McCubbin, M. A., McCubbin, H. I., & Thompson, A. I. (1994). The family problem solving communication index. In A. I. Thompson, *Gender, problem solving communication, and health risk: Considerations for adult education programing*. Unpublished Doctoral Dissertation. University of Wisconsin, Madison.

McGoldrich, M. (1989). Ethnicity and the family life cycle. In B. Carter & M. McGoldrich (Eds.), *The changing family life cycle* (2nd ed.). Boston, MA: Allyn & Bacon.

Miller, L. (1969). Child rearing in the kibbutz. In J. G. Howells (Ed.), *Modern perspectives in international child psychiatry*. Edinburgh: Oliver & Boyd.

Mokuau, N. (1992). A conceptual framework for cultural responsiveness in the health field. In J. Fischer (Ed.), *East-West directions: Social work practice, tradition, and change*. Honolulu, HI: School of Social Work, University of Hawaii.

Nanda, S. (1980). *Cultural anthropology*. New York, NY: D. Van Nostrand.

Pedhazur, E. (1982). *Multiple regression in behavioral sciences*. (2nd ed.). New York, NY: Holt, Rinehart & Winston.

Pelzel, J. (1970). Japanese kinship: A comparison. In *Family and kinship in Chinese society*. Stanford, CA: Stanford University Press.

Reiss, D. (1981). *The family's construction of reality*. Cambridge, MA: Harvard University Press.

Segal, Z. (1988). Appraisal of the self-schema construct in cognitive models of depression. *Psychological Bulletin, 103*(2), 147–162.

Taylor, S. E., & Crocker, J. (1981). Schematic bases of social information processing. In E. T. Higgins, C. P. Herman, & M. P. Zanna, (Eds.), *The Ontario symposium on personality and social psychology* (Vol. 1). Hillsdale, NJ: Lawrence Erlbaum.

Tseng, W. S., & Hsu, J. (1986). The family in Micronesia. In W. S. Tseng & C. A. Less (Eds.), *Culture and mental health in Micronesia*. Honolulu, HI: Department of Psychiatry, John A. Burns School of Medicine, University of Hawaii.

Tseng, W. S., & Hsu, J. (1991). *Culture and family: Problems and therapy*. New York, NY: The Haworth Press.

Werner, E. E., Bierman, J. M., & French, F. E. (1971). *The children of Kauai: A longitudinal study from the prenatal period to age ten*. Honolulu, HI: University of Hawaii.

II. Coherence and Families at Risk

Chapter 4

Theoretical Linkages

Family Meanings and Sense of Coherence[1]

Joan M. Patterson and Ann W. Garwick

Cognitive factors, which are related to the concept of coherence, have been an integral part of most, if not all, family stress theories that have been advanced to explain family response to stressful life events. The earliest family stress model, the ABCX Model, was developed by Reuben Hill (1949, 1958) to describe families' responses to war separation and reunion. In this model, the c factor was the family's definition of the stressor event, which interacted with the stressor itself (the a factor) and the family's crisis-meeting resources (the b factor). The interaction of these three factors was used to explain whether a family experienced a crisis (the x factor).

Building on Hill's ABCX Model, McCubbin and Patterson (1982, 1983a, 1983b) introduced the Double ABCX Model to describe post-crisis adaptation in families who had husbands/fathers missing in action in the Vietnam War. This model was subsequently used to study other family stressors, such as childhood chronic illness. In the Double ABCX Model, the c factor was expanded to the cC factor and defined as the family's perception of the original stressor event and the family's perception of the pile-up of other stressors and strains (the aA factor), plus the family's perceptions of its resources (bB factor). In addition, the concept of coping was incorporated into the Double ABCX Model and was viewed as a key adaptive process in families wherein resources, perceptions, and behavior interacted. Coping was defined to include both cognitive and behavioral strategies. Coping by altering the meaning of the situation was viewed as one way families coped with an unbalanced family situation where demands exceeded capabilities. Families could reduce their pile-up of demands and/or increase their resources for managing those demands by the way they viewed their situation. For example, expecting less than perfect performance as a parent would be a way to reduce parenting strains.

In addition, a more generalized meaning construct was introduced in the Double ABCX Model: a sense of coherence. Influenced by Antonovsky's (1979) work, a family's sense of coherence was defined as "the family's ability to balance control and trust—that is, knowing when to take charge and when to trust in or believe in the authority and/or power of others."

In an effort to emphasize *adaptation* as the central outcome of the stress process, the Double ABCX Model was called the Family Adjustment and Adaptation Response (FAAR) Model (Patterson, 1988, 1989a). This renaming emphasizes potential positive outcomes, which is consistent with the many studies now focusing on family and individual resilience, or what Antonovsky (1979, 1987) called a salutogenic perspective.

In the FAAR Model, two levels of meaning were differentiated: situational meanings and global meanings (Patterson, 1988, 1989a). Situational meanings referred to the individual's and family's subjective definition of their demands, their capabilities, and these two factors relative to each other. Global meanings were defined as transcending any given situation and comprising a more stable cognitive set encompassing beliefs about the relationships of family members to each other and the relationship of the family unit to the larger community. The work of Antonovksy (1979, 1987), as well as the work of Reiss (1981), Kobasa, Maddi, and Kahn (1982), and Fisher, Ransom, Kokes, Weiss, and Phillips (1984), was integrated in proposing five conceptual dimensions of the global meanings construct: shared purpose, collectivity, frame-ability, relativism, and shared control. The conceptual linkages between these five dimensions and the work of the four theoreticians are presented in Table 1.

These five dimensions of global family meanings have not been operationalized and tested with regard to family adaptation. However, through qualitative analyses of research interviews with families who have children with chronic illnesses and disabilities, there is evidence for each of these dimensions of family meanings. (See Patterson, 1993, for a discussion of these qualitative findings.)

In an effort to more fully understand how families are able to adapt to the chronic hardships and challenges associated with having a member with disability or chronic illness, the research proto-

Table 1
Comparison of Family Global Meanings
to Other Theoretical Models of the Meanings Construct

Family Global Meanings Conceptual Dimensions	Family Level		Individual Level	
	Family Paradigm (Reiss, 1981)	World View (Fisher et al., 1984)	Coherence (Antonovsky, 1979)	Hardiness (Kobasa et al., 1982)
Shared purpose: having family values, goals, and commitments that are shared; having a family ideology and identity			Meaningfulness: having values and commitments of emotional significance	Commitment vs. hopelessness and alienation in life
Collectivity: recognizing that the individual or family is part of something larger; a "we" vs. "I" orientation	Coordination: solidarity of unit: sensitivity to each other	Consensus vs. toleration of differences	Comprehensibility: life is ordered and just; it has continuity	
Frameability: viewing life situations optimistically and with hope as well as realism		Optimism vs. pessimism		Challenge: change is normative and a growth opportunity, not a disaster
Relativism: viewing life in the context of present circumstances, not in terms of absolutes	Closure: open to new information; here-and-now focus	Variety vs. sameness		
Shared control: balance of personal and family control with trust in others	Configuration: sense of mastery and belief that family can learn and gain control	Security vs. insecurity	Manageability: belief that things will work out by one's efforts and with help from others	Control: belief that one can influence experiences, not be powerless

From Patterson, J. M. (1988). Families experiencing stress. The FAAR Model. *Family Systems Medicine, 6(2),* 202–237.

cols generally ask families to tell their *stories* about what has happened to them in the wake of the diagnosis of chronic illness (Garwick, 1991; Patterson, 1989b; Patterson, Budd, Goetz, & Warwick, 1993; Patterson & Leonard, 1994; Patterson, Leonard, & Titus, 1992; Patterson, McCubbin, & Warwick, 1990). The stories families tell incorporate cognitive factors that go beyond the definition the family gives to the stressor (that is, the onset of disability) as families search for meaning in a life that, in many ways, has been shattered by the presence of added demands, multiple losses, and changed routines, roles, and expectations. From our research, it appears that there are multiple levels of family meanings. Furthermore, the meanings a family holds are often reconstructed after the experience of chronic stress, and conversely, the different levels of family meanings influence and shape the processes and outcomes of family adaptation to stressful situations.

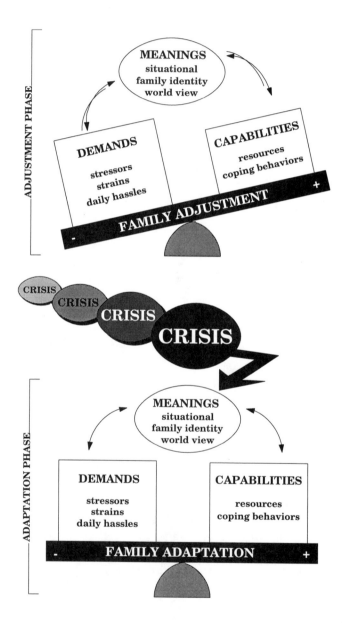

Based on these analyses, we propose that families, as a whole, construct and share meanings on three levels: (1) specific stressful situations; (2) their identity as a family; and (3) their view of the world (see Figure 1). These meanings represent three levels of abstraction and stability that are dynamically interrelated. The global meaning construct in the earlier versions of the FAAR Model has been redefined as family identity (level two) and family world view (level three). The family's world view is the most abstract, usually implicit, and often something the family is not consciously aware of nor readily able to articulate. It evolves slowly and is the most stable. It provides the framework for both the family's identity and for their style of defining stressful situations as they are encountered. Situational meanings are the most concrete and more immediately available in the family's consciousness. They are also the most responsive to change. From observations of families having a member with chronic illness, a major part of the adaptation process is defining the situation, attributing meaning to the illness event that has imposed itself on their lives. This is often followed by a change at the other two levels of meaning: The family's identity changes in a way that allows for the illness and its associated hardships to have a place in their family life, and this, in turn, often brings forth a change in the family's world view or how they see themselves in relation to the rest of the world.

Three Levels of Family Meaning

Level One: Situational Meanings

The first level of family meanings still involves situational meanings as defined in the FAAR Model (Patterson, 1988, 1989a). As family members talk with each other about a stressful situation, they begin constructing meanings about the stressor event or the pile-up of demands as well as their capabilities as a family to manage the demands. It may take time for a shared definition to emerge, which is part of the process of family adaptation (McCubbin & Patterson, 1983b). Because family members share social space, time, and experience, they influence each other in their ways of appraising situations. In cohesive families, joined by bonds of unity, there is likely to be mutual influence in arriving at these appraisals. It is highly unlikely that agreement will always occur among all family members, and it probably is not necessary for families to always agree and still function well. A shared definition does not necessarily imply agreement among family members. Family members may agree to disagree. There are many domains of family life where individuals act independently (although families have implicit rules for how much independence is tolerated, which is part of our second level of family meanings). However, when a coordinated family behavioral response is necessary for effective functioning, the need for agreement on situational definitions will be more important.

In families who have a member with chronic illness or disability, there are numerous examples of the role of situational meanings in the coping and adaptation process. In one study of families who have a child that is medically fragile (Patterson & Leonard, 1994), parents frequently reported the positive aspects of having a child with intense medical needs: the child's warmth and responsiveness; the tenacity and perseverance of the child to endure, making the parents want to invest more of their effort; the closeness felt in the family unit, pulling together to manage; the assertiveness and skill that they as parents developed in response to caring for the child and learning to deal with multiple providers and third-party payers; and the growth in empathy and kindness in their other children. In other words, parents selectively attended to the positive aspects of their child's personality and behaviors while minimizing the limitations or health problems. In addition, many parents emphasized the growth and development of the self or the family unit in response to the challenges.

Level Two: Family Identity

The second level of meaning refers to how families view themselves—the family identity. This global view about family relationships is more stable than situational meanings about demands and capabilities. How a family defines itself is reflected in both its structure (who is in the family) and its functioning (the patterns of relationship linking members to each other). Implicit rules of relationship guide family members in how they are to relate to each other. These rules include (1) definitions of external boundaries (who is in the family) and internal boundaries (for example, encouraging subsystem alliances), (2) role assignments for accomplishing family tasks, and (3) rules and norms for interactional behavior.

The construct of family identity is more abstract than situational meanings and if asked, family members probably would be unable to articulate their identity per se. However, it is through routines and rituals that family identity is developed and maintained and it is through observing these patterned interactions that an outsider may be able to gain insight into a family's identity. This construct builds on the work of several family scholars who have examined the role of family rituals in maintaining a family's sense of itself as a collective whole, in establishing shared rules, attitudes, and ways of relating, and in maintaining continuity and stability in family functioning over time (Bennett, Wolin, & McAvity, 1988; Bossard & Boll, 1950; Imber-Black, Roberts, & Whiting, 1988; Wolin & Bennett, 1984).

Included in the many types of family rituals are rituals for family boundary changes, such as when a child is born, when someone gets married, or when a family member dies. When family boundaries are *not* clear and the family identity is challenged, there is usually added strain that increases the pile-up of demands for the family.

Pauline Boss's (1977, 1987, 1988) work on boundary ambiguity is particularly relevant to this second level of family meanings. Boss emphasized two types of presence that members have in a family: physical presence and psychological presence. When there is incongruence between a family member's physical presence and psychological presence, the resultant ambiguity increases family distress; the boundary about who is "in" the family and who is "out" is unclear. Families experiencing chronic illness are particularly vulnerable to this kind of boundary ambiguity. For example, the birth of a premature infant who spends many months in a neonatal intensive care unit is an example of psychological presence but physical absence in the family system, which may be exacerbated even further by uncertainty about the infant's survival. Another example, related to the functional loss associated with some disabilities, can be seen in a family member who is cognitively impaired or demented. Is a person with Alzheimer's Disease, who is physically present but psychologically absent, "in" or "out" of the family system? Chronic illness or disability can and often does have a significant impact on a family's identity, challenging an old identity and calling for something new.

In her research on family caregiving, Garwick (1991) found that each family she studied had a unique construction of the reality of living with a member in the early stages of Alzheimer's Disease. The disease clearly disrupted the fabric of everyday life in these families. In listening to a family talk together about this impact, it was possible to identify the family's meaning of the ex-perience and a sense of their own changed identity in relation to it.

A family system also establishes a role structure for accomplishing basic tasks, such as earning the family income and providing child care, meal preparation, and household maintenance. Families vary in how segregated (each gender performing separate roles) or egalitarian (both genders sharing most roles) they are. When the family boundaries expand to include a new member or contract when someone leaves home or dies, these roles often have to be renegotiated. Similarly, the diagnosis of a chronic illness often calls for role changes.

In one study of families with a medically fragile child (Patterson & Leonard, 1994), many mothers had to leave the work force partially or totally in order to care for their ill child. This often led to fathers working longer hours to earn more income and/or to assure job security. In other words, bringing their child home led to a reorganization in the family's roles and rules, which impacted how the family defined itself. This family definition of itself, which we call the family identity, is more stable than level one situational meanings of stressors and capabilities, but it, too, can change over time.

Level Three: Family World View

It is at the third level of family meaning that Antonovsky's concept of coherence is particularly relevant. The third level of meaning focuses on the family's orientation toward the world, how they interpret reality, what their core assumptions are about their environment, as well as their existential beliefs, such as the family's purpose and place in life. This is the most abstract of the three levels of meaning and most families probably would not be able to directly report their world view if asked. It is important to remember that the world-view construct is much less about the content of beliefs and more about the process of relating or orienting to others. The construct of world view has been applied to persons, to families, and to cultures, recognizing that the views of each system are in part shaped by the larger context in which it is embedded.

At the level of an individual person, Antonovsky (1979, 1987) has suggested that a *sense of coherence* (SOC) is a personal trait associated with better individual health. He defined coherence as "the pervasive, enduring, though dynamic feeling of confidence that internal and external environments are predictable and there is a high probability that things will work out as well as can reasonably be expected" (Antonovsky, 1979, p. 123).

In addition to the work of Antonovsky, our conceptualization of the family world view has been influenced by the work of theorists who have focused on this global orientation as a way to explain what helps persons adapt to or manage challenging circumstances in life. In Table 1, the dimensions of Antonovsky's coherence concept are presented in relationship to the theoretical work of Reiss (1981), Fisher et al. (1984), and Kobasa et al. (1982). While there appears to be considerable similarity among these theorists in what constitutes the dimensions of world view, the unit of analysis—individual versus family—is different. Kobasa, in operationalizing the personal hardiness construct, clearly focused only on the individual. Antonovsky's work has related primarily to individuals, although he has suggested that family units can also be assessed as to their degree of coherence (Antonovsky & Sourani, 1988). From Antonovsky's perspective, family coherence involves both the degree to which the family unit (as well as the rest of the world) is seen as coherent and the degree to which family members share this orientation. In the first instance, the focus is on one individual's perception about the family unit as one aspect of the social world. In the second instance, family coherence seems to be defined as a combination of individual member orientations, especially the degree of consensus among family members.

Ransom, Fisher, and Terry (1992) have recently published some of their work on the relationship of family world view to health outcomes. They operationalized the family world-view construct, focusing on the husband-wife dyad as the unit of analysis, and used both spouses' self-report scores in an inter-battery factor analysis to create a family world-view score. In contrast, Reiss (1981), whose focus is also the collective family, has not used self-report methods to assess the family paradigm. Rather, his research group used a family interaction task, called the card-sort procedure, where family members work together to solve a problem. They are scored on the three paradigm dimensions of configuration, coordination, and closure based on their process of interacting during the card-sort problem-solving task.

Two important questions emerge from a review of this work. Is there a family world view that is the property of the collective family? If so, how does one measure it? Based on qualitative research with families who have a chronically ill member, preliminary evidence points to the existence of a collective family world view. This has been observed in conjoint family interviews, where the family members talk with each other about their ways of adapting to their changed life circumstances. Together, they talk about learning to let go, to trust each other and members of the health care team. At the same time, they talk about taking responsibility for managing their child's care and for teaching him or her how to take age-appropriate responsibility for his or her own care, for knowing when they can lean on each other for emotional support and tangible help, and for recognizing when they need to advocate and coordinate care with other service providers. Collectively, families often share their belief in the strength of their interpersonal bonds, their sense of being there for each other, and their belief that things will work out. They have a sense of themselves as a group, the ways they complement each other in their abilities, and how they share responsibility for their situation and draw strength and fortitude from each other. Perhaps it is the chronic nature of these illnesses along with the unrelenting demands that contribute to the group's shared orientation.

These results do not imply that all families have a shared, positive, hopeful world view or even that this is the case for the "best" families. Families can certainly have a world view that is pessimistic, cynical, or distrusting of others. Most of the dimensions of world view that have been posited by the theoreticians noted above acknowledge that these dimensions are bipolar or continuous, with one end usually being viewed as more optimal for adaptation to life. So the family's world view could vary along each dimension. The multidimensional nature of a world view would suggest several different types of families. For example, Reiss (1981) describes consensus-sensitive families as high on coordination and high on closure, and environment-sensitive families as high on configuration and low on closure.

The method utilized to learn about the variability in family world views has been through qualitative analysis of the language used in conjoint family interviews, where family members talk with each other about issues of consequence to them, such as a member's chronic illness and its impact on their lives. Due to the interest on a *family* world view, this chapter has emphasized an orientation and meanings that the family shares as a collective.

Meanings as Family-Level Constructs

Focusing on the family system as the unit of analysis has led to the idea that family meanings are distinct from the meanings held by an individual family member.[2] Furthermore, family meanings are distinct from consensus between individually held meanings. *Family meanings* are the interpretations, images, and views that have been collectively constructed by family members as they interact with each other; as they share time, space, and life experience; and as they talk with each other and dialogue about these experiences. They are the family's social constructions, the product of their interactions. They belong to no one member, but to the family as a whole. Berger and Luckmann's (1966) classic text, *The Social Construction of Reality*, provided the theoretical grounding for the premise that all meanings are created and maintained through social interaction. Berger and Luckmann argued that images of reality are created by human actors in the process of social interaction. Meanings are collectively constructed for these images and these meanings are expressed through language. According to cybernetician Humberto Maturana, people survive by fitting in with one another in social space, what he calls "structural coupling in a surrounding medium" (Dell, 1985). To maintain this coupling and to coordinate complex interaction patterns, implicit and shared assumptions and meanings emerge about individuals in relation to each other, and about individuals as units in relation to systems beyond their boundaries. This structural coupling is, in essence, an emergent family, which, over time, evolves an increasingly complex set of images, assumptions, and meanings to guide day-to-day behavior. Reiss (1981), who eloquently elaborated upon the theoretical basis for family constructions of reality, emphasized that shared explanatory systems play a crucial role in organizing and maintaining group process. Shared meanings reduce ambiguity and uncertainty about a complex array of stimuli and make coordination of response among group members possible. This, in turn, contributes to group stability. It also creates an identity for the group, which sets it apart from its context, creating a boundary between who is in and who is out of the group that we are calling the "family."

Reiss (1981) emphasized that these family constructions of reality emerge from the family's shared process and that this process is different from simple agreement or consensus among family members. In other words, the presence of disagreement does not imply the absence of sharing. If one were to ask a single family member to report about his or her family's meanings, that person's version would be his or her own story; the "family myth" (Wamboldt & Wolin, 1989) or the "represented family" (Reiss, 1989) is based on what one individual has internalized and can recall from his or her immersion in family experiences. The notion of consensus or disagreement between individual subjective accounts would be relevant to the report of one family member. This subjective account, or multiple individual accounts, should be differentiated from what actually happens when family members are engaged with each other—what Reiss (1989) called the "practicing family" and what Wamboldt and Wolin (1989) termed "family reality."

Wamboldt and Wolin (1989), who have been studying these family-level constructs, pointed out a critical difference between *interaction* and *transaction* that is relevant to family constructions. All interaction is not transaction. Interaction becomes transaction when the persons engaged in the interaction undergo internal change, allowing for individual beliefs, emotions, and behaviors to be modified during the interaction process. There is a kind of reciprocal transformation and something new is created or emerges. It belongs to no one person, but rather is a product of their transaction.

Measuring Family Meanings

How then can family meanings be measured? As suggested by the above discussion, different theoreticians and researchers have used different methods to measure family-level variables. In 1986, Ransom offered the following typology for classifying family data:

> *Type I:* data are based on some characteristic possessed by the family unit or one of its members and are usually categorical (e.g., single-parent family or family with a child with a handicap).
>
> *Type II:* data are derived from an individual family member about the family unit and are obtained by methods such as a self-report questionnaire or an interview. There are two kinds of Type II data: (a) information obtained from only one family member (e.g., mother), and (b) the same information obtained from two or more family members and then combined to create a relational score (e.g., couple discrepancy score).
>
> *Type III:* data are derived from family interaction in naturalistic or laboratory settings where (a) an outside observer rates or counts aspects of family process, or (b) a behavioral product score is derived directly from the interaction itself.

Examining the methods described above, Antonovsky and Sourani (1988) used Type IIa and IIb with husband and wife completion of a self-report questionnaire about coherence. Ransom et al.

(1992) used something approximating Type IIb when they combined husband and wife self-reports in a factor analysis. Reiss's (1981) card-sort procedure for assessing family paradigm is a Type IIIb method. Our method of qualitatively analyzing family narratives has varied depending on whether parents are being interviewed individually (Type II) or the family is being interviewed conjointly (Type III).

It is also interesting to consider the relationship between the levels of meaning we have proposed with regard to measurement. If we examine the beliefs or world view held by individual family members, the amount of consensus between members could vary from high to low. The family's rules of relationship (level two meaning) essentially determine the degree to which disagreement between family members on important matters like a world view will be tolerated. The family's identity will influence how synthetic its world view is. A family that is high on the need to agree, to coordinate and be cohesive, will relate to the world outside itself in a more synthetic, integrated way, and their world view will be more organized. In contrast, a family whose rules of relationship emphasize uniqueness, difference, and autonomy vis-à-vis each other will probably have a family world view that appears more disorganized to the observer because members will be oriented in different directions. In fact, in the aftermath of a major stressor and crisis, families often appear disorganized, as though members have differing orientations. In an earlier article, McCubbin and Patterson (1983b) argued that part of the process of adaptation following a crisis involved developing a shared family view of the situation. This article preceded the differentiation of meanings at three levels and hence referred only to situational meanings. However, one might speculate on the relationship between the three levels of family meaning, particularly whether and how they change in response to stressful life experience.

The Process of Changing Meanings

Clearly the three levels of family meanings are interrelated. World view includes an orientation, values, and beliefs that influence how relationships both within and outside the family are structured. Thus world view influences the formation of the family identity. Both family identity and world view will influence how a given situation is viewed. And moving in the other direction, a newly experienced event, especially one that is more severe, disastrous, or victimizing, is likely to lead to changed relationship structures and may even alter the family world view.

Several theorists have articulated a meaning-making process that evolves from an individual's experience of disastrous events. Janoff-Bulman and Frieze's (1983) assumptive world-view perspective held that persons see the world as benevolent and meaningful and the self as worthwhile. Disastrous events shatter this world view, which must be rebuilt to incorporate the negative events. In contrast, Taylor (1983) argued that persons who experience disastrous events adapt by selectively distorting negative views of self, relationships, and the world as a way to reduce the threat; they build illusions containing meaning, mastery, and self-enhancing cognitions. Thompson and Janigian (1988) proposed a life-scheme framework, which provides a sense of order and purpose in life. When negative events challenge the life scheme, persons search for new meanings and purpose and challenge their life scheme.

What evidence is there that families engage in a similar search for meaning? Research with families who have a medically fragile child has provided evidence that some parents change their world view regarding the meaning and purpose of their life so that it is consonant with the reality of their behavioral and emotional investment in their child. There may be too much cognitive dissonance for a parent to spend time and energy caring for a medically fragile child while viewing this as an undesirable person or set of circumstances. Some parents join together with other parents of children with disabilities to advocate for their rights, to improve services, and to change social policies. Many report that the meaning of life changes as parents develop more concern for living in the present, caring about people, and appreciating little things.

When a child is first diagnosed with chronic illness, family members may react in disbelief and deny the doctor's prognosis. They often search for a cause—"why did this happen?" Their present world view and their family identity will likely influence the definition they give this stressor—"we are being punished for our misdeeds," "the doctors made a mistake," "you didn't take care of yourself during the pregnancy," or "God knows that our family can handle this." In addition to interpretations about what caused the disease, the family will also have or develop expectations about who is responsible for managing the illness. A family's world view may influence this situational definition of capabilities for managing a stressor event. A family's orientation may vary from internal control, to external control via chance, to external control via powerful others (Levenson, 1981). This orientation about control has implications for behavioral compliance with treatment regimens and the relationships families develop with health providers. Belief in chance may result in marginal connections to the health care system. Belief in powerful others may lead to searches for cures or to passivity in managing disease processes. High internal control may lead to more active management.

At the second level of meaning, the family's identity will be impacted by the presence of illness or disability. Normal family regulatory processes will be disrupted (Gonzalez, Steinglass, & Reiss, 1989; Reiss, Steinglass, & Howe, 1993; Steinglass & Horan, 1987). Routines for managing the illness tasks, role reallocations, and rule changes will need to occur. The way in which the family restructures itself to accommodate the illness demands may have an impact on the family's identity and sense of purpose. Gonzalez et al. (1989) have emphasized that in some families faced with chronic illness, there may be a tendency to direct a disproportionate share of their resources toward the illness needs, reducing resources needed for normative family needs. This skew can lead to a family illness identity—"the diabetic family" versus the family who has a diabetic member.

If this skew toward the illness happens, family members may change their world view (the third level of meaning), redefining goals and purpose for their lives. The illness becomes the centerpiece for organizing all family activity. It is possible, of course, that one parent may orient this way, making the child with chronic illness the central focus, while the other parent resists, trying to maintain more balance in family functioning. Reiss and Oliveri (1985) have pointed out how stressful experience, especially a crisis, is likely to lead to a breakdown in a shared family paradigm. When the parents' orientations diverge, family members could change their relationship identity and agree to disagree, accepting less coordinated family behavior. Conversely, the divergence in relationship rules could extend to other values and beliefs, creating an inability to agree on a family relationship identity and ultimately resulting in the dissolution of the family system. In essence, family breakdown and dissolution occur when family members can no longer sufficiently agree on the rules for their relationship. The structure becomes uncoupled and two separate family units result.

However, the divergence in family members' orientations may cause the family system to restructure in a way that makes it stronger. It is a principle of physics that to "harden" steel, you place stress on it. In the sample of families with a medically fragile child, it was striking how frequently parents reported that having and caring for this child pulled their family unit together and made them stronger. This response may reflect the processes of coping and adaptation via shared social construing. Disastrous events shatter expectations, goals, and even world views, resulting in uncertainty and ambiguity. Individuals turn to their significant others in search of emotional comfort and an explanation for what is happening. The loss of a sense of personal control leads to joining more closely with others. Steinglass and Horan (1987) reported that families often pull together, giving up individual world views for a shared one. Support groups also serve this function for persons experiencing major illness. Part of the coping process involves enlarging the context—"We are not just a family who has a member with a disease; but a family with a history, an identity, and values who has a member with a disease; and we live in relationships with significant others and in a world where others have this disease, too."

Perhaps a synthetic family world view prior to the occurrence of a major stressor guides a family in crisis to reorganize its internal relationships more efficiently and satisfactorily. Or, as has been argued about chronic illness, perhaps the nature of the stressor and crisis is such that some family members change their world view. An important research question that has emerged is whether a synthetic family world view enhances adaptation to chronic stress.

Conclusion

This chapter has argued for the importance of the social context, particularly the family, in the search for meaning in response to crises. Theory suggests that there are at least three levels of family meaning that are interrelated and that each of these levels influences the process of family adaptation to stressful experience.

Families are complex social units and they vary widely in their adaptive capacities. One of the challenges social scientists face is to extend their understanding and describe the range of this variability. One of the most interesting questions remaining to be answered is why some families develop positive, adaptive beliefs and meanings and others do not. Further studies are needed to understand how families share and construct meanings about illness and disability. Longitudinal studies of family process are needed to learn how individuals and families successfully change meanings in the context of their natural support systems. In addition to continuing to build family stress theory, such findings would contribute to improved practices in working with families who are adapting to chronic stress, particularly the presence of disability or chronic illness.

Notes

1. Preparation of this chapter was supported by the National Institute on Disability and Rehabilitation Research Grant #H133890012.

2. *Family* should be thought of in the broadest possible sense as that group of persons with whom one shares a bond of connection by virtue of blood, marriage, adoption, or long-term commitment. Any person is likely to have membership in more than one family over the life course. For example, we are born into a family of origin; we create a new family of procreation at the time of marriage; and perhaps create a stepfamily at the time of remarriage, etc. In the case of chronic illness and disability, it is also quite probable that a *caregiving family* may emerge, distinct and separate from these other families. Most people have several families and our discussion is relevant to the widest definition of family structure.

References

Antonovsky, A. (1979). *Health, stress, and coping.* San Francisco: Jossey-Bass.

Antonovsky, A. (1987). *Unraveling the mystery of health: How people manage stress and stay well.* San Francisco: Jossey-Bass.

Antonovsky, A., & Sourani, T. (1988). Family sense of coherence and family adaptation. *Journal of Marriage and the Family, 50,* 79–92.

Bennett, L., Wolin, S., & McAvity, K. (1988). Family identity, ritual, and myth. A cultural perspective on life cycle transitions. In K. Falicov (Ed.), *Family transitions.* New York: Guilford Press.

Berger, P. L., & Luckmann, T. (1966). *The social construction of reality.* New York: Doubleday.

Boss, P. (1977). A clarification of the concept of psychological father presence in families experiencing ambiguity of boundary. *Journal of Marriage and the Family, 39,* 141–151.

Boss, P. (1987). Family stress. In M. Sussman & S. Steinmetz (Eds.), *Handbook of marriage and the family.* New York: Plenum.

Boss, P. G. (1988). *Family stress management.* Newbury Park, CA: Sage.

Bossard, J., & Boll, E. (1950). *Ritual in family living.* Philadelphia: University of Pennsylvania Press.

Dell, P. F. (1985). Understanding Bateson and Maturana: Toward a biological foundation for the social sciences. *Journal of Marital and Family Therapy, 11,* 1–20.

Fisher, L., Ransom, D., Kokes, R., Weiss, R., & Phillips, S. (1984, October). *The California family health project.* Paper presented at the Family and Health Preconference Workshop of the National Council on Family Relations, San Francisco, CA.

Garwick, A. (1991). Shared family perceptions of life with dementia of the Alzheimer's type (Doctoral dissertation, University of Minnesota). *Dissertation Abstracts International, 52-05A,* 1098.

Gonzalez, S., Steinglass, P., & Reiss, D. (1989). Putting the illness in its place: Discussion groups for families with chronic medical illnesses. *Family Process, 28,* 69–87.

Hill, R. (1949). *Families under stress.* New York: Harper.

Hill, R. (1958). Generic features of families under stress. *Social Casework, 49,* 139-150.

Imber-Black, E., Roberts, J., & Whiting, R. (Eds.). (1988). *Rituals and family therapy.* New York: Norton Press.

Janoff-Bulman, R., & Frieze, I. H. (1983). A theoretical perspective for understanding reactions to victimization. *Journal of Social Issues, 39,* 1–17.

Kobasa, S., Maddi, S., & Kahn, S. (1982). Hardiness and health: A prospective study. *Journal of Personality and Social Psychology, 42,* 168–177.

Levenson, H. (1981). Differentiating among internality, powerful others, and change. In H. Lefcourt (Ed.), *Research with the locus of control construct. Vol. I: Assessment methods.* New York: Academic Press.

McCubbin, H. I., & Patterson, J. M. (1982). Family adaptation to crises. In H. I. McCubbin, A. E. Cauble, & J. M. Patterson (Eds.), *Family stress, coping, and social support.* Springfield, IL: Charles C. Thomas.

McCubbin, H. I., & Patterson, J. M. (1983a). Family stress and adaptation to crises: A double ABCX model of family behavior. In D. Olson & B. Miller (Eds.), *Family studies review yearbook.* Beverly Hills, CA: Sage.

McCubbin, H. I., & Patterson, J. M. (1983b). The family stress process: The double ABCX model of family adjustment and adaptation. *Marriage and Family Review, 6,* 7–37.

Patterson, J. M. (1988). Families experiencing stress. The family adjustment and adaptation response model. *Family Systems Medicine, 6(2),* 202–237.

Patterson, J. M. (1989a). Illness beliefs as a factor in patient-spouse adaptation to coronary artery disease. *Family Systems Medicine, 7(4),* 428–442.

Patterson, J. M. (1989b). A family stress model: The family adjustment and adaptation response. In C. Ramsey (Ed.), *The science of family medicine.* New York: Guilford.

Patterson, J. M. (1993). The role of family meanings in adaptation to chronic illness and disability. In A. Turnbull, J. Patterson, S. Behr, D. Murphy, J. Marquis, & M. Blue-Banning (Eds.), *Cognitive coping, families, and disability.* Baltimore: Paul Brookes.

Patterson, J. M., Budd, J., Goetz, D., & Warwick, W. (1993). Family correlates of a ten-year pulmonary health trend in cystic fibrosis. *Pediatrics, 91,* 383–389.

Patterson, J. M., & Leonard, B. J. (1994). Caregiving and children. In E. Kahana, D. E. Biegel, & M. Wykle (Eds.), *Family caregiving across the lifespan* (pp. 133–158). Newbury Park, CA: Sage.

Patterson, J. M., Leonard, B. J., & Titus, J. C. (1992). Home care for medically fragile children: Impact on family health and well-being. *Developmental and Behavioral Pediatrics, 13*(4), 248–255.

Patterson, J. M., McCubbin, H. I., & Warwick, W. (1990). The impact of family functioning on health changes in children with cystic fibrosis. *Social Science and Medicine, 31*(2), 159–164.

Ransom, D. C. (1986). Research on the family in health, illness, and care—State of the art. *Family Systems Medicine, 4,* 329–336.

Ransom, D. C., Fisher, L., & Terry, H. E. (1992). The California family health project: II. Family world view and adult health. *Family Process, 31,* 251–267.

Reiss, D. (1981). *The family's construction of reality.* Cambridge, MA: Harvard University Press.

Reiss, D. (1989). The represented and practicing family: Contrasting visions of family continuity. In A. Sameroff & R. Emde (Eds.), *Relationship disturbances in early childhood. A developmental approach.* New York: Basic Books.

Reiss, D., Steinglass, P., & Howe, G. (1993). The family's organization around the illness. In R. Cole & D. Reiss (Eds.), *How do families cope with chronic illness?* Hillsdale, NJ: Lawrence Erlbaum.

Steinglass, P., & Horan, M. (1987). Families and chronic medical illness. *Journal of Psychopathology and the Family, 3,* 127–142.

Taylor, S. (1983). Adjustment to threatening events: A theory of cognitive adaptation. *American Psychologist, 38,* 624–630.

Thompson, S., & Janigian, A. (1988). Life schemes: A framework for understanding the search for meaning. *Journal of Social and Clinical Psychology, 7,* 260–280.

Wamboldt, F., & Wolin, S. (1989). Reality and myth in family life: Changes across generations. *Journal of Psychotherapy and the Family, 4,* 141–165.

Wolin, S., & Bennett, L. (1984). Family rituals. *Family Process, 23,* 401–420.

Chapter 5

Sense of Coherence and the Stress-Illness Relationship Among Employees

A Prospective Study

Lisa M. Fiorentino and Richard J. Pomazal

The relationship between stress and illness has received considerable attention. The relationship between stressful life events and subsequent illness, however, is far from straightforward (Antonovsky, 1987; Monat & Lazarus, 1985; Schafer, 1987). The current trend in stress-illness research is the examination of stress resistance variables. Prompted in part by the significant but rather weak relationship between stress and illness, this salutogenic orientation examines factors that keep individuals healthy despite the increased risk associated with highly stressful lives. Over recent years, numerous stress-resistant and health-inducing variables have been explored. These include: health practices, social support, coping strategies, and personal characteristics.

Salutogenic Factors

The relationship between health practices and wellness is self-evident and well established. Belloc and Breslow (1972) found that good health practices (regular meals, adequate sleep, near-average weight, physical activity, and avoidance of smoking and excessive drinking) were positively related to health. The relationship between exercise and health, and exercise, diet, and health, is also well documented (Brown, 1991; Koniz-Booher & Koniz, 1986; Williams, 1990).

The deleterious effects of chemical dependency are well established (Smith-Dijulio, 1990).

Moreover, numerous psychosocial resources have been shown to have a buffering effect on the stress-illness relationship (Broadhead, 1983; Turner, 1983), although exactly *how* they operate is still a question (Reis, 1984). Berkman and Syme (1979) conducted a nine-year follow-up study assessing the mediating effect of social contact (marriage, contact with friends and relatives, church membership, formal and informal group membership) on mortality. Kobasa and Puccetti (1983) reported a significant interaction among perceived boss support, stress, and illness. Male executives experiencing high stress reported lower symptomatology if they perceived their superior as supportive. Social support has also been shown to be related to decreased depression (Aneshensel & Ferichs, 1982) and reduced occupational stress (LaRocco, House, & French, 1980).

Various coping strategies also reduce the effects of stress (Menaghan, 1983). Folkman, Lazarus, Gruen, and DeLongis (1985) found that *actively* approaching a problem with a plan of action, as opposed to avoiding or distancing oneself from a problem, is positively related to health status. Meichenbaum and Cameron (1983) focused on the benefits of cognitive and behavioral coping skills—self-relaxation, defining problems as challenges, and creating a sense of curiosity and adventure. Ellis's (1973) rational-emotive approach to therapy has been found to be quite effective in dealing with negative emotional consequences (stress) initiated by precipitating events. Ellis encouraged actively disputing one's irrational beliefs about how life "should" or "must" be.

Finally, solitude, hobbies, and recreation can also serve as stress-managing techniques. Not only do they remove one from a stressful environment, but they also allow for diversion of attention and a chance for renewal (Schafer, 1987).

The Sense of Coherence

The buffering effect of personality variables on the stress-illness relationship has also received considerable attention: Kobasa (Kobasa, 1979; Kobasa & Puccetti, 1983) investigated the mediating effects of a "hardiness" dimension; Ben-Sira (1985) demonstrated the stress-buffering effects of a personality disposition termed "potency"; Folkman et al. (1985) focused on "mastery"; whereas Boyce, Schaefer, and Uitti (1985) investigated a construct that they termed "sense of permanence."

Using a salutogenic or health orientation, Antonovsky (1979, 1987) has researched the health-inducing attributes of one's sense of coherence. The sense of coherence (SOC) is a way of seeing the world and oneself within the world. A supposedly stable element of the personality structure, the SOC is shaped, reinforced, and refined throughout one's life. The stronger the SOC, the more adequately an individual is able to cope with ever-present stressors. A strong SOC lowers the probability that tension will be transformed into stress. Life is full of complexities, complications, failures, and frustrations, yet individuals with a strong SOC possess a feeling of confidence that things will, by and large, work out well. A strong SOC also provides the basis for participation in health-promoting behaviors and avoidance of health-endangering activities. People with a weak SOC have neither the motivation nor the cognitive basis for successful coping.

According to Antonovsky (1984), one's sense of coherence encompasses three components: (1) *comprehensibility*—the extent to which an individual perceives stimuli that confront him/her as making cognitive sense, that is, ordered and consistent rather than disordered and chaotic; (2) *manageability*—the extent to which an individual perceives he/she has resources at his/her disposal (or at the disposal of legitimate others upon whom one can count) to meet the demands posed by stimuli; and (3) *meaningfulness*—the extent to which an individual feels life makes sense, that at least some problems are seen as challenges and are worth investigating. The relationship between these three components is still unclear. Antonovsky (1987, p. 86) himself stated that they are "inextricably intertwined" and that examination of the nature of their interrelationship remains unfinished business.

Although the SOC concept is still in the early stages of development, recent investigations have shown support for its health-promoting properties in children (Margalit, 1985), adolescents (Antonovsky & Sagy, 1986), and production workers (Fiorentino, 1986).

Combinations

More recently, the importance of assessing the effect of combinations of variables on the stress-illness relationship has been recognized. To better understand how individuals remain healthy when confronted with stressful life events, the effects of two or more variables must be considered concurrently, such as: hardiness and exercise (Kobasa, Maddi, & Puccetti; 1982); personality characteristics, social support, and coping strategies (Holahan & Moos, 1986); and sense of control, smoking reduction, and alcohol moderation (Seeman & Seeman, 1983).

Present Study

Keeping with the current trend of combinations of predictors, the present study explored the mediating effects of numerous personal characteristics, health practices, resistance resources, and perception of health on subsequent illness. More specifically, the effects of Antonovsky's (1987) sense of coherence measure were studied in combination with three health practices (exercise, cigarette smoking, and alcohol consumption), resistance resources, and perception of health. Based on the previous discussion, it was hypothesized that workers scoring high on the SOC questionnaire would be the least likely to report various illnesses. Likewise, workers who scored low on the SOC scale should be the most likely to report various illnesses. The sense of coherence, health practices, resources, and perception of health were predicted to have a mediating effect on reported illnesses for workers with high stress. Specifically, workers who reported high levels of stress were predicted to report fewer illnesses if they scored high on the SOC scale, scored high on questions concerning resistance resources, and perceived themselves as being healthy.

Various demographic variables (gender, age, etc.) that have been purported to be related to one's sense of coherence were also investigated. The prospective nature of this study also allowed for an examination of the nature, structure, and predictive ability of the SOC measure at Time I and Time II.

Methodology

Phases I and II of this study were conducted in a medium-sized electronics company in western New York. At Time I, 165 potential subjects were randomly selected from the employee roster. Each potential subject was personally approached and given a standardized explanation of the study. If they agreed to participate, a consent form was completed and they were instructed when and where to return completed questionnaires. Of the 165 production workers approached to serve as subjects, 118 (72%) completed and returned usable questionnaires.

Phase II was conducted one year after Phase I. Of the 118 production workers who participated at Time I, at Time II ten had quit their job, four had retired, and two were terminated, leaving a sample size of 102. Ninety-three of the 102 production workers were personally approached by the investigator and given a standardized explanation of Phase II. The remaining nine workers who were not at the plant location, due to illness, vacation, or disability, were mailed questionnaires including a letter of explanation and a consent form. Of the 102 production workers approached to participate in Phase II, 74 (73%) completed and returned usable questionnaires.

At the end of each data collection period information was gathered from the company's personnel records about the worker's absenteeism behavior.

Sample

The sample of 74 production workers who participated in both phases of the study consisted of 55 females and 19 males. Their ages ranged from 21–67 years (Mean = 41). The majority were married (70%) and had completed high school (79%).

Measures

The measures used to test the hypotheses in this study were combined into a detailed 17-page questionnaire.

Sense of Coherence (SOC): Measured by the 29-item instrument developed and refined by Antonovsky (1979, 1987). Measured at Time I and Time II.

Stress: Refers to those events experienced over a one-year period, requiring some degree of change. Stressful life events were measured with the 42-item Schedule of Recent Experience (SRE) scale developed by Holmes and Rahe (1967). Measured at Time I and Time II.

Illness: The main dependent variable, measured by the Seriousness of Illness Rating Scale developed by Wyler, Masuda, and Holmes (1968). Workers indicated whether, during the previous year, they had suffered from 126 separate illnesses (from acne to whooping cough). Measured at Time II.

Resistance Resources: Refers to characteristics of an individual that are effective in combating stress. These include genetic makeup, food, wealth, shelter, intelligence, coping strategies, social support, and cultural, community, and governmental supports. The six components of the tool correspond to the six categories of resistance resources identified by Antonovsky (1979). Resistance resources were measured by a 64-item tool developed by Fiorentino (1986). Measured at Time I.

Health Practices: Refers to the individual behaviors regarding current and/or past smoking habits, alcohol consumption, exercise, and dietary intake. This five-item subscale was constructed from the resistance resources measure. Measured at Time I.

Perception of Health Status: Measured by the four-item instrument (Ease/Disease Continuum) developed by Antonovsky (1979). According to Antonovsky (1979), one's location on this continuum is not only "... a consequence of other variables but also serves as a resistance resource (if high on the scale) or as a stress (if one is low)" (p. 120). Measured at Time I.

In addition, workers were also asked to provide background demographic information regarding their gender, age, marital status, education, and income level. All workers were encouraged to answer the questions honestly and were assured their responses would be held in confidence and would not jeopardize their position at the company.

Results

The Total Illness Score ranged from 0 to 3,813 with a mean of 1,389 (SD = 930). Of the 126 illnesses for which data were obtained, a subscore was constructed for subsequent analyses. Illnesses were chosen for the subscore if they had a moderate base rate of occurrence (approximately 30%) or were significantly correlated with the overall SRE stress rating. The selected illnesses were heartburn (46%), acne (14%), diarrhea (45%), dizziness (31%), sinus infection (30%), increased menstrual flow (11%), painful menstruation (14%), hemorrhoids (5%), migraine (14%), overweight (39%), depression (24%), arthritis (10%), high blood pressure (10%), and chest pain (11%). For each illness, workers were assigned a score of 1 if they did not have it and 2 if they did. A 14-Illness Score was obtained by summing the scores across the 14 illnesses. The 14-Illness Score correlated (+ . 86, $p <$ .001) with the Total Illness Score.

At Time I the workers' SOC scores ranged between 68 and 189 with a mean of 133.7 (SD = 25.9). The Time II scores ranged between 58 and 194 with a mean of 135.2 (SD = 28.9). The correlation between the SOC measured at Time I and Time II was highly significant (r = .78, $p <$ .001), indicating that the measure was quite reliable, as previously reported (Antonovsky, 1987, p. 82).

The total stress scores (SRE) of the workers at Time I ranged from 0 to 591 with a mean of 163 (SD = 140.9). At Time II they ranged from 0 to 600 with a mean of 173 (SD = 141.5). The correlation between the SRE measure at Time I and Time II was highly significant $(+ .46, p < .001)$.

The total resistance resources score ranged from 76 to 124 with a mean score of 100.3 (SD = 10.79). The total perception of health score ranged from 4 to 15 with a mean score of 6.4 (SD = 2.44).

Table 1 presents the correlation coefficients of the SOC and stress measures with select variables at Time I and Time II. At Time I, the SOC score correlated $(-.51, p < .001)$ with the stress score. At Time II, the correlation between these two variables was $-.36$ $(p < .001)$.

Table 1
Correlations Between Sense of Coherence (SOC),
Stress, and Select Variables at Time I and Time II

Variable	Time I		Time II	
	SOC	Stress	SOC	Stress
Gender (1 = male, 2 = female)	− .07	− .01	− .08	+ .10
Age	+ .19**	− .22**	+ .19**	− .26**
Marital Status (1 = not married, 2 = married)	+ .11	+ .12	+ .25**	+ .09
Education	− .06	+ .18*	+ .23**	− .14
Income Level	+ .23**	− .18*	+ .23**	− .14
Home Ownership (1 = no, 2 = yes)	+ .19**	− .24**	+ .14	− .27**
Resistance Resources	+ .33**	− .24**	+ .16	+ .12
Habits	− .02	− .09	− .06	+ .10
Perception of Health (Time I)	− .27**	+ .11	− .13	+ .07
Absenteeism	− .20**	+ .16**	− .09	+ .05
14-Illness Score	− .33**	+ .36**	− .39**	+ .05
Total Illness Score	− .31**	+ .34**	− .32**	+ .42*

* $p < .10.$ ** $p < .05.$

To assess the relationship between the predictor variables (stress, the SOC, health practices, resistance resources, perception of health) and illness, numerous multiple regression analyses were performed.

First, with the Total Illness Score as the outcome variable, stress and the SOC (both at Time I and Time II) were entered as predictor variables. The best predictors of illness were stress at Time II and the SOC at Time I, as shown in Table 2. The same analyses were conducted using the 14-Illness Score as the outcome variable. Again, stress at Time II and the SOC at Time I were the best predictors of illness, as shown in Table 3. The same analyses were conducted adding the composite health practices score as the third predictor variable. In each analysis, health practices did not enter into the equation.

Table 2
Regression Table: Predictors of Illness

Predictor Variables	Outcome Variable Total Illness Score		
	Multiple R	R^2 Change	Significance
Stress Time II	.40	.16	.000
SOC Time I	.46	.22	.000

Table 3
Regression Table: Predictors of Illness

Predictor Variables	Outcome Variable 14-Illness Score		
	Multiple R	R^2 Change	Significance
Stress Time II	.49	.24	.0000
SOC Time I	.56	.32	.0000

Next, with the Total Illness Score as the outcome variable, stress and the SOC (at Time I) along with health practices, resistance resources, perception of health, and age were entered as the predictor variables. As shown in Table 4, the SOC, health practices, and age did not fall into the equation.

Table 4
Regression Table: Predictors of Illness

Predictor Variables	Outcome Variable Total Illness Score		
	Multiple R	R² Change	Significance
Stress Time I	.45	.21	.000
Perception of Health	.57	.32	.000
Resistance Resources	.60	.37	.000

When the 14-Illness Score was substituted as the outcome measure, stress, perception of health, and age fell into the equation—the SOC, health practices, and resistance resources did not (Table 5).

Table 5
Regression Table: Predictors of Illness

Predictor Variables	Outcome Variable 14-Illness Score		
	Multiple R	R² Change	Significance
Stress Time I	.48	.23	.000
Perception of Health	.54	.30	.000
Age	.60	.36	.000

Finally, with the Total Illness Score as the outcome variable, stress and the SOC (at Time II) along with health practices, resistance resources, perception of health, and age were entered as predictor variables. As shown in Table 6, the SOC, health practices, and age did not fall into the equation.

Substituting the 14-Illness Score as the outcome measure, the procedure was run again. As shown in Table 7, the SOC, perception of health, health practices, and age did not fall into the equation. When the health practices measure was removed as a predictor variable, stress, resistance resources, and perception of health fell into the equation (Table 8).

Table 6
Regression Table: Predictors of Illness

	Outcome Variable Total Illness Score		
Predictor Variables	Multiple R	R^2 Change	Significance
Stress Time II	.42	.17	.000
Resistance Resources	.61	.37	.000
Perception of Health	.65	.43	.000

Table 7
Regression Table: Predictors of Illness

	Outcome Variable 14-Illness Score		
Predictor Variables	Multiple R	R^2 Change	Significance
Stress Time II	.50	.25	.000
Resistance Resources	.58	.33	.000

Table 8
Regression Table: Predictors of Illness

	Outcome Variable 14-Illness Score		
Predictor Variables	Multiple R	R^2 Change	Significance
Stress Time II	.45	.24	.000
Resistance Resources	.58	.34	.000
Perception of Health	.61	.38	.000

Table 9
Correlation Coefficients Between Comprehensibility, Manageability,
and Meaningfulness Scores at Times I and II with Illness at Time II

Illness	Comprehensibility		Manageability		Meaningfulness	
	I[a]	II[b]	I	II	I	II
Heartburn	−.11	−.12	.01	−.15	.03	−.01
Acne	−.06	−.19*	−.13	−.18*	−.03	−.18*
Diarrhea	−.11	−.18*	−.10	−.16*	−.02	−.10
Dizziness	−.27**	−.23**	−.27**	−.18*	−.16*	−.11
Sinus Infection	−.23**	−.21**	−.13	−.13	−.04	−.02
Increased Menstrual Flow	−.23**	−.31**	−.42**	−.31**	−.31**	−.36**
Painful Menstruation	−.23**	−.45**	−.32**	−.36**	−.18**	−.31**
Hemorrhoids	−.01	−.02	.04	−.02	.02	−.05
Migraine	−.25**	−.15	−.19**	−.14	−.15	−.12
Overweight	−.15	−.28**	−.16*	−.17*	−.18*	−.14
Depression	−.31**	−.30**	−.38**	−.40**	−.44**	−.42**
Arthritis	−.15	−.20**	−.10	−.12	−.17*	−.10
High Blood Pressure	−.03	−.02	−.08	−.12	−.07	−.05
Chest Pain	−.17*	−.11	−.17*	−.28*	−.22**	−.23**

[a]$n = 74$. [b]$n = 71$.
*$p < .10$. **$p < .05$.

To examine the predictive powers of each of the three proposed components of the SOC scale, comprehensibility, manageability, and meaningfulness scores were computed for each worker by summing the items from the SOC scale that were identified by Antonovsky (1987) as comprising each of these dimensions. Table 9 presents the correlation coefficients between the comprehensibility, manageability, and meaningfulness scores at Times I and II with illnesses at Time II.

As with the SOC scale itself, the relationship between the measures of the components of the SOC construct at Time I were as predictive of reported illnesses at Time II (a full year later) as were the measures of the components taken concurrently at Time II. Of the 42 pairs of comparisons between Time I and II, 23 of the correlations were slightly stronger at Time II, 18 of them were slightly weaker at Time II, and 1 pair of correlations was the same.

According to Antonovsky (1987, p. 22), the meaningfulness component (followed by comprehensibility and manageability) is the most crucial element for successful coping in life. The correlations in Table 8 indicate that the comprehensibility component was somewhat better at predicting resistance to illnesses at Time I *and* Time II. At Time I, the comprehensibility component correlated significantly with six illnesses, whereas the manageability and meaningfulness components correlated with five and three, respectively. At Time II the comprehensibility component correlated significantly with seven illnesses, compared to only four for both the manageability and meaningfulness components.

A principal component factor analysis was performed on the 29-item SOC scale at Time I. Using a varimax rotation, seven factors were isolated, accounting for 70% of the variance.[1] Each of the factors was comprised of a mixed combination of comprehensibility, manageability, and meaningfulness items and none could be identified. Three SOC items (4, 15, 20) did not weigh on *any* of the 7 factors. At Time II, the factor analysis revealed six factors which also accounted for 70% of the variance. Again, each factor was comprised of a mixed combination of comprehensibility, manageability, and meaningfulness items and none could be meaningfully understood. At Time II, one item (21) did not weigh on any of the factors. Moreover, there was no similarity whatsoever between the factor structure of the SOC variable at Time I and II. For example, of the eight items on Factor 1 at Time I and the nine items that comprised Factor 1 at Time II, there were only three items in common. Factor 2, which was comprised of five items at Times I and II, had only one item in common. Similar patterns of disarray were found for the remaining factors. Factor analyses also were performed for the 13-item modified version of the SOC scale at Time I and Time II. In each analysis, three factors which emerged from the weightings of the items did not correspond to Antonovsky's proposed three components.

Discussion

In terms of means and standard deviations, the workers' sense of coherence scores at Time I and Time II were similar to those obtained in previous studies (Antonovsky, 1987; Fiorentino, 1986). The relatively high reliability also compares to past research. The results presented in Table 1 are in general agreement with Antonovsky's reasoning. A worker receiving a high SOC score tended to be an older, married, upper-income person who owned his/her home. This person was less likely to be absent from work and also less likely to report illnesses in general. As expected, the SOC measure was not related to gender. Surprisingly, the SOC tended to be negatively related to education, although not significantly.

The significant correlations are also in keeping with the current literature concerning stress and health. Those workers scoring high on the stress scale tended to be younger, less well-to-do, and did not own their homes. Although they were not necessarily more likely to be absent from work, they were more likely to report various illnesses.

The numerous significant relationships between the predictor variables and subsequent illness strongly suggest the importance of resistance resources and the perception of health, yet the results do not support the sense of coherence. Theoretically, resistance resources shape the SOC. The sense of coherence is the intervening variable between resistance resources and health status. Thus resistance resources should not be needed in the chain of reasoning. The results, however, did not support this notion, except in one instance. When resistance resources and perception of health were added as predictor variables, the SOC no longer entered into the equation. Perhaps the sense of coherence is a type of a resistance resource. Antonovsky (1987, p. 24) stated that the SOC questionnaire "... was designed to be applicable to the life situation of all adults cross-culturally." While this may be the case, if future research does not support this contention, the SOC scale could be modified for various subpopulations.

The stable nature of the SOC measure and its predictive power both concurrently and a full year into the future is impressive. Antonovsky (1987, p. 107) stated that "... in the early period of adulthood ... one's location on the SOC continuum becomes more or less fixed." Longitudinal studies could clarify this point.

The SOC may prove to be reasonably flexible. If so, experimental work could serve to identify possible experiences, working conditions, and/or intervention strategies that would strengthen one's SOC and thus further reduce the stress-illness relationship.

The factor analytic results of the present study suggest that one's sense of coherence may not be encompassed by, and/or made up of, the three components as proposed by Antonovsky. Not only were there seven distinct factors of the sense of coherence scale revealed at Time I, six were obtained at Time II. More puzzling was the varied and unexplainable combination of items that comprised each factor at both time periods and for both versions of the scale. Admittedly, the disarray may be due in part to the present relatively small sample size. Further research could help clarify this crucial structural issue.

Note

1. Items chosen for each factor were those with factor loadings greater than .50, eigenvalue = 1.

References

Aneshensel, C., & Ferichs, R. (1982). Stress, support, and depression: A longitudinal causal model. *Journal of Community Psychology, 10*, 363–376.

Antonovsky, A. (1979). *Health, stress, and coping.* New York: Jossey-Bass.

Antonovsky, A. (1984). The sense of coherence as a determinant of health. In J. Matarazzo, S. Weiss, J. Herd, N. Miller, & S. Weiss (Eds.), *Behavioral health: A handbook of health enhancement and disease prevention.* New York: John Wiley & Sons.

Antonovsky, A. (1987). *Unraveling the mystery of health.* San Francisco: Jossey-Bass.

Antonovsky, A., & Sagy, S. (1986). The development of a sense of coherence and its impact on responses to stress situations. *Journal of Social Psychology, 126*, 213–225.

Belloc, N., & Breslow, L. (1972). Relationship of physical health status and health practices. *Preventive Medicine, 1*, 409–421.

Ben-Sira, Z. (1985). Potency: A stress-buffering link in the coping-stress disease relationship. *Social Science and Medicine, 21*, 397–406.

Berkman, L., & Syme, L. (1979). Social networks, host resistance, and mortality: A nine-year follow-up study of Alameda County residents. *American Journal of Epidemiology, 109*, 186–204.

Boyce, W., Schaefer, C., & Uitti, C. (1985). Permanence and change: Psychosocial factors in the outcome of adolescent pregnancy. *Social Science and Medicine, 21*, 1279–1287.

Broadhead, W. (1983). The epidemiologic evidence for a relationship between social support and health. *American Journal of Epidemiology, 117*, 521–537.

Brown, J. (1991). Staying fit and staying well: Physical fitness as a moderator of life stress. *Journal of Personality and Social Psychology, 60*(4), 555–561.

Ellis, A. (1973). *Humanistic psychotherapy*. New York: McGraw-Hill.

Fiorentino, L. (1986). Stress: The high cost to industry. *Occupational Health Nursing, 345*, 217–220.

Folkman, S., Lazarus, R., Gruen, R., & DeLongis, A. (1985). Appraisal, coping, health status, and psychological symptoms. *Journal of Personality and Social Psychology, 50*, 571–579.

Holahan, C., & Moos, R. (1986). Personality, coping, and family resources in stress resistance: A longitudinal analysis. *Journal of Personality and Social Psychology, 51*, 389–395.

Holmes, T., & Rahe, R. (1967). The social readjustment rating scale. *Journal of Psychosomatic Research, 11*, 213–218.

Kobasa, S. (1979). Stressful life events, personality, and health: An inquiry into hardiness. *Journal of Personality and Social Psychology, 37*, 1–11.

Kobasa, S., Maddi, S., & Puccetti, M. (1982). Personality and exercise as buffers in the stress-illness relationship. *Journal of Behavioral Medicine, 5*, 391–404.

Kobasa, S., & Puccetti, M. (1983). Personality and social resources in stress resistance. *Journal of Personality and Social Psychology, 45*, 839–850.

Koniz-Booher, P., & Koniz, M. (1986). Nutrition and lifestyle. In C. Edelmen & C. Manelle (Eds.), *Health promotion throughout the lifespan*. St. Louis: C. V. Mosby Co.

LaRocco, J., House, J., & French, J. (1980). Social support, occupational stress, and health. *Journal of Health and Social Behavior, 21*, 202–219.

Margalit, M. (1985). Perceptions of parents' behavior, familial satisfaction, and sense of coherence in hyperactive children. *Journal of Social Psychology, 23*, 355–364.

Meichenbaum, D., & Cameron, R. (1983). Stress-inoculation training: Toward a general paradigm for training coping skills. In D. Meichenbaum & M. Jarenko (Eds.), *Stress prevention and management*. New York: Plenum.

Menaghan, E. (1983). Individual coping efforts: Moderators of the relationship between life stress and mental health outcomes. In H. Kaplan (Ed.), *Psychosocial stress: Trends in theory and research*. New York: Academic Press.

Monat, A., & Lazarus, R. (Eds.). (1985). *Stress and coping: An anthology*. New York: Columbia University Press.

Reis, H. (1984). Social interaction and well-being. In S. Duck (Ed.), *Personal relationships V: Repairing personal relationships*. London: Academic Press.

Schafer, W. (1987). *Stress management for wellness*. New York: Holt, Rinehart & Winston.

Seeman, M., & Seeman, T. (1983). Health behavior and personal autonomy: A longitudinal study of the sense of control in illness. *Journal of Health and Social Behavior, 24*, 144–160.

Smith-Dijulio, K. (1990). People who depend upon alcohol. In E. Varcarolis (Ed.), *Foundations of psychiatric mental health nursing*. Philadelphia: W. B. Saunders.

Turner, R. (1983). Direct, indirect, and moderating effects of social support on psychological distress and associated conditions. In H. Kaplan

(Ed), *Psychosocial stress: Trends in theory and research*. New York: Academic Press.

Williams, S. (1990). *Essentials of nutrition and diet therapy*. Boston: Times Mirror/Mosby Publishing.

Wyler, A., Masuda, M., & Holmes, T. (1968). The seriousness of illness rating scale. *Journal of Psychosomatic Research, 11,* 363–374.

Chapter 6

Sense of Coherence as a Predictor of Family Functioning and Child Problems

Preliminary Findings Among Homeless, Substance-Abusing Women With Children[1]

Louise H. Flick and Sharon M. Homan

This chapter describes preliminary findings from an exploratory study of the sense of coherence (SOC) within a larger research demonstration project. The larger project evaluates several programmatic approaches to serving homeless, substance-abusing women with children, using a semi-randomized, longitudinal, experimental design. The interventions and the study design have been described elsewhere (Homan, Flick, Heaton, Meyer, & Klein, 1993; Smith, North, & Heaton, 1993).

A major component of this research demonstration is a randomized trial to compare the existing 60-day case management (CM) approach used at two Salvation Army family shelters to an enhanced CM approach. The enhanced CM approach has three unique elements: (1) a public health nurse/social worker team approach to CM; (2) extension of the CM services to the client to 12 months post shelter entry; and (3) structuring the CM approach to working with clients along the three SOC dimensions. This third element impacts the nature of the CM-client relationship and may affect the success of the client in achieving greater manageability, comprehensibility, and meaningfulness in her life. While the sense of coherence does not dictate CM practice, the case managers use the SOC dimensions to guide client assessment, setting goals with clients and focusing the intervention on what is meaningful to clients. Thus, case managers may establish priorities amongst seemingly overwhelming needs.

Within the larger study we ask four questions related to the sense of coherence:

1) Are women with a higher SOC better able to nurture their children in the face of extreme circumstances?

2) Does the SOC predict a client's (and her children's) ability to benefit from intervention?

3) Can intervention strengthen the SOC?

4) Can the SOC provide a useful guide to intensive, year-long case management with this population?

While preliminary data to be presented here address the first question, some background on all of the questions helps set the study context. Antonovsky (1984) conceptualized the sense of coherence as an orientation that influences one's response to challenges from the environment. This response includes the appraisal of stimuli, the recognition of stress, and the ability to make use of available resources to cope with stress. More than a style of coping, the SOC includes the potential for reorganization in response to challenges so that the individual is left strengthened by the experience. In Antonovsky's (1984, 1987) formulation, the SOC develops gradually through childhood and early adulthood and is a characteristic determined by genetics, culture, life experience, and an individual's access to structural resources such as money, services, and transportation.

The sense of coherence influences how one responds to events and crises, with the low SOC person tending to respond with a feeling of hopelessness and burden and the high SOC person with a sense that he or she can apply some structure to seemingly chaotic events (Antonovsky, 1987). Within a family, a high SOC parent (or a high SOC family) would be more successful at creating a stable and adaptive environment in spite of challenges within or outside the family (Antonovsky & Sourani, 1988). Quality of interaction between parent and child would be influenced both by the family environment and by the parent's SOC. A high SOC parent would be better able to cope with events and the resulting quality of nurturing would be less affected by internal or external stressors than that provided by a low SOC parent. If one accepts that the SOC is a developmental construct, as Antonovsky (1984) argued, and that, therefore, the sense of coherence develops with age into early adulthood, then indirect support for this proposed relationship appears in a previous study of adolescent and adult mothers. When life stresses were low there was little difference in the observed quality of mother-child interaction of adolescent mothers when compared to older mothers. When life stresses were high, adolescent mothers displayed significantly more negative behavior than did older mothers (Flick, 1980).

It is important to note, however, that the sense of coherence does not allow prediction of what one will do in a specific situation; it influences quality of behavior. For example, a high SOC and a low SOC parent may both choose to discipline a young child for a particular act, both may understand the behavior is common for that age child, and both may believe spanking is acceptable. The high SOC parent, however, might be more likely to instruct the child matter-of-factly about the limits of behavior and inform the child of the consequences (such as a spank) should the behavior continue. The low SOC parent, overwhelmed and feeling out of control of the child and of life in general, might be more likely to yell and hit as a first response.

While Antonovsky (1984) viewed the SOC as largely stable and established by early adulthood, he argued that there is evidence that change, even significant change, can occur if people can be enabled to alter their lives significantly, encouraging SOC-enhancing experiences to occur with greater frequency over a sustained period (Antonovsky, 1987). Long-term intensive drug-abuse treatment accompanied by removal from a drug-infested neighborhood and the breaking off of associations with a drug-using social group could theoretically strengthen the SOC. The last two study questions, and the design of our experimental case management intervention, are based on the assumption that, while a major portion of one's sense of coherence is a stable, enduring characteristic of the individual based on heredity and early life experiences, lived adult experience has the potential to alter the sense of coherence (Antonovsky, 1984, 1987).

The effect that substance abuse has on a "true" SOC and, separately, on our ability to accurately measure the SOC, raises three related questions:

1) Does chemical dependence so shrink the sphere of what is meaningful that the true SOC can remain close to previous levels in spite of the disintegration of role performance and interpersonal relationships? Antonovsky argued that " ...no one can so narrow the boundaries as to put beyond the pale of significance four spheres—one's inner feelings, one's immediate interpersonal relations, one's major activity, and existential issues—yet maintain a strong SOC" (Antonovsky & Sourani, 1988, p. 80). Yet this appears to occur with substance abuse. Children go hungry and unsupervised, rent money is spent on drugs, jobs are lost, and relationships with non-substance-using family and friends are severely strained.

2) Does the true SOC fall but measurement remain artificially high when the highly developed denial that can be a characteristic of substance abuse is fully operating? Or is this a truly high but rigid/ fragile SOC, such as described by Antonovsky (1987), that can be shattered? If either of these held, then such clients would evidence a drop in the SOC early in recovery as they became fully aware of, and could acknowledge, their inability to control their substance use and the damage done to what had previously given their lives meaning.

3) Or, does the true SOC stay essentially stable in spite of the development of substance abuse and its consequences?

In any of the above scenarios, the ability to effectively recover might be related to the SOC, as might the relative ability to nurture children in spite of the effects of substance abuse.

The present study explores evidence for a relationship between the sense of coherence and a mother's ability to nurture her children in the extreme circumstances of homelessness and substance abuse. The "ability to nurture" in this case includes the quality of the family environment within which the children are cared for and the quality of interactions between the mother and her children. Figure 1 models the expected relationships between variables. Indirect indicators of the ability to nurture include the child's behavioral and emotional problems. Preceding variables that may influence child problems include the length of time homeless, the length and severity of a mother's substance abuse, and a mother's past psychological/psychiatric problems. Each of these could affect child problems directly, or indirectly through their influence on child development or on the mother's current level of substance abuse or psychiatric symptoms. The sense of coherence is assumed to influence child problems indirectly through its effect on family functioning and mother-child interaction. Many of the relationships with the SOC are reciprocal. For example, heavy cocaine use during a past pregnancy could produce a child with behavioral problems that would tax the quality of mother-child interaction and family functioning under the best of circumstances. Under such circumstances the sense of coherence would be expected to decrease.

Figure 1

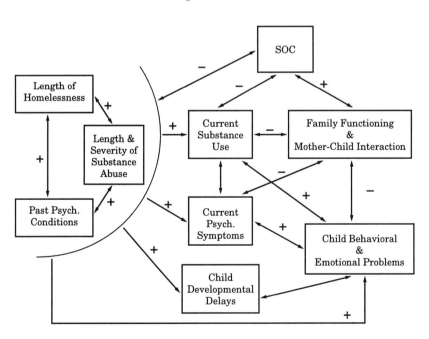

Note. Variables are for mother unless specified.

Methods

Sample

Analyzed for this study were data from the 72 women and their children who had been enrolled in the Salvation Army component of the project as of September 15, 1992, and for whom a baseline SOC measure was available. This represents slightly over half of the projected sample size at study completion. Eligible women had current or past substance abuse or dependence and were residents of one of two family shelters, one in the inner city and one in the surrounding area of a large Midwestern metropolitan region. The women were predominately young (mean age was 29 years), African-American women (97%), who on the average had 2.9 children. Cocaine was the most frequent primary substance of abuse (69%), followed by alcohol (13%).

Measures

Sense of Coherence. The 29-item Orientation to Life Questionnaire (Antonovsky, 1987) was self-administered to provide a single summary measure of the SOC. A Cronbach's Alpha of .85 indicated adequate internal reliability in our sample.

Family Environment Scale (FES). The FES (Form R) includes 90 true-false questions that elicit the respondent's perception of the social environment in the nuclear or conjugal family (Moos & Moos, 1991). Examples of the ten subscales include Conflict, Expressiveness, Cohesion, and the family's orientation toward Achievement and toward Independence (see Table 1 for the complete list). Six of the subscales achieved acceptable Cronbach's Alphas of .70–.80 but the remaining four subscales showed low internal reliability (.36–.59).

Clarke-Stewart Rating Scales (C-S). The C-S Rating Scales of mother-child interaction were derived from Ainsworth's (1969) concept of a syndrome of optimal maternal care that enhances child competence. Observers rate 12 global dimensions of behavior such as tone of voice, closeness of physical contact, and effectiveness of parental behavior. Ratings are made on a five-point Likert scale (Clarke-Stewart, 1973). Trained observers completed C-S Ratings for interactions between the mother and two of her children between the ages of three months and four and a half years. Observations were made in a client's room at the family shelter or in a private interviewing room. Raters considered all observed interaction between mother and child in the course of all data collection and during three "teaching tasks." Mothers were asked to teach each child to perform three simple tasks based on the child's age and development.

Child Behavior Checklist (CBCL). The CBCL for children aged 4–18 was used to collect standardized data from the mother or a parent surrogate on children's problems (Achenbach & Edelbrock, 1991). These analyses used age and sex standardized summary scale scores (t scores) for the following subscales: Externalizing Problems (includes items describing delinquent or aggressive behavior), Internalizing Problems (describes children who are withdrawn, anxious, or depressed), and Total Problems (includes externalizing, internalizing, and problems that do not fit into either category, such as social, attention, and thought problems). The CBCL was self-administered.

Table 1
Child and Family Variables

Family Environment Scales	X	SD	Clarke-Stewart Scales	X	SD
Cohesion	5.48	2.65	Tone of Voice	5.19	0.82
Expressiveness	4.80	1.86	Amount of Expressed Positive Emotion	3.81	0.98
Conflict	4.51	2.48	Attitude to Child Behavior	3.80	0.77
Independence	5.77	1.90	Amount of Physical Contact	4.11	0.81
Achievement Orientation	6.17	1.44	Closeness of Physical Contact	4.11	0.81
Intellectual/Cultural Orient.	4.59	2.43	Vigor of Physical Contact	3.80	0.88
Activity/Recreation Orient.	4.46	2.27	Amount of Auditory/Verbal Contact	3.71	0.73
Moral/Religious Orientation	6.06	1.75			
Organization	5.25	2.19	Amount of Eye-to-Eye Contact	3.61	0.72
Control	5.39	1.54	Amount of Social Stimulation	3.18	0.84
			Amount of Communicative Stimulation	3.59	0.90
Child Behavior Checklist			Effectiveness of Behavior	3.43	0.76
Externalizing	53.61	10.81	Appropriateness for Age and Ability	3.36	0.87
Internalizing	50.48	11.15			
Total Problems	53.52	11.38			
Child Depression Inventory	38.07	5.00			

Beck Depression Inventory (BDI). The BDI is a 21-item, self-report measure of the depth and intensity of depression symptoms (Beck, 1970). A child version of the BDI has been developed and was also administered to children age seven and older (Kovacs & Beck, 1977). Both the adult and child versions were self-administered when the respondent could read well. Analyses of internal reliability showed adequate levels for both the adult and child versions (Cronbach's Alpha = .86 and .80).

Self-Esteem. Rosenberg's (1965) 10-item, self-report rating scale measured the mother's self-esteem. A Cronbach's Alpha of .76 indicated this scale was internally reliable in our sample.

Current Substance Use. This was defined as a self-report of any drug use or drinking of alcohol to the point of feeling high, within the last 30 days.

Length of Substance Use. Additional data were collected on the total number of years of regular consumption of alcohol or regular use of drugs, whichever was longer. "Regular use" was defined as use at least three times per week.

Analyses

The exploratory (nonhypothesis testing) analyses consisted of Pearson correlations, *t* tests, and inspection of box and whisker plots to detect nonlinear relationships between pairs of variables in the proposed model and to compare the heterogeneity/homogeneity in the distribution of SOC scores within different categories. Systematic variation in heterogeneity can be as revealing as summary statistics such as means or correlations. For example, if an artificially high SOC for some of the most distressed individuals is distorting the results, a wider distribution (greater heterogeneity) in SOC scores would be expected for the most negative category for a characteristic. A linear comparison like a correlation may obscure important relationships that appear only at one end of the distribution when an important threshold has been passed.

Continuous variables were categorized into low, medium, and high for the box and whisker plots, based on their distributions. The lowest 25% of the distribution represents the "low," the middle 50% the "middle," and the highest 25% the "high" category. The C-S Ratings, which had a narrow distribution skewed toward the positive end of the scale, were classified into "low" or "high" based on visual inspection. The "low" category indicates a negative rating while the "high" includes both neutral and positive ratings.

Analyses of child data, such as the CBCL, the Child Depression Inventory, or the C-S Ratings, were run for a single child-mother pair. For each child instrument, a single child was selected within each family from among those who had received that instrument (each child received only those that were age-appropriate). If there were two children for a given measure, the youngest was chosen; if there was an odd number, the middle child was chosen; if there was an even number greater than two, the youngest who was closest to the middle of the ages represented was selected. Consequently our analyses represent more of a composite view of the children than they do a systematic look at the relationship between the mother and a single child.

Figure 2
Family Environment Cohesion Scale by SOC

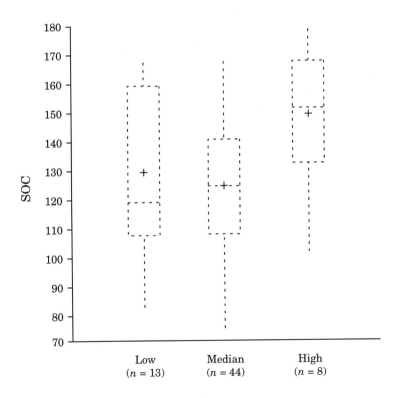

Results

Pearson correlations between the sense of coherence and the Family Environment Scales and between the SOC and the C-S Ratings of mother-child interaction were nonsignificant. However, two correlations approached significance. As SOC scores increased so did ratings on how accepting the mother was of the child's behavior ($r = .25$, $p < .10$, $n = 40$) and on the amount of social stimulation that was observed ($r = .27$, $p < .10$, $n = 40$). The box and whisker plots indicated higher mean and median SOC scores with scores in the more positive categories on 6 of the 10 FES scales. These included Cohesion, Conflict, Organization, Independence, Intellectual/Cultural Orientation, and Activity/Recreation Orientation. The plots for Cohesion and Organization are presented in Figures 2 and 3.

Figure 3
Family Environment Organization Scale

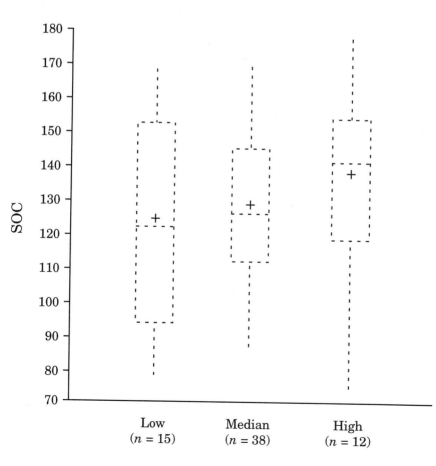

Organization

Figure 4
Observed Tone of Voice by SOC

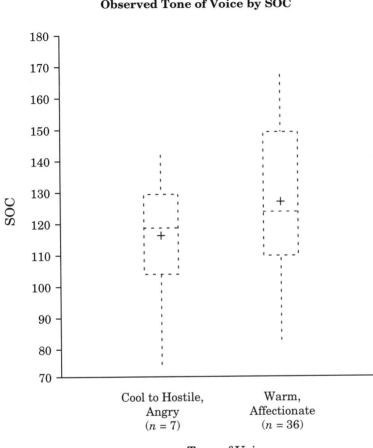

Cool to Hostile,
Angry
(*n* = 7)

Warm,
Affectionate
(*n* = 36)

Tone of Voice

Similar results were obtained for the C-S Ratings. Ten of the 12 ratings showed higher mean and median SOC scores for the "high" category. Figure 4 illustrates the plot for the SOC and Tone of Voice.

Of the two rating scales that did not show this association, Amount of Eye-to-Eye Contact was unrelated and Amount of Auditory/Verbal Contact increased with lower SOC scores. This latter finding may result from our particular sample. Among extremely distressed families, criticism or belittling may make up a significant proportion of the communication with children. Consequently, families with higher SOC scores may display less rather than more verbal interchange.

A *t* test comparing mean SOC scores for women reporting current substance use with those claiming no current use did not reach significance (*t* = 1.34). However, a box and whisker plot indicated greater heterogeneity among the SOC scores within the nonuser group and equal lower boundaries to the 25th percentiles in both groups (Figure 5). Interviewers often suspected that women falsely denied current use. Current substance use was negatively associated with only one C-S Rating and none of the FES Scales. Women reporting current use were observed to be less accepting of their child's behavior (Current User, X = 3.59, SD = .80; Not Current User, X = 4.11, SD = .68; *t* = 2.23, *p* < .05). None of the child problem variables (CBCL scores or the BDI) were associated with current substance abuse.

Figure 5
Current Substance Use by SOC

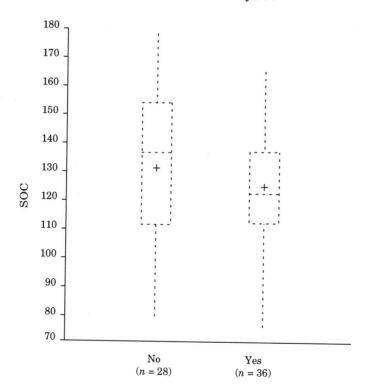

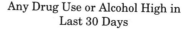

Any Drug Use or Alcohol High in
Last 30 Days

As others have found, the sense of coherence was highly correlated with Self-Esteem ($r = .57, p < .001$) and the BDI ($r = -.51$, $p < .001$), our measures of current psychological state. Both associations linked higher SOC scores with more positive states of mind. Nonsignificant correlations were obtained between "years of substance use" and the SOC, Self-Esteem, and the BDI. But "years of substance use" was positively associated with "length of homelessness" ($r = .27, p < .05$) and depression symptoms (BDI) increased in association with length of homelessness ($r = .27, p < .05$).

We found modest evidence of an association between a mother's depression and the environment within the family. More depressed mothers showed less social stimulation ($r = -.36, p < .05$) and more close physical contact with their children ($r = .34, p < .05$). Two FES subscales, Cohesion and Expressiveness, showed nonsignificant trends toward less positive scores in more depressed mothers ($r = -.23, p < .10; r = -.23, p < .10$). Child problems proved unrelated to the mother's psychological status.

Since the mechanism for an effect of the sense of coherence on child problems is through the ability of higher SOC mothers to create a family environment that is nurturing and shields the child from her experience of stress, the proposed relationship between family variables and child problems is of particular importance. The results, however, do not present a clear picture. Only with child Internalizing Problems do any of the family variables reach or approach significance. Correlations with the FES subscales Intellectual/Cultural Orientation and Control reach significance ($r = .34, p < .05; r = .34, p < .05$). But only the association with Control is in the expected direction. Families with greater Control (considered by Moos to be a negative family characteristic) have children with more Internalizing Problems. An Intellectual/Cultural Orientation is supposed to be a positive characteristic yet our results indicate it is associated with more child problems. Similar results were found for nonsignificant trends with Independence and a Moral/Religious Orientation ($r = .27, p < .10; r = .28, p = .10$).

Only one correlation between Internalizing Problems and a C-S Rating is significant and one approaches significance. Mothers who show less Auditory/Verbal Contact have children with more problems ($r = -.42, p < .05$). Mothers who touch their children less are also more likely to have children with more problems ($r = -.38$, $p < .10$).

Surprisingly, when a direct association between the sense of coherence and child problems is examined, there is a clear relationship. Mothers with low SOC scores are more likely to have children with more problems on all 3 scales explored: Internalizing ($r = -.26$, $p < .10$), Externalizing ($r = -.40$, $p < .01$), and Total Problems ($r = -.37$, $p < .05$).

Figure 6
CBCL Internalizing Problems by SOC

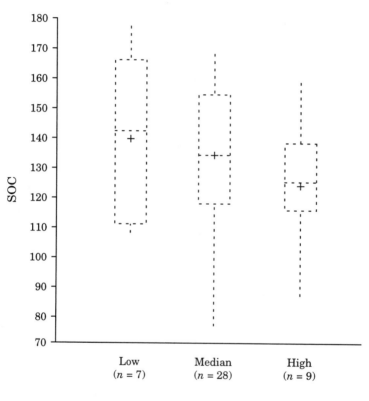

Internalizing Problems
(Age & Sex Standardized)

The final step in the analyses was the inspection of the box and whisker plots of SOC scores plotted against the categorized family and child variables. If there were inflated (high/rigid) SOC scores among distressed individuals who deny both use and the consequences of that use, then these plots should show greater variability in SOC scores within the more negative categories. This is consistently the case for 6 of the 10 FES subscales (see Figures 2 and 3 for examples); in only one of the remaining 4, Control, does the opposite pattern appear. The plot for the SOC with Current Substance Use/Not Current Use is also consistent with the presence of some inflated scores in that the distribution of SOC scores shows greater heterogeneity among those who deny use than among those who acknowledge use (Figure 5).

However, the results for the CBCL scales and the C-S Ratings contradict this pattern. The Externalizing and Total Problems scores show no differences in heterogeneity by category, while the Internalizing scores show greater heterogeneity when children have fewer problems (Figure 6). Likewise, greater heterogeneity in SOC scores consistently occurs when the C-S Ratings indicate neutral/positive observed interactions (see Figure 4 for an example).

Discussion

These preliminary, exploratory analyses address the first of the four sense of coherence questions to be addressed in the larger study: Are women with a higher SOC better able to nurture their children in the face of extreme circumstances? Figure 7 summarizes the proposed relationships and the results from these analyses.

Even in this highly distressed population of homeless shelter residents, the sense of coherence is positively associated with perceived family environment and observations of mother-child interaction. While active substance use, a mother's self-esteem, and depression symptoms (psychological state) are each negatively associated with some subscales of the Family Environment Scale or the C-S Ratings, neither the psychological state variables nor current substance abuse appear to account for the strength of these relationships with the SOC. "Current abuse" is not associated with the SOC, suggesting that each of these variables has an independent impact on the family/interaction variables. Both self-esteem and depression symptoms are strongly correlated with the SOC, but self-esteem is not associated with either set of family variables. There are some negative associations between a mother's depression, family environment, and interaction variables, but these do not seem adequate in number or strength to account for the observed relationships with the sense of coherence. However, multivariate analyses with the final sample may reveal that depression symptoms do account for some of the apparent associations between the SOC and family variables.

Figure 7

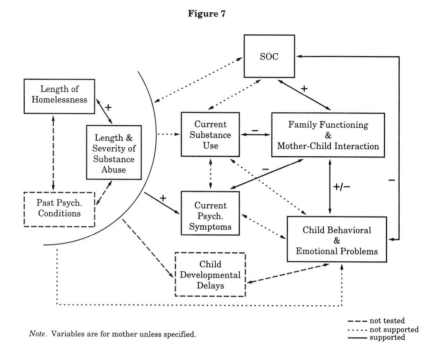

Note. Variables are for mother unless specified.

The suggested relationships between the sense of coherence and observations of mother-child interaction are of particular importance. If further work can demonstrate that the SOC influences the quality of mother-child interaction independent of any depression effect, it will provide important validation of the construct. These observations cannot be accounted for by any effect of the mother's perception that might also influence the SOC. For example, associations between perceived family environment and the sense of coherence could be due to a single underlying factor, such as negativism/positivism, which affects perception. A bias in perception could account for any association between the two measures. Observations of behavior made by an independent observer, unaware of the SOC score, could not be attributed to such a bias in perception.

The proposed model held that the sense of coherence would influence child problems through its effect on the family environment and the quality of mother-child interaction. The results suggest the SOC is strongly related to child problems, but they do not support family environment or interaction as the mechanism for that relationship. The family/interaction variables related to only one of the three child problem variables (CBCL, Internalizing), and the results indicated both negative and positive associations depending on the specific family variable. The sense of coherence was strongly associated with both the Externalizing and the Total Problems scales on the CBCL, accounting for 16% of the variance in both scales, and approached significance with Internalizing Problems. Neither current substance use nor the psychological variables were associated with child problems, so they cannot account for the results.

Examination of heterogeneity in the distribution of SOC scores provides mixed results regarding the presence of inflated or rigid SOC scores among some clients. It is plausible that women with advanced substance abuse, who deny use and its consequences when direct evidence is obvious, might report an SOC score that is unnaturally high. But the data do not provide consistent evidence to support this.

All of these results must be viewed cautiously as they represent a partial sample and an exploratory analysis. They do support the sense of coherence as an important construct in explaining family environment, mother-child interaction, and child problems in an extremely distressed population. The results support using the sense of coherence as a predictor of positive treatment outcome, in that women with higher SOC scores report more positive family attributes, display more positive interaction with their children, and have children with fewer significant problems. Such women would have a more stable base from which to make use of drug treatment and family support services. These findings also suggest that interventions that change a mother's sense of coherence, if that is possible, would influence a number of dimensions that support sobriety and increase family stability.

Note

1. This research is supported by the National Institute on Alcohol Abuse and Alcoholism under the Cooperative Agreements for Research Demonstration Projects on Alcohol and Other Drug Abuse Treatment for Homeless Persons.

References

Achenbach, T. H., & Edelbrock, C. (1991). *Child Behavior Checklist/4–18 and 1991 Profile*. Burlington, VT: University of Vermont, Department of Psychiatry.

Ainsworth, M. (1969). *Maternal behavior and infant initiative.* Paper presented at the Symposium on Maternal Behavior in Mammals. Organized by the International Union of Biological Sciences, London.

Antonovsky, A. (1984). The sense of coherence as a determinant of health. In J. D. Matarazzo, S. M. Weiss, J. A. Herd, N. E. Miller, & S. Weiss (Eds.), *Behavioral health: A handbook of health enhancement and disease prevention* (pp. 114–130). New York: Wiley.

Antonovsky, A. (1987). *Unraveling the mystery of health: How people manage stress and stay well.* San Francisco: Jossey-Bass.

Antonovsky, A., & Sourani, T. (1988). Family sense of coherence and family adaptation. *Journal of Marriage and the Family, 50,* 79–92.

Beck, A. T. (1970). *Depression: Causes and treatment.* Philadelphia: University of Pennsylvania Press.

Clarke-Stewart, A. (1973). Interactions between mothers and their young children: Characteristics and consequences. *Monographs of the Society of Research in Child Development, 38* (6), Serial No. 7, 1–109.

Flick, L. (1980). *Psychosocial development as a determinant of adolescent maternal behavior.* Unpublished doctoral dissertation, University of North Carolina at Chapel Hill, Chapel Hill, NC.

Homan, S. M., Flick, L. H., Heaton, T. M., Meyer, J. P., & Klein, M. (1993). Reaching beyond crisis management: Design and implementation of extended shelter-based services for chemically dependent homeless women and their children. *Alcoholism Treatment Quarterly, 10*(3/4), 101–112.

Kovacs, M., & Beck, A. T. (1977). An empirical-clinical approach toward a definition of childhood depression. In J. G. Schulterbrandt & A. Raskin (Eds.), *Depression in childhood: Diagnosis, treatment, and conceptual models* (pp. 1–25). New York: Raven Press.

Moos, R. H., & Moos, B. S. (1991). *Family environment scale manual* (2nd ed.). Palo Alto, CA: Social Ecology Laboratory, Stanford University and the Veterans Administration Medical Center.

Rosenberg, M. (1965). *Society and the adolescent self-image.* Princeton, NJ: Princeton University Press.

Smith, E., North, C., & Heaton, T. (1993). A substance abuse recovery program for homeless mothers with children: St. Louis. *Alcoholism Treatment Quarterly, 10*(3/4), 91–100.

Chapter 7

The Salutogenic Effect of an MBA Program

Sense of Coherence and the Academic Experience of U.S. and Foreign MBA Students[1]

Elisabeth K. Ryland, Linda F. Tegarden, and Jeanne C. King[2]

In this study, we examine two issues raised by Aaron Antonovsky in his chapter in the present volume: the developmental aspects of the sense of coherence (SOC), and the nature of cultural differences in the SOC (see Chapter 1). These issues are investigated by comparing the SOC scores of new and returning U.S. and foreign students enrolled in the Master of Business Administration (MBA) program at California State University, San Bernardino (CSUSB). We also relate MBA students' SOC scores to other demographic and psychological measures, including alienation from the university and perceptions of the quality of the academic program. In sum, this study assesses the value of the MBA experience in relation to the sense of coherence of students with very different backgrounds and needs.

It is well established that the sense of coherence predicts numerous outcomes related to health and well-being (see Antonovsky, 1992). Possible theoretical bases for the development of the SOC also have been discussed in several places (Antonovsky, 1987; see Chapter 1), but empirical work using the SOC as an outcome variable is only just beginning (Antonovsky, see Chapter 2). The main focus of our research is the developmental substrate of the SOC. Specifically, we believe that a structured course of graduate study—such as the one offered by the CSUSB MBA program—will have a positive effect on students' sense of coherence.

The sense of coherence is formally defined as "a global orientation that expresses the extent to which one has a pervasive, enduring though dynamic feeling of confidence that (1) the stimuli deriving from one's internal and external environments in the course of living are structured, predictable, and explicable; (2) that resources are available to one to meet the demands posed by these stimuli; and (3) these demands are challenges, worthy of investment and engagement" (Antonovsky, 1987, p. 18).

The sense of coherence is comprised of three components corresponding to aspects of the definition: comprehensibility, manageability, and meaningfulness. According to Antonovsky, a strong SOC is associated with a high level of all three components. A greater sense of comprehensibility is developed by repeatedly experiencing that things fit together and that unknowns are explained to one's satisfaction in an ordered pattern. A stronger sense of manageability is determined by experiences of an appropriate load balance, or the availability of resources with which to meet the demands of a given situation. Specific experiences that contribute to greater meaningfulness include continued participation in socially valued decision making. (For more discussion of the theory of how the three components develop, see Antonovsky, 1987, chap. 6.)

How might a structured curriculum, such as an MBA program, contribute to the development of the three components of the SOC? The description of an MBA program offers some suggestions. According to the 1992-93 *Bulletin*, the major objectives of the CSUSB MBA program are "to provide the student with the tools of decision making, an understanding of the total administrative system, a capability for understanding interrelationships, and specialized training in a functional field of administration" (California State University, San Bernardino, 1993, p. 338).

Classes that provide students with the "tools of decision making" may affect the manageability component. Course work in the MBA program progresses from learning tools in specialized areas (such as accounting, finance, and management) to policy and strategy courses that challenge students to integrate these tools. This incremental approach increases students' confidence over time in their ability to handle more and more complex business and management problems.

Course work that leads to an "understanding [of] the total administrative system [and] ... a capability for understanding interrelationships . . ." may influence the comprehensibility component of the SOC. Much MBA teaching is devoted to helping students develop an understanding of the operation of complex systems. The third component of the SOC—meaningfulness (also referred to by Antonovsky as the motivational component)—may be a function of successive and successful completion of individual assignments, courses, and ultimately of attaining the degree itself. The MBA degree usually opens the door to advancement into the upper echelons of the corporate world, enabling the best students to become major participants in socially valued managerial decision making.

The relationships between the typical MBA curriculum and the components of the sense of coherence suggest that an MBA program may potentially have a "salutogenic" effect, which will be reflected in higher SOC scores among individuals as they advance in their studies and complete their degrees.

Cultural Differences in the Sense of Coherence

Increasing numbers of students from abroad are flocking to universities in the U.S. to obtain training in business and management. Foreign students have been reported to experience disproportionately high levels of academic dissatisfaction, stress, and general adaptation problems during their stay in this country. Ryan, Raffel, and Lovell (1987) reported that foreign students in U.S. public administration programs experience financial problems, social isolation from Americans, difficulty in speaking and reading English, time pressure during exams, and difficulty understanding class examples drawing on American business culture. They are also victims of ethnocentrism, discrimination, and alienation from the dominant group. There is almost no information in the literature on foreign business students beyond our initial efforts (see Ryland & King, 1992). However, the literature on foreign students in other disciplines suggests that U.S. academic programs do not adequately address the needs of non-U.S. students, especially with respect to English language skills, cross-cultural communication, study and test-taking skills, and, notably, women's issues (Surdam & Collins, 1984).

Based on such findings, we believe that foreign students will be less likely to experience the "salutogenic" effect of an MBA program as reflected in their SOC scores. For example, foreign students' sense of comprehensibility may be quite low. They are often unfamiliar with the rules of the U.S. academic system, which is quite different from academic systems in many other countries. The English language itself is a barrier to comprehensibility, and many foreign students are accepted with a very poor background and little speaking experience in English. In terms of the sense of manageability, foreign students are cut off from their habitual sources of support, such as networks of family and friends, while they are still unfamiliar with university support services, such as counseling and tutoring programs. It is worth noting that foreign business students are much more critical than U.S. students of those academic support systems that they do use extensively, especially the library and computer facilities (see Ryland & King, 1992).

Meaningfulness is more difficult to assess. In previous research (Ryland & King, 1992), we found that foreign students rated instruction to be extremely important, as did U.S. students. But they were also very dissatisfied with the quality of instruction and their overall educational experience, while U.S. students were generally satisfied. This is consistent with students' written comments to open-ended questions in the surveys from which the data for this chapter were derived; that is, foreign MBA students complained that the content of some courses was not relevant to their experiences or needs.

Purpose of the Research

This study emerged from our ongoing program of research on the characteristics, needs, and adjustment problems of foreign students majoring in business. The complete research program includes CSU system level survey data [from the 1989 Student Needs and Priorities Survey (SNAPS)] on undergraduate and graduate business students collected by the Chancellor's Office (California State University, 1989), which we analyzed and reported on in an earlier article (Ryland & King, 1992). After this effort, we designed a questionnaire to collect more detailed information from undergraduate and graduate business students at the San Bernardino campus. This survey was administered on two separate occasions, and included measures of social psychological factors such as the sense of coherence, self-esteem, alienation from the university, and social contact—not included in the CSU SNAPS data—which we believed might explain foreign students' reported dissatisfaction with their academic experiences (Ryland & King, 1992).

Thus far, our research has had a problem focus; we realized, however, that our data on the SOC scores of MBA students—especially of foreign students—offered us the opportunity to probe some conceptual issues in this chapter. Thus, we limit our presentation mainly to analyses of SOC scores and selected survey variables that may be linked to the SOC, both as precursors and as consequences, including "developmental" markers such as age, experience in the MBA program, alienation from the university, and perceptions of the MBA instructional program. However, we remind the reader that the research design was not originally conceived of in terms of existing theory on the SOC. We have chosen these measures because they are convenient; that is, they were included in the surveys administered to CSUSB MBA students and were readily analyzable. Although they may have some conceptual promise, the entire set of factors that might account for differences in the SOC scores of U.S. and foreign MBA students is not represented in this investigation. In addition, despite the fact that we have "repeated" measures of the SOC and other factors, very few of the respondents who completed the survey the first year also provided us with data the following year. Consequently, the research design uses a cross-sectional indicator of MBA program experience (all "new" MBA students versus all "returning" MBA students, pooled over both years) rather than a longitudinal (pre-post) factor.

To summarize, we believe that the reported problems of foreign students in U.S. academic settings suggest that these students are less likely than U.S. students to respond to the possible salutogenic effect of a two-year course of graduate study in business, and that this difference should be reflected in their SOC scores. In other words, language and cultural differences may reduce the ability of foreign students to comprehend and attach meaning to the curriculum and related activities during their U.S. educational experience. In the absence of such an integrated experience, foreign students' sense of coherence is unlikely to increase and may in fact deteriorate. Thus, this study addresses the question of whether an MBA program can produce a salutogenic effect among all students. Our belief is that it cannot, and we therefore predict that the SOC scores of U.S. MBA students will be significantly higher than the SOC scores of foreign students. Further, when the SOC scores of MBA students returning for their second year of study are compared to first-year students, we expect experience and citizenship to interact. Specifically, we predict that the SOC scores of returning versus new U.S. MBA students will be higher than the SOC scores of returning versus new foreign MBA students.

Method

Design

The research design is a 2 x 2 nonexperimental, nonorthogonal design based on two subject factors: MBA program experience (new or returning student) and citizenship status (U.S. citizen or foreign visa student). New students are those who are in the first year of the MBA program; returning students are those in the second or subsequent years of the curriculum. Because the experience factor is part of a larger developmental process, the overlapping effect of age is statistically controlled in the factorial analysis. Again, it should be noted that experience is a cross-sectional factor (that is, it refers to independent groups of students) rather than a longitudinal one.

The primary dependent variable is the SOC. In addition, a standard measure of alienation from the university and a composite measure of perceived instructional quality, based on perceptions of specific components of the MBA program, are included. In a follow-up analysis, gender is added to the design to further untangle the MBA experience and citizenship effects.

Respondents

The study population was defined as all students enrolled in the MBA program at California State University, San Bernardino, during the academic years 1991–92 and 1992–93. During the fall quarter of the first academic year, questionnaires were distributed to instructors of several MBA classes. Those students who were not captured during the in-class administration were mailed a survey shortly thereafter. During the second year, questionnaires were mailed in the fall to the local mailing address of all MBA students. The total number of students contacted each fall was 324 and 343, respectively. Questionnaires were returned by 232 students the first year and, due to the difference in procedure, by 157 students the second year. Nevertheless, for a survey largely requiring a return by mail, the response rates for both years (72% and 46%) are quite respectable. The final sample consisted of 338 MBA students and was achieved by pooling the survey data across both years.[3] To eliminate the pre-testing effect, students who completed the survey both times (as new students in 1991–92 and as returning students in 1992–93) were dropped from the sample.

The sample of 338 MBA students includes nearly equal numbers of males and females (57% vs. 43%), and of U.S. and foreign visa students (57% vs. 43%). MBAs (both U.S. and foreign) who identify their ethnicity as "Asian" slightly outnumber Anglo students (47% vs. 42%); the remaining respondents are small numbers of Latinos, African-Americans, and others. Not surprisingly, the sample is comprised of an older group of college students; the MBA students' average age is 30 years. Foreign MBAs, however, are significantly younger ($M = 26.7$ years) than U.S. MBAs [$M = 33.1$ years; $t(317) = -9.54$, $p < .01$], and their ages are less variable (SD = 3.06 vs. 8.20, respectively).

Four out of five MBAs (79%) are returning for their second or subsequent year of study.[4] Thus, when MBA program experience is crossed with citizenship, the resulting group sizes are unequal and—from smallest to largest—are: new U.S. MBAs (22), new foreign MBAs (50), returning foreign MBAs (95), and returning U.S. MBAs (171).[5] Therefore the analysis is based on a hierarchical regression method, which is recommended for nonorthogonal designs (see Tabachnick & Fidell, 1989).

Questionnaire

The survey instrument was developed from our experience working with the CSU Student Needs and Priorities Survey (SNAPS) data. About half of the questionnaire consisted of measures from the SNAPS that we adapted for the CSUSB MBA population. These included standard demographic items (gender, age, citizenship, ethnicity) as well as a measure of the student's experience in the MBA program ("is this your first quarter at CSUSB?"). Another set of items adapted from the SNAPS asked students to rate the importance of 15 factors (such as instruction, faculty, courses, library, and so on) in relation to their educational goals. We then asked them to rate the *quality* of the same factors (on five-point scales) in the CSUSB School of Business and Public Administration and in the University as a whole. Seven items from this set were used to form a composite Perceptions of Instructional Quality scale: quality of instruction, accessibility of faculty, advising from faculty, variety of courses offered, fairness of testing and grading, intellectual stimulation from faculty, and content of courses. This composite measure of instructional quality was reliable and had a respectable degree of internal consistency, as indicated by Cronbach's Alpha (.86, $n = 285$).[6]

The remainder of the questionnaire contained standard measures of four social psychological constructs. Two of these constructs, the SOC and alienation from the university, are the focus of the present research. The sense of coherence was measured by the 13-item version of the Orientation to Life scale (Antonovsky, 1987). The 13 statements in the scale refer to a wide variety of stimuli and situations and are multifaceted measures of the three SOC components. The statements are rated on seven-point scales with relevant anchors, such as: "Do you have the feeling that you don't really care about what goes on around you?" (very seldom or never to very often); "Has it happened that people whom you counted on disappointed you?" (never happened to always happened). Consistent with research using other populations, the standard criterion (.80) for measurement reliability was exceeded with our sample of MBA students (Cronbach's Alpha = .84, n = 325).

Our measure of student alienation was adapted from Burbach's (1972) University Alienation Scale. The scale contains 24 items loaded by three factors (powerlessness, meaninglessness, and social estrangement); however, because the factors are highly correlated, the scale can also be used as a unidimensional measure of alienation in a university context. In order to reduce the length of the questionnaire, we selected 11 items appropriate for our population (such as, "I feel that I am a part of this university community," and "Classes at this university are so regimented that there is little room for the personal needs and interests of the student"). Each of the items is rated on a four-point scale (strongly disagree to strongly agree). The reliability of our shortened version of the alienation scale was clearly acceptable (Cronbach's Alpha = .80, n = 297).

Results and Discussion

Age, MBA Program Experience, and the Sense of Coherence

The sense of coherence can be argued to be a maturational construct; that is, it is responsive to how people manage and master challenges and situations over the course of their lives (see Antonovsky, 1987). The most global and direct index of a maturational process is of course chronological age and, in nonexperimental research, it is difficult to disentangle the effects of an experiential factor—such as the MBA program experience—on some outcome variable from the general process of maturation.

Thus, before proceeding with the main analyses, we examined the Pearson correlations between age, MBA program experience, and SOC scores. As expected, significant zero-order correlations between age and SOC scores [$r(308) = .27$, $p < .01$], and between experience and SOC scores [$r(308) = .16$, $p < .01$] were found, although the magnitude of the relationship is modest in both cases. Not surprisingly, the correlations indicate that older and returning MBA students tend to have higher SOC scores than younger and new MBA students.

Since age and experience are also correlated [$r(308) = .20$, $p < .01$], we examined the first-order partial correlations between age, experience, and SOC scores. When age is statistically controlled, the magnitude of the correlation between MBA program experience and SOC scores drops slightly—from .16 to .12. By contrast, when experience is controlled, the partial correlation between age and the SOC (.25) is of virtually the same magnitude as the zero-order association (.27). Thus, age in general accounts for a large amount of the variability in SOC scores. But more interesting for our purposes, when age is statistically eliminated, experience continues to have a significant positive association with the sense of coherence.[7]

In simpler terms, the results suggest that the SOC is indeed associated with maturation and that specific experiences can have an impact within the general developmental process. We discuss some general methodological issues bearing on the interpretation of our results in the concluding section. For the moment, we again mention that the age-SOC and experience-SOC relationships are modest in magnitude—an indication that variability in the sense of coherence of MBA students is not explained simply by age and maturation-related processes. Further, foreign MBA students are much younger on average and tend to be more homogeneous in age as a group than U.S. MBA students, and in both groups the age range is restricted because the entire life span is not represented. Differences between groups in age ranges—and especially the highly restricted age range for the foreign MBAs—may be suppressing the magnitude of the age-SOC correlation. Nevertheless, a low magnitude age-SOC correlation is consistent with our expectation that cultural differences will have a substantial impact on students' SOC scores—a topic that we consider next.

MBA Program Experience, Citizenship Status, and the Sense of Coherence

To assess the relationships between MBA program experience, citizenship status, and SOC scores, a two-way analysis of covariance (ANCOVA) was performed, using age as the covariate. Since age is significantly correlated with SOC scores, it is appropriately included as a way to statistically remove the effects of age on the experience factor.[8] The ANCOVA was made using the hierarchical regression method recommended by Tabachnick and Fidell (1989) for nonorthogonal designs. This method provides a solution based on partialling the variance due to the covariate before the variation due to the main effects, which are then removed sequentially before the interaction term. Since the group sizes are unequal, the factors are correlated and the order of entry of the main effects becomes important. We report the results of both orderings of the main effects to illustrate the consistency of the solution.

As expected, age is a significant covariate of the sense of coherence when it is entered first to be statistically eliminated from the other systematic effects [$F(1,305) = 30.32$, $p < .01$]. In strict terms, after controlling or removing the variability in a measure due to a covariate, the measure is said to be "adjusted" for that covariate. Thus, the SOC score is "age-adjusted" in the significance tests of the other factors, and the results should be interpreted with this transformation in mind.

Citizenship status has a significant main effect on age-adjusted SOC scores irrespective of order of entry [entered first, $F(1,305) = 62.08$, $p < .01$; entered second, $F(1,305) = 57.20$, $p < .01$]. The average SOC score of U.S. MBA students (both new and returning) is much higher ($M = 69.05$) than that of foreign MBA students ($M = 58.05$). MBA program experience has a significant main effect on SOC scores only when entered after the age covariate and before the citizenship main effect [$F(1,305) = 4.93$, $p < .05$]. However, the means indicate that returning MBA students do tend to have higher average SOC scores than new MBA students irrespective of citizenship status (Means = 65.30 vs. 60.74, respectively).

Further examination of the results revealed that the effect of the MBA program experience combines with citizenship status in a most interesting way. The two-way interaction of these factors over and above the main effects is significant ($F[1,305] = 6.20$, $p < .025$), and the age-adjusted SOC scores for this effect are shown in Figure 1. The figure shows differences in the SOC as a function of MBA program experience for U.S. and foreign students separately (simple main effects). As predicted, SOC scores for returning U.S. MBA students are much higher on average than SOC scores for new U.S. MBA students. By contrast, SOC scores are *lower* for returning versus new foreign MBAs, although the magnitude of the difference is not as great.

The experience-citizenship interaction is evidence that our primary hypothesis is supported. As we predicted, the SOC scores

Figure 1
Two-way interaction of MBA program experience and
citizenship status on age-adjusted SOC scores.

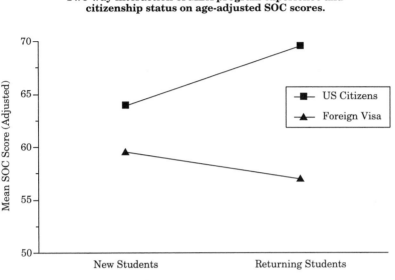

MBA Program Experience

of returning versus new U.S. MBA students are *higher* and the SOC scores of foreign MBA students are generally *lower*. We also suspected that the SOC scores of returning foreign MBAs might be lower than those of new foreign MBAs, and this pattern emerged in our analysis.[9] These results are consistent with our expectation that the MBA program has a salutogenic effect only on the sense of coherence of U.S. students, and they suggest some distressing consequences of the U.S. academic experience among students from abroad.

Gender, the MBA Program Experience, and the Sense of Coherence

After interpreting our primary findings, we began to speculate about whether we should also expect gender differences in SOC scores and, if so, about the direction these differences might take. Specifically, we wondered whether the salutogenic effect of the MBA program suggested by the higher SOC scores of returning versus new U.S. MBA students would be reflected in equal measure among males and females. Adding gender to the analysis was easily accomplished, but it also magnified the differences in group sizes, which range from 8 (new U.S. females) to 94 (returning U.S. males). A three-way ANCOVA with age as the covariate and citizenship, MBA program experience, and gender as the factors was performed, again using the hierarchical regression method in order to accommodate the unequal group sizes, and varying the entry order of the main effects. The findings should be considered tentative, however, until results based on a longitudinal design with larger group sizes are available.

This analysis revealed some provocative gender differences in SOC scores as a function of the other factors. Although gender failed to have a significant main effect (irrespective of being entered first, second, or third), it did contribute to the emergence of a marginally significant three-way interaction [$F(1,300) = 3.70, p < .06$]. The cell means for this interaction are plotted in Figure 2. The top half of the figure shows the MBA program experience-citizenship interaction for males, the bottom half shows the same interaction for females.

Figure 2 clearly shows that differences in SOC scores between new and returning MBA students depend on gender as well as citizenship status. Most notable is the fact that the difference (that is, higher SOC scores among returning vs. new students) occurs *only* among U.S. males. Similarly, only foreign males show the opposite effect—lower SOC scores among returning as compared to new MBAs. The means for U.S. and foreign females are striking because there is essentially *no difference* in age-adjusted SOC scores between new and returning females. U.S. females have consistently high SOC scores while foreign females have consistently low scores. Interestingly, this also means that new female MBAs from the U.S. have a much higher SOC than new U.S. male MBAs. This difference favoring females appears to reverse, however, because the SOC for returning U.S. males is higher than for returning U.S. females. By contrast, mean SOC scores are lower for both new and returning female versus male foreign students.

Thus, differences in SOC scores are further clarified when gender is added to experience and citizenship status. It is notable that the SOC scores of returning foreign male and female MBAs are never higher than the scores of new foreign male and female MBAs. However, the average SOC score for returning versus new foreign male MBAs is lower while no difference exists in the SOC scores of new and returning foreign female MBAs. Gender differences among the U.S. MBA students also raise some interesting questions.

Figure 2
Three-way interaction of MBA program experience, citizenship
status, and gender on age-adjusted SOC scores.

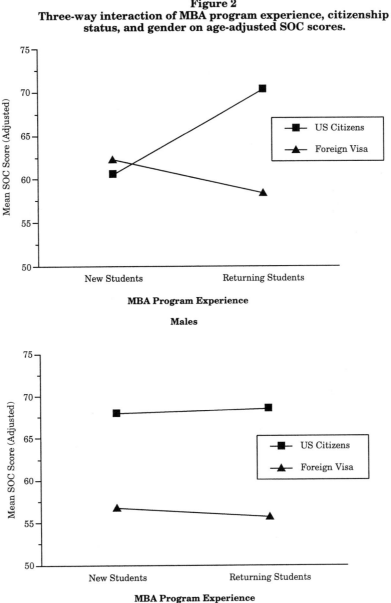

Males

Females

Returning U.S. male MBAs have higher SOC scores, while among U.S. females, no difference exists. In the United States, business—as an academic discipline and as a vocation—has been and continues to be dominated by Caucasian males; thus, the MBA program may be "validating" for these individuals. That the MBA program is not universally salutogenic in effect is suggested by the fact that the SOC scores of returning U.S. female MBAs are no higher than those of new U.S. female MBAs. Based on this evidence, we suspect that U.S. female MBAs with high SOC scores may be "self-selecting" into the male-dominated MBA program. That is, only those women with a strong sense of coherence may be willing to enroll in a male-dominated academic discipline such as business.

The Sense of Coherence, Alienation From the University, and Perceptions of Instruction

Thus far, our results suggest that the MBA program experience is associated with distinct differences in students' SOC scores. The contrast in SOC scores of U.S. and foreign students is especially noteworthy. By comparison with new MBAs, the SOC scores of returning U.S. students are higher and those of returning foreign students are lower. Further probing suggests that this pattern is more evident among male students. The SOC scores of U.S. and foreign females appear to be maintained at—in the first case—the same high level or—in the second—the same low level, irrespective of whether they are new or returning to the MBA program.

The final issue to be explored concerns the implications of an individual's SOC score for further positive experiences. That is, does a strong SOC positively influence a person's attitudes and perceptions of his or her experience? And if so, does the enhanced SOC gained from a structured academic experience then influence a person's perception of the value of that experience?

At this time, we can offer a tentative answer, after examining both the relationship between experience in the MBA program and the SOC, and relationships between the SOC and two other measures included in our survey: alienation from the university and perceptions of instruction. We constructed a simple path model and determined the direct and indirect path coefficients between the four measures.[10] To control for the interaction of experience, citizenship, and gender on the sense of coherence, we constructed separate models for U.S. and foreign males and females. Consistent with the results of the ANCOVA of SOC scores, the most interesting relationships occurred for U.S. versus foreign male MBA students. The path diagrams for these two groups are shown in Figure 3.[11]

As previously demonstrated, the salutogenic effect of the MBA program appears to be limited to U.S. males, because only returning U.S. males have higher SOC scores than their first-year counter-

Figure 3
Direct and indirect paths between MBA program experience, SOC, alienation, and perceptions of instruction for U.S. and foreign males.

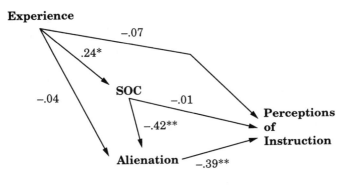

U.S. Males ($n = 87$)

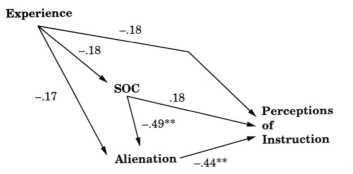

Foreign Males ($n = 63$)

* $p < .05$.   ** $p < .01$.

parts. This relationship is represented in the path model by the significant direct effect of experience on SOC scores (.24). Experience fails to have a direct effect either on self-reported feelings of alienation or perceptions of instruction. Thus, of the three possible social psychological outcomes—the SOC, alienation from the university, and judgments of the quality of instruction—only SOC scores are directly altered by U.S. males' experiences in the MBA program.

What is also clear is that experience has an *indirect* influence on both alienation from the university and perceptions of instruction through its effects on the SOC. The path model for U.S. males further shows that the direct effect of the SOC on feelings of alienation (–.42) is significant and *negative* (that is, U.S. males with higher SOC scores report that they feel *less* alienated). The sense of coherence also affects perceptions of instruction indirectly through alienation, which has a significant and negative direct effect on instruction (–.39). In other words, the coefficients in the path model for U.S. males suggest that the MBA program experience leads to an increase in SOC. Individuals with higher SOC scores feel less alienated and consequently evaluate the quality of the instruction they are receiving more favorably.

The path coefficients in the model for foreign males tell a different story. Although only the coefficients for the SOC/alienation/perceptions-of-instruction path are significant, it would be premature, given the small sample size, to conclude that the other effects are irrelevant. For purposes of exploring the underlying differences, it is worth contrasting the magnitude and direction of the relationships between MBA program experience and the other variables for U.S. males and foreign males. By contrast with the former group, the direct effect of experience on the SOC scores of foreign males is *negative* (–.18), a pattern consistent with the results of the ANCOVA reported earlier. Returning foreign males also are more alienated (–.17) and have poorer perceptions of the quality of instruction (–.18).

Given the opposite effect of experience on the SOC of foreign males, it is nevertheless noteworthy that foreign males with higher SOC scores also have lower feelings of alienation from the university and more favorable perceptions of instruction. The direct effects of the SOC on alienation (–.49) and of alienation on perceptions of instruction (–.44) are negative and significant for these students as well. Among foreign males, the SOC has a stronger direct effect on perceptions of instruction (.18), whereas SOC has no direct effect on these perceptions among U.S. males.

One could conclude from these patterns that the MBA program has a "self-propagating" salutogenic effect on U.S. males. That is, the MBA program experience may serve to reinforce or strengthen these students' sense of coherence, which consequently "primes" them for further experience in the form of favorable perceptions or attitudes toward the endeavor. The results for foreign males suggest that, for some, the sense of coherence will deteriorate, while for others, the negative aspects of living and studying in a foreign language and culture will be mitigated. Foreign males who enter the program with a strong sense of coherence may be more likely to at least feel that their experience is worthwhile, irrespective of whether it further enhances their SOC.

Conclusions and Implications

Our results suggest that the salutogenic effect of the MBA experience occurs only among certain individuals—namely U.S. males, who still comprise the dominant group in U.S. business culture. Within the non-dominant constituencies (women and foreign males), only those individuals with initially high SOC scores may be able to derive some benefit (although our data suggest that the "benefit" for these individuals provides only SOC-*maintenance* rather than SOC-*enhancement).* Our data of course do not indicate why or how some women and foreign males come to have higher SOC scores, but perhaps these individuals are more "like" U.S. males in terms of their socialization and experience. At greatest risk seem to be the foreign females. Their SOC scores are much lower than those of their U.S. counterparts and the scores do not appear to change as a function of experience. From our informal observations, these women seem to cope by being "invisible students"—neither losing nor gaining anything from their educational experience. Still other possible explanations are worth noting and investigating in the future.

We of course hesitate to draw strong causal conclusions about results based on a nonexperimental design. Our cross-sectional data suggest that the MBA program has a "developmental" effect on students' SOC scores, but this conclusion must remain somewhat speculative until a longitudinal study with more rigorous control of extraneous factors is conducted. We were able to control for the effect of repeated testing by dropping respondents who completed the survey both times. Other well-known threats to the validity of our findings, including statistical regression, other correlates of maturation, historical events, instrument decay, selection bias, and differential attrition, cannot be ruled out. Of these, differences based on gender and citizenship in selection (decision to enroll in and the fact of being accepted into an MBA program) and attrition (dropping out before graduating) are probably the most serious concerns, and should be minimized in future studies.

Further, to our knowledge, the existing literature does not address the issue of whether the Orientation to Life (OTL) scale is a valid measure of the SOC for non-Western cultures. In other words, the existing version of the OTL scale may yield a valid measure of an individual's SOC only among native English speakers who share common cultural experiences (which might of course differ between generations). We have interpreted our findings under the assumption that foreign students taking the SOC questionnaire employ frames of reference similar to those of U.S. students. To accept this assumption without debate is obviously ethnocentric. Thus, it may actually be the case that foreign students do not have lower SOC scores than U.S. students—they simply don't understand or relate to the dimensions of the OTL scale the same way. Focus-group discussions involving foreign students from different cultures might reveal whether the components of the SOC as represented in the OTL scale are generalizable across cultures.

Other differences between U.S. and foreign MBA students have interesting implications. U.S. students tend to be older, and over half of those in our sample are enrolled in the MBA program only on a part-time basis, mainly because they have full- or part-time jobs. Thus, many U.S. MBA students can immediately apply the concepts and tools they acquire in the MBA program to facets of their work lives, which may favor the development of a stronger SOC. Foreign MBAs holding student visas are not permitted to work during their stay in the U.S. Since they can only be full-time students, they spend the majority of their time studying and attending class. Business and management concepts, though well learned, may remain abstractions for these students until some years later. Thus, relative immaturity coupled with the absence of a concurrent opportunity to apply their knowledge may lead to a lesser sense of the comprehensibility, meaningfulness, and manageability of their MBA experience among foreign students. Separating the effects of age and MBA program experience on the various groups of students will require further research where cohorts are tracked longitudinally, with additional control measures to account for pre-existing differences in the groups.

In conclusion, our findings justify further research into the sources of sense of coherence development. Clearly, educational experience is an important influence that shapes people's lives. We have also identified other important issues related to the development of the sense of coherence—culture, gender, and experience associated with the maturation process—to be considered in future research.

Notes

1. This research was supported by a California State University, San Bernardino, Faculty Professional Development minigrant. We are grateful to Zack Loukides and Marion McHugh for assistance in entering and analyzing the data.

2. The authors' contributions to this chapter are equal.

3. In the analyses reported subsequently, the total sample size drops below 338 when cases are dropped due to missing data. In all analyses, listwise deletion of missing responses is used.

4. Although there is clearly a disproportion in the number of returning vs. new MBAs, such a disproportion is mainly of concern when the number of cases in one of the groups exceeds 90% of the total and when that variable is then correlated with another dichotomous variable skewed in the opposite direction. None of the distributions for the other measures used in the study are so highly skewed and, in the analysis, the appropriate adjustments for unequal group sizes are made.

5. From these numbers, it can be easily deduced that the proportion of foreign students among new MBAs is higher than the proportion of foreign students among returning MBAs. The cross-sectional data do not allow us to determine the reason for this difference but at least one or both of the following are possibilities: (1) foreign students may be dropping out after the first year in greater numbers (differential attrition); and/or (2) as full-time students, foreign students are more likely to complete their degrees in a timely fashion (within the two-year period) and graduate. More U.S. MBA students are attending part-time; thus, because it is taking them more total years to complete their degrees, their proportion in the population of returning students is higher.

6. Statistics based on sample sizes smaller than the total (338) have been adjusted to exclude cases with missing responses.

7. Due to the large sample size, the .12 correlation is still significant at the .05 level.

8. In nonexperimental designs, covariates are often used to make nonequivalent (i.e, pre-existing, nonrandomized) groups equivalent on one or more dimension believed to be related to the dependent variable. Such an extensive adjustment requires a covariate that correlates quite strongly (usually .80 or higher) with the dependent measure. The age covariate is not used in this more rigorous sense here.

9. Even if foreign students are dropping out of the program at a higher rate than U.S. students, it seems highly likely that students with the lowest SOC scores are leaving. In other words, if an entire starting cohort of foreign students returned for a second year, the drop in SOC scores might be even greater than is suggested by the difference in SOC scores for new vs. returning foreign students in the present study.

10. We used a series of hierarchical regressions to determine the path coefficients. This method assumes that the concepts are measured by single indicators with uncorrelated

errors. Though this assumption may not be tenable, we believe that a simple path analysis is more appropriate for an initial exploration of causal relationships than the increasingly popular linear structural equation modeling approach (such as LISREL or EQS). We excluded age from the model because it tends to be colinear with experience. Nevertheless, it should be kept in mind that part of the "experience" effect is due to age.

11. We note that the group sizes are relatively small for a path analysis at this level of disaggregation, although they do not violate the standard ratio of cases to variables of 10 to 1. Obviously the results need to be replicated with large sample sizes before a judgment about the stability of the relationships can be made.

References

Antonovsky, A. (1987). *Unraveling the mystery of health.* San Francisco: Jossey-Bass.

Antonovsky, A. (1992, February). Salutogenesis. In A. Antonovsky (Ed.), *The sense of coherence newsletter* (No. 4). Jerusalem, Israel: Author.

Antonovsky, A. (See Chapter 1). *The sense of coherence: An historical and future perspective.*

Antonovsky, A. (See Chapter 2). *The structure and properties of the sense of coherence scale.*

Burbach, H. J. (1972, April). The development of a contextual measure of alienation. *Pacific Sociological Review,* 225–234.

California State University. (1989). *A survey of student needs and priorities (SNAPS).* Long Beach, CA: California State University, Office of the Chancellor.

California State University, San Bernardino. (1993). *Bulletin 1992-93.* San Bernardino, CA: California State University.

Ryan, R. W., Raffel, J. A., & Lovell, C. (1987). International students in U.S. public administration programs: Profile, needs, and program response. *International Journal of Public Administration, 10*(1), 51–76.

Ryland, E. K. (1992). International students in management: From silence to synergy. *Journal of Management Education, 16,* 116–128.

Ryland, E. K., & King, J. C. (1992). Dissatisfied customers: International students in U.S. business management programs. In J. L. Wall & L. R. Jauch (Eds.), *Academy of Management best paper proceedings '92* (pp. 133–137). Madison, WI: Omnipress.

Surdam, J. C., & Collins, J. R. (1984). Adaptation of international students: A cause for concern. *Journal of College Student Personnel, 25*(3), 240–245.

Tabachnick, B.G., & Fidell, L. (1989). *Using multivariate statistics* (2nd ed.). New York: Harper & Row.

Chapter 8

Sense of Coherence in Adolescents With Cystic Fibrosis

Lois K. Baker

Cystic fibrosis (CF), a genetic disease that results in chronic respiratory infections and improper digestion of nutrients, is a major chronic illness affecting over 5,800 adolescents ages 12–22 years in the United States (Cystic Fibrosis Foundation, 1993). Until recently, few children with CF ever lived to reach puberty. Now, with recent medical advances, the median life expectancy is 29 years (Cystic Fibrosis Foundation, 1993). Consequently, at a time when major developmental changes are occurring, adolescents with CF are faced with the challenge of assuming greater independence in the performance of self-care behaviors that are critical to life itself. Some adolescents do engage in self-care while others perform self-care only sporadically. Little has been known about the factors that enhance or impede self-care behaviors in this population.

A study was undertaken to identify the predictors of self-care in adolescents with CF (Baker, 1991). The sense of coherence (SOC), along with nine other research variables, was examined for its ability to explain and predict self-care variance. The purpose of this chapter is to summarize the SOC findings in the context of the overall study results and to discuss the importance of the sense of coherence to adolescents who have a progressive and fatal disease.

Theoretical Framework

The theoretical framework for this theory-testing/theory-explication research was derived from Orem's theories of self-care and self-care deficit (1991). The theory of self-care focuses on those learned behaviors that individuals perform in the regulation of life, health, development, and well-being. The theory of self-care deficit explains the need for nursing when individuals experience health-related limitations in the continuous performance of self-care. Three major concepts from these two theories were examined: self-care, self-care agency, and basic conditioning factors.

Self-Care

Orem (1991) defined self-care as "the practice of activities that individuals initiate and perform on their own behalf in maintaining life, health, and well-being" (p. 117). Two types of self-care were examined in this research: universal and health-deviation self-care. Universal self-care consists of actions to maintain health that are required of everyone, such as eating a nutritious diet. Health-deviation self-care consists of actions that are required because of a specific disease and are thus not universally required of all persons. An example of health-deviation self-care in adolescents with CF is the infusion of tube feedings during the night in order to promote normal adolescent growth.

Figure 1
The Substantive Structure of Self-Care Agency

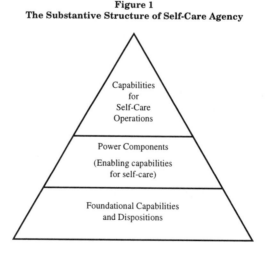

Taken from: Gast, H. L., Denyes, M. J., Campbell, J. C., Hartweg, D. L., Schott-Baer, D., & Isenberg, M. (1989). Self-care agency: Conceptualizations and operationalizations. *Advances in Nursing Science, 12* (1), 26-38.

Self-Care Agency

Orem (1991) defined self-care agency as "the *complex acquired ability* to meet one's continuing requirements for care that regulates life processes, maintains or promotes integrity of human structure and functioning and human development, and promotes well-being" (p. 145). Recent conceptual work has resulted in the clarification of this construct as consisting of three related but theoretically distinct human capabilities or traits (Gast et al., 1989). These three components, arranged in hierarchical order, are: (a) foundational capabilities and dispositions; (b) power components; and (c) capabilities to perform estimative, transitional, and productive self-care operations (Figure 1).

Foundational capabilities and dispositions. Foundational capabilities and dispositions are those human characteristics that are most basic to the performance of any type of deliberate action and which are foundational to the other two dimensions of self-care agency. As such, one would expect these abilities to be distinct from, yet related to the other components of self-care agency. Two concepts, general intelligence and the SOC, were conceptualized by the researcher as foundational abilities essential to the self-care of adolescents with CF.

General intelligence is defined by Wechsler (1981) as "... the global capacity of the individual to act purposefully, to think rationally, and to deal effectively with his environment" (p. 7). It is obvious that a certain degree of intelligence is necessary if adolescents with CF are to knowledgeably plan and perform the self-care necessary to the maintenance of life. However, the manner in which intelligence interacts with the other dimensions of self-care agency and its relationship to self-care has not been previously examined.

Antonovsky (1979, 1987) developed the salutogenic model of health to explain the fact that individuals remain healthy despite the ubiquity of stressors in everyday life (Figure 2). Central to this theory is the sense of coherence concept, which Antonovsky proposed as foundational to the maintenance or improvement of one's health status. The SOC affects health through its facilitation of tension-management behaviors. This conceptual relationship between the SOC and tension-management behaviors is similar to that proposed by Orem (1991) between self-care agency and self-care behaviors. Furthermore, successful tension-management behaviors and therapeutic self-care behaviors are both postulated to influence one's health in a positive way (Antonovsky, 1987; Orem,

Figure 2
The Salutogenic Model

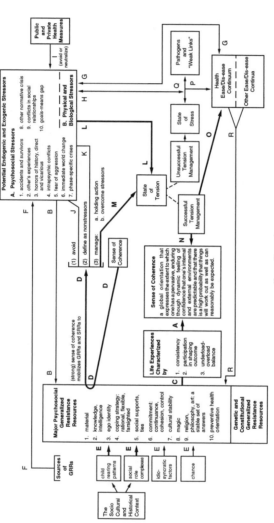

Key to Figure 2

Arrow A: **Life experiences shape the sense of coherence.**

Arrow B: Stressors affect the generalized resistance resources (GRRs) at one's disposal.

Arrow C: **By definition, a GRR provides one with sets of meaningful, coherent life experiences.**

Arrow D: **A strong sense of coherence mobilizes the GRRs and specific resistance resources (SRRs) at one's disposal.**

Arrows E: **Childrearing patterns, social role complexes, idiosyncratic factors, and chance build up GRRs.**

Arrow F: The sources of GRRs also create stressors.

Arrow G: Traumatic physical and biochemical stressors affect health status directly; health status affects extent of exposure to psychosocial stressors.

Arrow H: Physical and biochemical stressors interact with endogenic pathogens and "weak links" and with stress to affect health status.

Arrow I: Public and private health measures avoid or neutralize stressors.

Line J: A strong sense of coherence, mobilizing GRRs and SRRs, avoids stressors.

Line K: A strong sense of coherence, mobilizing GRRs and SRRs, defines stimuli as nonstressors.

Arrow L: **Ubiquitous stressors create a state of tension.**

Arrow M: **The mobilized GRRs (and SRRs) interact with the state of tension and manage a holding action and the overcomming of stressors.**

Arrow N: **Successful tension management strengthens the sense of coherence.**

Arrow O: **Successful tension management maintains one's place on the health ease/dis-ease continuum.**

Arrow P: **Interaction between the state of stress and pathogens and "weak links" negatively affects health status.**

Arrow Q: Stress is a general precursor that interacts with the existing potential endogenic and exogenic pathogens and "weak links".

Arrow R: Good health status facilitates the acquisition of other GRRs.

Note. The statements in **bold** type represent the core of the salutogenic model.

From: Antonovsky, A. (1979). *Health, stress, and coping* (p. 184-185). San Francisco: Jossey-Bass.

1991). Because of this conceptual congruence and because of the need to further explicate those factors that are critical to the performance of self-care, it was proposed that the sense of coherence is a foundational capability. Antonovsky (1987) defined the SOC as:

> A global orientation that expresses the extent to which one has a pervasive, enduring though dynamic feeling of confidence that (a) the stimuli deriving from one's internal and external environments in the course of living are structured, predictable, and explicable; (b) the resources are available to one to meet the demands posed by these stimuli; and (c) these demands are challenges, worthy of investment and engagement (p. 19).

Antonovsky (1987) further clarified the substantive structure of the SOC as being comprised of three components: (a) comprehensibility, (b) manageability, and (c) meaningfulness. These components of a sense of coherence develop as one's patterns of life experiences are influenced by consistency, underload-overload balance, and participation in shaping outcomes, respectively. Although adolescence is almost stereotypically known as a "storm and stress" period of development, Antonovsky (1987) did not preclude adolescents from the possibility of developing a sense of coherence. The central issue is the degree to which the adolescent has life experiences that are characterized by consistency, underload-overload balance, and participation in shaping outcomes.

Power components. Next in the hierarchy of the conceptual elements or dimensions of self-care agency are the power components (Gast et al., 1989). Unlike the foundational capabilities and dispositions, which are fundamental to any type of deliberate action, the power components are enabling for specific types of health self-care actions. The six power components examined in this research were: (a) ego strength; (b) valuing of health; (c) health knowledge and decision-making capability; (d) attention to health, or the degree to which the adolescents think about their health and what it might be like in the future; (e) energy; and (f) the ability to talk about one's feelings.

Capabilities to perform estimative, transitional, and productive self-care actions. Third in the hierarchical structure of self-care agency are the capabilities for performing three types of self-care operations (Gast et al., 1989). Estimative operations include the ability to investigate those internal and external factors significant to the performance of self-care. Transitional operations include the ability to make decisions concerning what can, should, and will be done to meet the self-care requirements. Productive operations include the capabilities necessary to the actual performance of self-care. This dimension of self-care agency was not examined in the present study.

Basic Conditioning Factors

Orem (1991) described basic conditioning factors as factors that influence an individual's self-care agency in a positive or negative way. Seven basic conditioning factors were examined in this study: (a) age; (b) gender; (c) family income; (d) family socioeconomic status; (e) egocentric thought, or the degree to which the adolescent's thinking was characterized by the personal fable or imaginary audience (Elkind, 1984); (f) the adolescent's satisfaction with his or her family; and (g) severity of illness.

In summary, Orem (1991) stated that individuals who engage in *self-care* possess specialized capabilities for actions (*self-care agency*). The individual's self-care agency is influenced in a positive or negative way by variables known as *basic conditioning factors*. The relationship between these three concepts is depicted in the Theoretical Model (Figure 3).

Figure 3
Theoretical Model

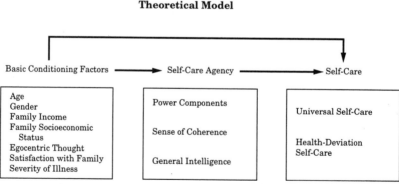

Hypotheses

The research hypotheses that were relevant to the purpose of this chapter were:

1) Basic conditioning factors (age, gender, family income, family socioeconomic status, egocentric thought, satisfaction with family, and severity of illness) will account for a significant amount of variance in the foundational capability and disposition dimension (general intelligence and the SOC) of self-care agency in adolescents with CF.

2) There will be positive relationships between general intelligence and the SOC; between general intelligence and power components; and between the SOC and power components in adolescents with CF.

3) There will be positive relationships between the SOC and universal and health-deviation self-care in adolescents with CF.

4) In combination, basic conditioning factors (age, gender, family income, family socioeconomic status, egocentric thought, satisfaction with family, and severity of illness) and self-care agency (general intelligence and the SOC) will account for a greater amount of variance in both universal and health-deviation self-care in adolescents with CF than will basic conditioning factors or self-care agency alone.

Review of Literature

Cystic fibrosis is one of the most common genetically transmitted diseases found in children and adolescents, affecting 1 in 1,600 births. Because CF dramatically shortens one's life, the majority of CF research has been devoted to genetic aspects, treatment, and cure. Although clinicians frequently witness more rapid disease progression in individuals who do not engage in self-care, no studies were found in which the self-care of persons with CF was examined. However, the current state of knowledge about self-care in healthy and ill children, adolescents, and adults has been enhanced by a growing number of studies in which self-care, self-care agency, and basic conditioning factors have been examined in other populations. Results of these studies have provided support for the proposed relationships between these three major concepts.

Self-Care

There is now considerable evidence that self-care agency dimensions are related to self-care. Low-moderate to strong positive relationships have been reported between the power component dimension of self-care agency and self-care (Denyes, 1988; Gaut & Kieckhefer, 1988). The power component dimension of self-care agency has also been found to be a significant predictor of universal self-care (Denyes, 1988). The foundational capability and disposition dimension of self-care agency, although examined less often in relationship to self-care than self-care agency, has been reported to account for a significant amount of variance in self-care when added to measures of basic conditioning factors (Saucier, 1984).

There is growing evidence that demonstrates support for Orem's proposed relationships between the various dimensions of self-care agency. Self-concept and coping dispositions, two newly conceptualized foundational abilities, have been examined in relationship to the power component dimension of self-care agency and the relationships have been moderately strong and positive (Haas, 1990; Harvey, 1986).

Sense of Coherence

Although the SOC concept has begun to receive widespread interdisciplinary examination as both an independent and dependent variable, there were no studies found in which the SOC had been examined in relation to self-care behaviors. However, a variety of studies have provided support for Antonovsky's (1979, 1987) salutogenic model of health. A cross-sectional study of 297 Israeli adults provided tentative support for the predictive value of the SOC in relationship to health status (Antonovsky, 1987). Additional support for the SOC/health link was provided by Fiorentino's (1986) study of 121 production workers. A significant but small negative correlation ($r = -.191, p = .05$) was found between SOC scores and health scores as measured by Antonovsky's (1979) health ease/dis-ease continuum.

Only two studies could be identified in which the SOC was examined in an adolescent population. Antonovsky and Sagy (1986) studied the development of the SOC and its impact on responses to stress situations in 418 adolescents, grades 9 through 12. Seventy-eight of these adolescents were soon to be evacuated from their homes in the Sinai region. Age, sex, and community stability (all of which are basic conditioning factors according to Orem, 1991) accounted for 8% of the variance in SOC scores. With anxiety used as a general measure of mental health, the SOC was found to be negatively correlated with trait anxiety ($r = -.555$ in the Sinai group; $r = -.621$ in the remaining sample). Further analysis demonstrated that the SOC was negatively correlated with state anxiety in "normal" ego-threatening situations ($r = -.165$ to $-.426$), but showed no relationship to state anxiety associated with the evacuation ($r = -.062$). The authors suggested that the lack of relationship between the SOC and state anxiety associated with the evacuation might be reflective of the times in life that are so overwhelming that one's SOC is challenged.

In Antonovsky and Sagy's (1986) sample, males reported significantly higher SOC scores than females and their scores increased through adolescence. However, no relationship was found between the parent-adolescent relationship and SOC scores—a finding that the authors suggested might be due to inadequate operational measure of the parent-adolescent relationship.

LaLiberte (1989) examined the SOC in a sample of 48 children, ages 9 through 13, who attended public schools. Unlike Antonovsky and Sagy's (1986) results, there were no significant differences in SOC scores by gender or chronological age. However, a significant difference emerged between those who attended the elementary versus middle schools [$t(46) = 2.50$, $p = .02$]. The authors suggested that these differences reflect the multiple changes that occur in the transition of moving from elementary to middle school—another example of life experiences that potentially challenge one's sense of coherence.

In summary, preliminary support for the validity of Orem's theories of self-care and self-care deficit (Orem, 1991) and Antonovsky's salutogenic model of health (1979, 1987) has been presented. The present investigation involved further testing of Orem's theories and was built on the foundation laid by previous theory-testing efforts. In order to account for a greater amount of variance in self-care than has been previously accounted for, two new foundational capabilities and dispositions—general intelligence and the SOC—were examined in the present study.

Methods

Design/Sample

A descriptive multivariate correlational design was used to examine the relationships between basic conditioning factors, self-care agency, and self-care, and to determine which variables were significant predictors of self-care. Adolescents, ages 12 through 22 years, who had CF and who were inpatients or attended the outpatient clinics at three children's medical centers in the Midwestern United States comprised the sample. According to Cohen (1977), with an alpha set at .05 and power at .80, a sample of 121 adolescents was necessary in order to detect a small effect size when using multivariate analyses.

Table 1
Theoretical Concepts and Operational Measures

Theoretical	Operational
1. Basic Conditioning Factors	
a. Age	Age in years as reported by adolescent
b. Gender	Subject's self-report status as male or female
c. Family income	Annual gross income of:
	a. parent(s) of adolescent who is not self-supporting or
	b. self-supporting adolescent/adolescent spouse
d. Family socioeconomic status	Four Factor Index of Social Status (Hollingshead, 1975)
e. Satisfaction with family	Family APGAR (Smilkstein, 1978)
f. Egocentric thought	Adolescent Egocentrism-Sociocentrism Scale (Enright, Shukla, & Lapsley, 1980)
2. Self-Care Agency	
a. Foundational capabilities and dispositions	
(i) General intelligence	Vocabulary subtest (Wechsler Adult Intelligence Scale–Revised) (Wechsler, 1981)
(ii) Sense of coherence	Sense of Coherence Questionnaire (Antonovsky, 1987)
b. Power components	Denyes Self-Care Agency Instrument-90 (Denyes, 1981)
3. Self-Care	
a. Universal self-care	Denyes Self-Care Practice Instrument (Denyes, 1981)
b. Health-deviation self-care	Cystic Fibrosis Self-Care Practice Instrument (Baker, 1991)

Instruments

Table 1 depicts the instruments chosen to measure the research variables. The construct or content validity of each of these measures has been documented. For the present study, the internal consistency reliabilities met or exceeded the minimum standards determined by Nunnally (1978).

The 29-item SOC questionnaire (Antonovsky, 1987) was used with one minor alteration. Item 10 was altered to reflect a time reference more appropriate to the research subjects' chronological age. "In the past ten years" was changed to "in the past five years." The Cronbach's Alpha coefficient for the present sample was .92.

Data Collection

The self-report operational measures were compiled into a master questionnaire booklet. Each of the 134 questions was formatted on a Likert or ratio scale.

Letters explaining the research and inviting participation were sent to potential subjects from the three medical centers. In the outpatient clinic or inpatient unit, the researcher met the adolescent and/or adolescent and parent and offered a verbal invitation to participate. After obtaining consent, the researcher gave the questionnaire booklet to the adolescent to complete in the waiting room, clinic examining room, or inpatient room. It took an average of 25 to 35 minutes to answer all of the written questions. Upon completion of the questionnaires, the researcher verbally administered the vocabulary subtest. Procedures to protect human subjects were strictly followed at all three research sites.

All data were analyzed by means of the Statistical Package for Social Sciences/Personal Computer Software (SPSS/PC). The SPSS default for listwise deletion of missing data was used. The significance level for each statistical test was set at .05.

Results

One hundred and twenty-three adolescents participated in this study. The subjects ranged in age from 12 through 22 years, with a mean age of 18.4 and standard deviation of 3.2; 51% of the subjects were male; 49% were female; 40% of the subjects had normal lung function as measured by forced vital capacity, while 18% had forced vital capacity less than 50% predicted. Although a convenience sample, the sample distribution by gender and severity of illness closely resembled the profile of all adolescents with CF in the United States.

The mean family income was between $30,000 and $35,000 with a range of less than $10,000 to over $50,000. The Hollingshead socioeconomic status scores for this sample ranged from 11 to 66, with a mean of 36.9. The summary statistics for the remaining research variables are contained in Table 2.

Table 2
Summary Statistics and Potential Range
of Values for Major Variables

Research Variable	n	Mean	SD	Min	Max	Potential Range
Egocentric thought	119	49.8	9.8	25.0	70.0	15 – 75
Satisfaction with family	123	6.6	2.7	0.0	10.0	0 – 10
Severity of illness	122	75.7	26.9	17.0	152.0	12 – 152
General intelligence	122	29.6	14.7	3.2	57.2	0 – 70
Sense of coherence	116	134.9	25.4	62.0	199.0	29 – 203
Power components[a]	110	73.4	13.7	29.8	99.3	0 – 100
Universal self-care	119	68.1	17.0	8.3	98.9	0 – 100
Health-deviation self-care	123	60.9	14.0	18.5	95.6	0 – 100

[a] Total scores.

Sense of Coherence Scores

The mean SOC score for this sample was 134.9 with a standard deviation of 25.4 and a range of 29 to 203. There were no significant age or gender differences in SOC scores.

Hypothesis 1: Relationships Between Basic Conditioning Factors and Self-Care Agency (General Intelligence and Sense of Coherence)

Hypothesis 1 stated that *basic conditioning factors* (age, gender, family income, family socioeconomic status, egocentric thought, satisfaction with family, and severity of illness) *will account for a significant amount of variance in the foundational capability and disposition dimension* (general intelligence and the SOC) *of self-care agency.* This hypothesis was supported. Prior to completing the regression analysis, zero-order correlations were computed between the basic conditioning factors and foundational abilities. Stepwise regression analysis was then used to assess the collective ability of the basic conditioning factors to account for self-care agency variance.

Basic conditioning factors and general intelligence. First, the basic conditioning factors were entered stepwise with the criterion variable being the level of general intelligence. Age entered first, accounting for 15% of the variance in general intelligence. Next socioeconomic status entered, accounting for an additional 16% of the variance. Together, age and family socioeconomic status accounted for 31% of the variance in general intelligence; both were significant predictors of general intelligence (Table 3).

Table 3
Stepwise Multiple Regression: Basic Conditioning Factors Predicting General Intelligence (n = 99)

Source of Variation	Step Enter	Multiple R	R Square	RSQ Change	F Change	Beta
Age	1	.38	.15	.15	16.76***	.45***
Socioeconomic status	2	.55	.31	.16	22.19***	.41***

***p < .001.

Basic conditioning factors and sense of coherence. Three moderately strong and significant zero-order relationships were detected between the SOC and the basic conditioning factors of family income (r = .38, p < .001), family socioeconomic status (r = .30, p < .001), and satisfaction with family (r = .50; p < .001). When the basic conditioning factors were entered stepwise into the regression equation with the SOC as the criterion variable, satisfaction with family entered first, accounting for 25% of the variance in SOC scores. Socioeconomic status entered next, accounting for an additional 9% of the variance. Together these two variables accounted for 35% of the variance in SOC scores; both were significant predictors (Table 4).

Table 4
Stepwise Multiple Regression: Basic Conditioning Factors
Predicting Sense of Coherence ($n = 96$)

Source of Variation	Step Enter	Multiple R	R Square	RSQ Change	F Change	Beta
Satisfaction with family	1	.50	.25	.25	31.63	.44***
Socioeconomic status	2	.59	.35	.09	13.37	.31***

***$p < .001$.

Hypothesis 2: Relationships Among Dimensions of Self-Care Agency

Hypothesis 2 stated *there will be positive relationships among the three dimensions of self-care agency in adolescents with CF.* There was partial support for this hypothesis. As seen in Table 5, the only significant relationship was a strong positive relationship between SOC scores and the overall score on power components of self-care agency.

Table 5
Correlation Matrix: Dimensions of Self-Care Agency

	1	2	3
1. General intelligence	1.00	.07	.11
2. Sense of coherence	—	1.00	.74***
3. Power components[a]	—	—	1.00

[a] Total scores.
***$p < .001$.

When Pearson product moment correlations were computed among the foundational dimensions and power component subscales, low positive relationships were detected between general intelligence and the two subscales of health knowledge and decision-making capability, and energy. The SOC was positively correlated with each of the power component subscales; these correlations were moderately strong to strong. General intelligence was not significantly related to either the overall power components score or to the SOC (see Table 6).

Table 6
Correlations Among Dimensions of Self-Care Agency
Using Power Component Subscale Scores

Foundational Capab/Disp	Power Components of Self-Care Agency					
	Ego Strength	Valuing Health	Health Know & Decision-Making Capability	Energy	Feelings	Attn Health
General intelligence	−.01	.02	.18*	.16*	.07	−.06
Sense of coherence	.76***	.49***	.62***	.38***	.51***	.46***

*p < .05.   ***p < .001.

Hypothesis 3: Relationships Between Sense of Coherence and Self-Care

Hypothesis 3 predicted *positive relationships between the SOC and universal and health-deviation self-care*. This hypothesis was supported. The sense of coherence was moderately and positively correlated with universal self-care ($r = .66$, $p < .001$) and with health-deviation self-care ($r = .51$, $p < .001$).

Hypothesis 4: Combined Effect of Basic Conditioning Factors and Self-Care Agency on Self-Care

Hypothesis 4 stated *in combination, the basic conditioning factors* (age, gender, family income, family socioeconomic status, egocentric thought, satisfaction with family, and severity of illness) *and self-care agency* (general intelligence, SOC, and power components) *will account for a greater amount of variance in both universal and health-deviation self-care in adolescents with CF than will basic conditioning factors or self-care agency alone.* This hypothesis received partial support. Since ability should theoretically be the best predictor of self-care, the power component subscale scores were entered first into the regression equation. Following the entry of the power components, the foundational capabilities and dispositions were entered stepwise as a set. Finally, the basic conditioning factors were also entered stepwise as a set.

At step one with *universal self-care* as the criterion variable, the power component subscales were entered into the regression equation (Table 7). Ego strength entered first, accounting for 55% of the variance. Next, attention to health entered, explaining an additional 9% of the variance. Finally, health knowledge and decision-making capability entered, explaining an additional 3% of the variance. Together, power components of self-care agency accounted for 67% of the variance in universal self-care.

Table 7
Summary of Hierarchical Regression for Predicting
Universal Self-Care in Adolescents with CF (*n* = 84)

Source of Variation	Step Enter	Multiple R	R Square	RSQ Change	F Change	Beta
Set 1: Power Component Subscales						
Subscale 1: Ego strength	1	.74	.55	.55	98.55***	.281***
Subscale 6: Attn health	2	.80	.63	.09	19.35***	.23**
Subscale 3: Health know & decision-making capability	3	.82	.67	.03	8.29**	.21*
Set 2: Foundational Capab/Disp (Stepwise)						
Sense of coherence	1	.84	.70	.03	8.01**	.28**
Set 3: Basic Conditioning Factors (Stepwise)						
None entered						

*$p < .05$. **$p < .01$. ***$p < .001$.

At step two, general intelligence and the SOC were entered stepwise into the equation. The sense of coherence was the only foundational ability to enter, accounting for an additional 3% of the variance in universal self-care. Finally, the basic conditioning factors were entered stepwise into the equation. None of the basic conditioning factors added significantly to the amount of variance explained. Together, ego strength, attention to health, health knowledge and decision-making capability, and the SOC accounted for 70% of the variance in universal self-care; each of these variables was a significant predictor.

Table 8
Summary of Hierarchical Regression for Predicting
Health-Deviation Self-Care in Adolescents with CF ($n = 84$)

Source of Variation	Step Enter	Multiple R	R Square	RSQ Change	F Change	Beta
Set 1: Power Component Subscales						
Subscale 6: Attn health	1	.56	.32	.32	39.23**	.36***
Subscale 3: Health know & decision-making capability	2	.61	.37	.06	7.64**	.17 ns
Set 2: Foundational Capab/Disp (Stepwise)						
Sense of coherence	1	.64	.40	.03	4.34*	.23*
Set 3: Basic Conditioning Factors (Stepwise)						
None entered						

$*p < .05.$ $**p < .01.$ $***p < .001.$

To assess the cumulative ability of self-care agency and basic conditioning factors to predict variance in *health-deviation self-care*, a second hierarchical regression analysis was run (Table 8). At step one, the power component subscales were entered stepwise as a set. Attention to health entered first, accounting for 32% of the variance. Next, health knowledge and decision-making capability entered, explaining an additional 6% of the variance. Together, the power components of self-care agency accounted for 37% of the variance in health-deviation self-care. At step two, general intelligence and the SOC were entered stepwise as a set. The SOC explained an additional 3% of the variance. Finally, at the third step the basic conditioning factors were entered stepwise into the equation. None of the basic conditioning factors met the requirements for entry into the equation. Together, attention to health, health knowledge and decision-making capability, and the SOC accounted for 40% of the health-deviation self-care variance. Only attention to health and the SOC emerged as significant predictors.

Discussion

The sense of coherence data obtained from this study are relevant to the support of Orem's theories of self-care and self-care deficit (1991) as well as Antonovsky's salutogenic model of health (1979, 1987). In addition, they provide the health care practitioner with a description of how a sense of coherence operates in adolescents with CF. Thus the findings have both theoretical and practical applications for those who wish to promote self-care in this group of young people.

Sense of Coherence in Adolescents With Cystic Fibrosis

In the context of having a disease that is progressive and fatal, it was interesting to see that the sample mean SOC score was within the range of means (125 to 170) that characterizes most samples (Antonovsky, personal communication, February 26, 1990). Antonovsky has suggested that only very unique samples fall outside of this range. However, individuals who face death issues during adolescence would certainly seem to represent a unique category. Therefore, further investigation of the salutogenic model was undertaken in an attempt to explain this phenomenon.

Antonovsky (1987) has suggested that the SOC develops out of life experiences that provide consistency, participation in shaping outcomes, and overload/underload balance. Although adolescents with CF may face developmental and death issues concomitantly, it appears that many of them also have life experiences that may promote the development of a sense of coherence. Their lives are often structured around the health-deviation self-care requirements of CF. In addition, most adolescents are seen in the outpatient clinic every two months. Both of these factors help to promote *consistency*. In spite of the progressive nature of CF, the adolescent can *participate* in self-care and can thus influence health outcomes. What was interesting was how often the interaction with nurses and other health professionals seemed to contribute to the adolescent's perception of life as being meaningful. On many occasions, it appeared obvious that the adolescents viewed the clinic staff as "family," often seeking their advice and confiding in them. In addition, it became apparent that many families helped to share the burden of self-care with the adolescent, providing an *overload/underload balance*. Therefore, even though these adolescents had a progressive and fatal disease, it seemed that many of them had life experiences that promoted the development of a sense of coherence.

Relationship Between Basic Conditioning Factors and Sense of Coherence

As seen in Table 4, the basic conditioning factors of satisfaction with family and family socioeconomic status accounted for 35% of the variance in SOC scores. Both were significant predictors of the SOC. This predictive relationship is congruent with Antonovsky's (1979, 1987) conceptualization of social support and material resources as generalized resistance resources that provide life experiences that strengthen one's SOC (Figure 2). At this juncture, it is interesting to ask whether satisfaction with family is more closely related to the generalized resistance resource of social support as previously suggested or whether it is related to child-rearing practices that Antonovsky (1979) conceptualized as a *source* of generalized resistance resources. Further theoretical and methodological work will be needed to answer this question.

Relationship Between Two Foundational Abilities

As seen in Table 5, the Pearson product moment correlation between general intelligence and the SOC was in the expected direction, but was small and nonsignificant. This lack of relationship was unexpected in light of the placement of intelligence as a generalized resistance resource in Antonovsky's model (1979). Perhaps the unidimensional nature of the vocabulary subtest contributed to this finding. Since general intelligence in adolescents is not fully developed, it is possible that a more generalized aptitude measure that is not as age dependent might have permitted a relationship to be detected.

Relationship Between Power Components and Sense of Coherence

As seen in Table 6, the SOC was positively correlated with each of the power components of ego strength, valuing of health, health knowledge and decision-making capability, attention to health, energy, and the ability to talk about one's feelings ($p < .001$). Theoretical similarities between Orem's (1991) power components and Antonovsky's (1979, 1987) generalized resistance resources show that these moderate to strong positive relationships between power components and the SOC are supportive of Antonovsky's proposed relationships between generalized resistance resources and the sense of coherence.

Table 9
Similarities Between Orem's and Antonovsky's
Conceptual Catagories

Orem	Antonovsky
Basic Conditioning Factor	**Generalized Resistance Resource**
Satisfaction with family	Social support
Family socioeconomic status	Material resources
Power Component	**Generalized Resistance Resource**
Ego strength	Ego identity
Health knowledge & decision-making capability	Knowledge/intelligence
Valuing of health	Preventive health orientation

Summary of Theoretical Similarities

In the present study, family income and family socioeconomic status were conceptualized as basic conditioning factors. Ego strength, valuing of health, health knowledge and decision-making capability, attention to health, energy, and the ability to talk about one's feelings were conceptualized as power components needed for the performance of self-care in adolescents with CF. The two basic conditioning factors and three of the power components are theoretically similar to five variables conceptualized as generalized resistance resources within Antonovsky's model (1979). Table 9 summarizes these conceptually similar variables.

In both Orem's and Antonovsky's models, specific resources/ abilities are postulated to be necessary for engaging in either tension-management or self-care behaviors. According to Antonovsky (1987), generalized resistance resources, when mobilized by a strong SOC, are necessary for successful tension management. Orem (1985, 1991) has defined power components as specific abilities necessary for health self-care action. In turn, basic conditioning factors are conceptualized as variables that influence one's ability to engage in self-care in a positive or negative manner.

Sense of Coherence and Universal Self-Care

The sense of coherence, even though strongly and positively correlated with ego strength ($r = .76, p < .001$), still emerged as a predictor of universal self-care and, relatively speaking, was as strong a predictor as ego strength, the beta weights being .280 and .281, respectively ($p < .001$). A closer look at how the sense of coherence operates within Antonovsky's salutogenic model of health (1979, 1987) assists in the interpretation of this finding.

According to Antonovsky (1979), having a sense of coherence mobilizes the general and specific resistance resources that one has for dealing with stressors (Figure 2). Interestingly, ego identity is identified as one of the generalized resistance resources. A sense of coherence provides a view of one's world which includes a view of oneself, whereas ego identity is more specifically a view of oneself. Having a sense of coherence is postulated to mobilize one's ego identity for dealing with life experiences. In addition, having a strong identity is believed to be essential to the development of a sense of coherence. In the present study, the strong correlation between the SOC and ego strength suggests this bidirectional influence.

The fact that the SOC emerged as a significant predictor of universal self-care, even with the power components in the regression equation, supports Antonovsky's (1987) notion that the SOC is related to but conceptually distinct from ego identity. In addition, the fact that the SOC was more strongly correlated with power components than with universal self-care suggests that it is "foundational" to the power components, a more specific type of ability for engaging in health self-care. This pattern of relationships supports both Orem's (1979, 1991) conceptualization of foundational capabilities and Antonovsky's (1979, 1987) distinction between the broad perspective of the world associated with the SOC and the more specific view of oneself indicated by ego identity.

Sense of Coherence and Health-Deviation Self-Care

The sense of coherence was also a predictor of health-deviation self-care, accounting for 3% of health-deviation self-care variance. However, the predictive pattern was different from the one for universal self-care, suggesting that the two types of care, although conceptually related, are still distinct. This finding is not unexpected since there is no doubt that the types of CF self-care behaviors that are required are indeed different from and more complex and time consuming than those actions associated with universal self-care.

Sense of Coherence and Severity of Illness

The Pearson product moment correlation between severity of illness and the SOC was $r = .06, p > .05$. Although this relationship was in the expected direction, it was small and nonsignificant.

The severity of illness measure may explain the lack of relationship between the SOC and severity of illness in the present study. The operational measure for severity of illness was the percent predicted forced vital capacity, the maximum amount of air that can be forcibly exhaled after a forcible inhalation (lower forced vital capacity indicated more severe illness). Since the SOC was a significant predictor of both types of self-care and since the projected outcome of self-care is maintenance or improvement of one's health status, it was expected that there would be a negative relationship between the SOC and severity of illness.

However, the unidimensional nature of forced vital capacity may have constrained the detection of any such relationship. While the most frequent cause of death in adolescents with CF is deterioration in pulmonary function, there is also a significant nutritional component to the disease. Perhaps the inclusion of nutritional status in addition to pulmonary function would have provided a more comprehensive measure of severity of illness.

Another consideration is the cross-sectional nature of the severity of illness measure. A longitudinal study might have permitted the detection of a relationship between the SOC and severity of illness.

Summary

In summary, the data presented suggest theoretical linkages between Orem's theories of self care and self-care deficit (1991) and Antonovsky's salutogenic model of health (1979). In addition, the data support Antonovsky's propositions about the bidirectional influence between generalized resistance resources and the SOC. Further conceptual and methodological work will be needed to clarify the lack of expected relationships between the SOC and the variables of general intelligence and severity of illness. Finally, the data suggest that having a sense of coherence is very important to the self-care of adolescents with cystic fibrosis. In spite of the strong positive relationships between the sense of coherence and power components of self-care agency, the sense of coherence still emerged as a significant predictor of both universal and health-deviation self-care.

References

Antonovsky, A. (1979). *Health, stress, and coping.* San Francisco: Jossey-Bass.

Antonovsky, A. (1987). *Unraveling the mystery of health: How people manage stress and stay well.* San Francisco: Jossey-Bass.

Antonovsky, H., & Sagy, S. (1986). The development of a sense of coherence and its impact on responses to stress situations. *Journal of Social Psychology, 126,* 213–225.

Baker, L. K. (1991). *Predictors of self-care in adolescents with cystic fibrosis—A test and explication of Orem's theories of self-care and self-care deficit.* Unpublished doctoral dissertation, Wayne State University, Detroit, MI.

Cohen, J. (1977). *Statistical power analysis for the behavioral sciences.* New York: Academic Press.

Cystic Fibrosis Foundation. (1993). *Cystic Fibrosis Foundation, patient registry, 1992 annual data.* Bethesda, MD: Author.

Denyes, M. J. (1981). Development of an instrument to measure self-care agency in adolescents (Doctoral dissertation, University of Michigan, 1980). *Dissertation Abstracts International, 41,* 1716B.

Denyes, M. J. (1988). Orem's model used for health promotion: Directions from research. *Advances in Nursing Science, 11*(1), 13–21.

Elkind, D. (1984). Teen-age thinking: Implications for health care. *Pediatric Nursing, 10,* 383–385.

Enright, R. D., Shukla, D., & Lapsley, D. K. (1980). Adolescent egocentrism-sociocentrism and self-consciousness. *Journal of Youth and Adolescence, 9,* 101–116.

Fiorentino, L. M. (1986). Stress—The high cost to industry. *American Association of Occupational Health Nursing, 34,* 217–220.

Gast, H. L., Denyes, M. J., Campbell, J. C., Hartweg, D. L., Schott-Baer, D., & Isenberg, M. (1989). Self-care agency: Conceptualizations and operationalizations. *Advances in Nursing Science, 12*(1), 26–38.

Gaut, D. A., & Kieckhefer, R. N. (1988). Assessment of self-care agency in chronically ill adolescents. *Journal of Adolescent Health Care, 9,* 55–60.

Haas, D. (1990). *The relationship between coping dispositions and power components of dependent-care agency in parents of children with special health care needs.* Unpublished doctoral dissertation, Wayne State University, Detroit, MI.

Harvey, M. J. (1986). *A nursing study of self-concept and self-care agency in adolescents with diabetes.* Unpublished master's study, Wayne State University, Detroit, MI.

Hollingshead, A. B. (1975). *Four factor index of social status.* Unpublished manuscript, Yale University, Department of Sociology, New Haven, CT.

LaLiberte, M.C. (1989). *Sense of coherence in school-aged children and adolescents.* Unpublished master's thesis, University of Michigan, Ann Arbor, MI.

Nunnally, J. C. (1978). *Psychometric theory* (2nd ed.). New York: McGraw-Hill Book Company.

Orem, D. E. (1985). *Nursing: Concepts of practice* (3rd ed.). New York: McGraw-Hill Book Company.

Orem, D. E. (1991). *Nursing: Concepts of practice* (4th ed.). St. Louis: Mosby Year Book.

Saucier, C. P. (1984). Self-concept and self-care management in school-age children with diabetes. *Pediatric Nursing, 10,* 135–138.

Smilkstein, G. (1978). The family APGAR: A proposal for a family function test and its use by physicians. *Journal of Family Practice, 6,* 1231–1239.

Wechsler, D. (1981). *Wais-R manual: Wechsler adult intelligence scale— Revised.* San Antonio, TX: The Psychological Corporation.

Chapter 9

The Relationship Between Family Sense of Coherence and Family Quality of Life After Illness Diagnosis

Collective and Consensus Views[1]

Kathryn Hoehn Anderson

Serious illness affects the lives of the ill individual and his or her family members (Campbell, 1986; Chesler & Barbarin, 1987; Litman & Venters, 1979; Schwenk & Hughes, 1983). The onset of a serious illness in the family adds a set of demands, strains, and hardships that interact with the normative changes experienced by families (Anderson, 1993b; McCubbin & McCubbin, 1991; Tomlinson, Kirschbaum, Anderson, & Fitzgerald, 1987; Udelman & Udelman, 1980). The additive stressors of illness may increase the family's vulnerability to the development of secondary problems in family relationships or family adaptation as well as lead to the development of health problems in individual family members (Boss, Caron, Horbal, & Mortimer, 1990; Reiss & Klein, 1987; Rolland, 1990; Turk & Kerns, 1985). Not all families, however, experience a crisis in response to illness. Some may demonstrate growth as an outcome of the illness experience (Boss, 1988; Knafl & Deatrick, 1987; McCubbin & McCubbin, 1991).

Most of the stress literature discussing illness deals with either long-term chronic illness or acute life-threatening illness. Family response, family dynamics, and family outcomes are all important elements in the early adjustment phase after the diagnosis of an illness, but the relationships between these aspects have not been clearly defined. Without identifying how family dynamics influence adjustment to the stress of illness, and thus family life and ultimately family health (Anderson & Tomlinson, 1992), it is difficult to formulate appropriate responses to family health needs.

This chapter explores the family sense of coherence (FSOC) as a family resistance resource and investigates its link with family regenerative or risk responses to illness. The purpose of this chapter is to examine the relationship between the collective family sense of coherence and family quality of life (FQOL) during the post-diagnosis time of a serious illness and to explore aspects of family consensus within the family members' FSOC scores. This chapter reports a segment of a larger study (Anderson, 1993b) that examined the influence of illness stress and family resource variables on family quality of life. The earlier paper reinforced previous research demonstrating that family system resources influence the family response to stress (Boss, 1988; Hill, 1958; Lavee & Olson, 1989; McCubbin & McCubbin, 1991; McCubbin & Patterson, 1983).

Conceptual Framework of the Study

Common aspects of family stress theory derived from Hill's (1958) ABCX Model of Family Crisis include the impact of a stressor event (a) in interaction with family resources (b) and the family perception of the event (c) leading to a family crisis (x). Studying family resources helps to indentify a profile of families who may be considered most adaptive or most at risk to the demands of the onset of serious illness.

The Family Illness Stress Model (FIST) (Anderson, 1993b) was used in the larger study. This model expands the concept of stressor event hardships or event demands to examine illness stress, including ongoing family strain, illness demands, and illness severity (see Figure 1). Selected family variables that may mediate the relationship of stressors to family quality of life are also integral to this model. The FIST model focuses on the stressors and resulting stress that families encounter at the time of illness diagnosis and considers the particular family demands which occur as a result of the illness experience and the illness itself.

Hill (1958) proposed that the adaptation of the family to stressors is heavily influenced by family resources. Family resources are traits, characteristics, or competencies of each family member or the family system as a whole that can be used to manage or meet family demands (Hill, 1958; McCubbin & McCubbin, 1991;

McCubbin & Patterson, 1983; Patterson, 1988). These resources reduce the impact of the demands on the family and/or help the family adapt to changes (Antonovsky, 1979; Lavee, McCubbin, & Patterson, 1985). This chapter focuses on the family resource of the family sense of coherence, its function in the adjustment to serious illness, and its relationship to family quality of life during illness.

Figure 1

Family Illness Stress Model (FIST)

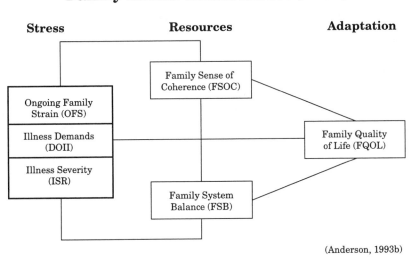

(Anderson, 1993b)

The adaptational ability of the family determines the family's vulnerability or resiliency to stressor events (McCubbin & McCubbin, 1989). Health is often cited as one of the most important determinants of overall quality of life (QOL), which underscores the relevance of using QOL as an ultimate outcome of health situations. The quality of family life is important to the resilience of the family in the face of stress (McCubbin et al., 1980). Research that examines the influence of chronic disease and family factors on quality of life is needed (Anderson, 1993b; Jassek & Knafl, 1990; Packa, 1989).

Background of the
Family Sense of Coherence

Since illness may intensify the sense of vulnerability of the family, it is important to examine how the family sense of coherence functions as a family resistance resource. Limited research has examined the FSOC (Antonovsky & Sourani, 1988; Brown, 1992).

Individual Sense of Coherence

The original work on the sense of coherence (Antonovsky, 1979, 1987) explained individual successful coping with stressors. Using a salutogenic model of health, Antonovsky (1987) defined the sense of coherence (SOC) as a construct that explains the motivational and cognitive bases for transforming one's potential resources into actuality, thereby facilitating coping with stressors and promoting health. Antonovsky (1987) proposed that the SOC is a dispositional world view that expresses one's dynamic feeling of confidence that the world is comprehensible (internal and external environments are structured, predictable, and explicable), manageable (resources are available to meet demands), and meaningful (life demands are challenges worthy of investment).

Studies have also used the individual sense of coherence measure to describe how the SOC can affect family life (Brown, 1992; Margalit, Leyser, Avraham, & Levy-Osin, 1988; Sagy & Antonovsky, see Chapter 11). Sagy and Antonovsky (see Chapter 11) found that it was sufficient to know the SOC score of one family member or the separate scores of several family members to determine the family level of the sense of coherence.

Family Sense of Coherence

Antonovsky's work has also pointed to the importance of a collective SOC. Proposing that the SOC may well function as a group property, Antonovsky (1987) introduced the idea of the family sense of coherence as a significant factor in shaping and modifying the individual sense of coherence. He argued that "in the face of collective stressors, the strength of the collective SOC is often decisive in tension management" (Antonovsky, 1987, p. 179). Antonovsky (1987) argued that the consensus of the family members or the group affects the collective sense of coherence and postulated possible interpretations of differences versus consensus in the SOC scores among family members.

Antonovsky and Sourani (1988) expanded the SOC construct to the family sense of coherence (FSOC). In their study on disabled Israeli retirees, they focused on family life as the object of the perception of coherence. The family sense of coherence was viewed as a factor that might attenuate the relationship between life events, stressors, and psychological risk factors that eventuate in physical and/or emotional pathology (Antonovsky & Sourani, 1988). In that study, they defined the FSOC as spouse agreement about perceptions of the family's ability to manage the demands of life and to see life as meaningful and comprehensible. Taking a narrower view than the original SOC, the FSOC refers to the "stimuli generated by interaction among family members and between family members and non-family units to what is perceived as more or less coherent" (Antonovsky & Sourani, 1988, p. 86). However, when closely examining the FSOC questionnaire (Anton-ovsky & Sourani, 1988), coherence in the family holds inherent linkages to a larger world view that influences family life behavior.

Antonovsky and Sourani (1988) determined that the strength of the FSOC was central to successful coping with family stressors and was associated with perceived satisfaction in intrafamily and family-community fit. Families with a high FSOC are theoretically more likely to be well adapted and to reach a high level of reorganization after a period of crisis. Conversely, families with a low FSOC are expected to be less likely to be able to adapt in crisis situations. The question yet to be conclusively answered is whether the FSOC defined as the family *collective* or as family *consensus* predicts family adjustment to stressful events.

The family sense of coherence can be viewed as a perceptual family resistance resource to the impact of stress and crisis on the family and thus may mediate the relationship between illness stress and family quality of life. The FSOC represents a resource involving the appraisal of the family's ability to function in its daily family world, the meaning the family gives to all the situations it encounters, and the sense of the family's ability to manage demands. The family's views and beliefs are crucial resources for family adaptation to crisis events (Boss, 1987; Patterson & Garwick, see Chapter 4).

In using a similar conceptual construction, Lavee, McCubbin, and Olson (1987) found that the FSOC, defined as the family general orientation to overall circumstances, acted as a stress-buffering variable. Patterson and Garwick (see Chapter 4) expanded the family sense of coherence to three levels: the situational meaning, the family identity, and the family world view. McCubbin and McCubbin (1991) and McCubbin (1993) used a conceptualization similar to the FSOC in their description of family hardiness. Carey, Oberst, McCubbin, and Hughes (1991) found that family caregivers who reported high family hardiness were less likely to appraise an illness situation negatively and more likely to view caregiving as challenging and beneficial.

Since Antonovsky and Sourani's (1988) article is the only published research documenting the use of the FSOC measure, further study exploring the influence of the FSOC in different situations is necessary. Two important aspects need further examination: the patient's FSOC response in relation to FQOL during the early adaptation phase after the diagnosis of a serious illness, and the consensus responses of family members' FSOC scores. If families differ in their quality of life responses to illness stress based on their FSOC, then health care interventions need to be geared to each particular family's SOC level.

Methodology

To qualify for the study, the person diagnosed with a serious illness had to be an adult between the ages of 18 and 60. The age 60 cutoff eliminated those persons over 60 who were likely to have more than one serious medical condition that might cloud the results of new illness demands. Ten pre-selected illnesses, based on incidence figures of major illness diagnoses (Massachusetts Medical Society, 1992), were included in the study. Each patient designated one family member, who was over 18 and who resided in the household, to complete the family member portion of the survey.

Setting

The research was conducted at two outpatient private general medical clinics serving a medium-sized city and the surrounding rural area (with a radius of about 70 miles) in the Midwestern United States.

Sample

The sample consisted of 78 families. Developmental stages of the participating families ranged from the stage I childrearing family to the stage VI empty nest family (Olson et al., 1983). Family configurations included married, remarried, cohabiting, single-parent, and two-generation families residing in one household. The sample included 52 married families, 10 cohabiting families, 9 single-parent families, and 7 parent/adult-child family configurations. One family participating in the study was African-American; the remaining families were Caucasian.

Distribution of family income ranged from under $5,000 to over $100,000, with 20.8% of incomes falling under $15,000, 31.2% between $15,000 and $29,999, 26% between $30,000 and $49,999, and 22.1% over $50,000. Family mean income was $25,716, the median family income was $25,000, and the modal family income was $40,000. The majority (68%) of patients were employed, with 41 (52.6%) working full-time and 12 (15.4%) working part-time. Of the remaining 25, 14 (18%) were homemakers and 11 (14.1%) were unemployed. The patient job positions, using Duncan Reiss classifications (Reiss, Duncan, Hole, & North, 1961), were spread across seven major areas of employment, with service workers accounting for the highest category. The family member job positions covered nine major areas of employment, with the professional category listed as the most prevalent.

The mean age of the patients was 42.5 (SD = 10.6), ranging from 21 to 60 years of age. The mean age of the family members was 40.7 (SD = 10.0), ranging from 21 to 64 years of age. The gender distribution for patients was 38 males and 40 females; incomplete demographic information prevented an accurate family member gender distribution. The mean education level for patients and family members was 13.4 years (SD = 2.5). The average length of the family relationship was 19.3 years (SD = 11.8), ranging from 1 year to 42 years.

Data Collection

Subjects diagnosed with a new serious illness in the outpatient clinic were approached by clinic personnel. They were contacted either in person or by letter indicating they met the criteria to participate in the study. Subjects were considered to be recruited when they agreed to receive the study questionnaire packet. Two months after the diagnosis of the patient's illness, the designated family member was sent a mailed survey. Family members completed the surveys in their homes and mailed the study packets to the researcher. The return response rate was 60%. Health care providers completed information about the diagnosed illness.

Variables and Measures

The variables and measures listed in Table 1 were used in the larger study. The variables of concern in this discussion are the family sense of coherence and family quality of life.

Table 1
Summary Table of Variables and Measures

Variable	Measure	Method
Illness Stress		
Ongoing family strain	Family Inventory of Life Events (FILE) (McCubbin, Patterson, & Wilson, 1983)	Self-report
Illness demands	Demands of the Illness Inventory (DOII) (Woods, Haberman, & Packard, 1987)	Self-report
Illness severity	Illness Severity Rating Scale (ISR) (Anderson, 1993a)	Determined by a panel of health experts
Family System Variables		
Family sense of coherence	Family Sense of Coherence (FSOC) Questionnaire (Antonovsky & Sourani, 1988)	Self-report
Family system balance	Family Adaptability and Cohesion Evaluation Scales (FACES III) (Olson, Portner, & Lavee, 1985)	Self-report
Demographic information	Family Information Form (FIF) (Anderson, 1993b)	Self-report
Family Quality of Life	Quality of Life (QOL) Parent Form (Olson & Barnes, 1982)	Self-report

The primary method of scoring selected to represent the collective or relational family view (Ransom, Fisher, Phillips, Kokes, & Weiss, 1990) on all of the major variables was the family mean score, the average of the patient and family member's individual scores. The family mean score was used because the researcher was interested in the overall family response to the illness experience; the family mean score is interpreted as representing the behavior of the family as a unit (Larsen & Olson, 1990). Mean scores also allow the inclusion of families with a single respondent (the patient) as the only eligible family member. In addition, patient and family member means for the entire sample were used to divide the family consensus scores into high and low categories.

The family sense of coherence from a collective perspective was measured using the mean family score on the 26-item Family Sense of Coherence (FSOC) Questionnaire (Antonovsky & Sourani, 1988). The FSOC scale has an internal reliability (Cronbach's Alpha) of .92. Internal consistency estimates (Cronbach's Alpha) for this study sample were .84 for patients and .65 for family members, with an overall reliability coefficient of .75. In this chapter, family quality of life reflected the family's adaptation and overall satisfaction with aspects of their family life (Olson & Barnes, 1982) since the diagnosis of a serious illness.

Demographic data on family income, length of family relationship, age, gender, education level, employment status, and occupation were also collected. All measures demonstrated very good reliability in this sample, except the Family Inventory of Life Events (FILE) (McCubbin, Patterson, & Wilson, 1983). The lower reliability of the FILE (.51) was due to the wide variability in life event occurrences. Results were considered significant at $p < .05$.

Results

This chapter focuses on (1) the contribution of the family sense of coherence to family quality of life at the time of illness, and (2) an examination of the FSOC from a consensus viewpoint.

Family Sense of Coherence
From a Collective View

The Family Sense of Coherence Questionnaire total scale mean score and the subscale scores are illustrated in Table 2. Using the family mean score for the family score, the higher the score, the stronger

Table 2
Comparison of Sample and Normative
Subscale and Scale Scores on the
Family Sense of Coherence (FSOC) Scale

Family Scores	Sample			Norm		
	Mean	SD	Range	Mean[a]	SD[a]	Range
Meaning	44.38	8.44	30 – 81			18 – 126
Manageability	43.10	9.78	30 – 81			18 – 126
Comprehensibility	37.08	8.97	20 – 72			16 – 112
Family mean score	124.56	25.64	82 – 182	129.74	33.67	52 – 362

[a] No normative data for subscales.

the FSOC. The sample mean (124.56) was slightly lower than the normative mean (129.74) but not significantly different.

The associations of the FSOC with the major variables were explored. Using Pearson's r and point bi-serial correlations, the family, patient, and family member correlations depicting the rela-

Table 3
Correlations of Major Variables with FSOC:
Family, Patient, and Family Member

Variable	Family FSOC	Patient FSOC	Family Member FSOC
Illness stress	– .37***	– .36***	– .31**
Family system balance	.10	.26*	.08
Family quality of life	.55****	.56****	.40****
Income	.18	.31***	– .02
Patient full-time job	.33**	.37***	.22*
Family member full-time job	.25*	.25*	.20

*$p < .05$. **$p < .01$. ***$p < .001$. ****$p < .0001$.

tionship of the FSOC to the major variables and selected contextual variables are found in Table 3. The relationship between the FSOC and family quality of life was found to be strongly and significantly positively correlated ($r = .55; p < .0001$). This indicates that the greater the FSOC, the greater the level of family quality of life. The family sense of coherence and illness stress were significantly negatively correlated; the greater the illness stress, the lower the FSOC. The family FSOC was positively correlated with patient and family members working full-time. There was no relationship between the FSOC and income or family system balance. The correlation values of the total family and the patient were somewhat similar on family quality of life, illness stress, and family employment status.

Predictors of Family Quality of Life

To determine which variables best predicted family quality of life, the relationship of all of the variables with FQOL was first examined. Based on the Pearson correlations of the major and contextual variables with FQOL, the independent variables of the FSOC ($r = .55; p < .0001$), illness stress ($r = -.45; p < .0001$), family system balance ($r = .33; p < .01$), length of relationship ($r = .24; p < .05$), family income ($r = .29; p < .01$), and patient and family member employment status were selected as candidates for entrance into the regression analysis. A multiple regression analysis was performed to determine which of the independent variables were most predictive of the dependent variable, family quality of life. Stepwise regression techniques selected a set of predictors from candidates previously identified.

Table 4 summarizes the individual variable results at each step of the analysis, as the variable entered the equation during the stepwise regression analysis.

The final equation indicated that the FSOC, illness stress, family system balance, length of family relationship, patient full time job status, and family income accounted for 57.6% of the variance that predicted family quality of life. The FSOC was the largest predictor of FQOL and accounted for over 30% of the variance in the final multiple regression equation ($p < .000$). The other variables in the equation each accounted for less than 10% of the variance individually. The beta weights show the relative contribution and the direction for each variable found in Table 4.

Table 4
Summary of Stepwise Regression Analysis
at Each Step with Family Quality of Life

Variable	R	R^2	F-ratio	Sig. T	Beta
Family sense of coherence	.55	.305	32.45	.000	.45
Family system balance	.61	.378	22.19	.004	.29
Illness stress	.68	.462	20.59	.001	-.34
Length of relationship	.71	.509	18.43	.011	.16
Patient full-time job	.74	.552	17.22	.012	-.31
Family income	.76	.576	15.63	.050	.18

Family Sense of Coherence
From a Consensus View

FSOC Individual and Family Member Scores. After the family collective FSOC scores had been examined, the individual patient and family member FSOC scores were examined to obtain a family consensus score. Table 5 shows the patient and family member FSOC values. The mean score for patients was 137.53 (SD = 28.36) and for family members 111.59 (SD = 28.41), or 5.29 and 4.29 per item, respectively. There was a significant difference in the patient and family member group scores [$t(77)$ = 9.41; p < .0001]. The correlation between patient and family member FSOC scores was .63 (p < .0001), indicating a strong and significant relationship. The individual FSOC ratings indicated that the FSOC was in the high optimistic range for the patients and the moderately optimistic range for family members. In this study, the patient FSOC scores were consistent with Antonovsky and Sourani's (1988) reported husband and wife scores; however, the family member FSOC scores were considerably lower than previously reported scores.

Family Consensus. Family consensus is another way of interpreting a family's FSOC score. Based on Antonovsky and Sourani's (1988) discussions about family consensus, families with consensus or agreement in FSOC scores have a strong family sense of coherence. Families who are in disagreement by definition have a weak FSOC (Antonovsky & Sourani, 1988, p. 83).

Table 5
Statistics for Patient and Family Member FSOC Scores

Variable	Mean	Median	Mode	SD	Range
Patient FSOC	137.53	135.50	117.00	28.36	87 – 182
Family member FSOC	111.59	103.00	92.00	28.41	72 – 182

To obtain family consensus scores, the patient and family member scores were dichotomized at each sample mean. Those individuals with scores above the mean were placed in the high FSOC group and those with scores below the mean were placed in a low FSOC group. Of the 71 families with FSOC consensus data, 54 (76%) families had consensus between family members, with 23 in the high patient (P)/high family member (FM) range and 31 in the low(P)/low(FM) range; according to Antonovsky's and Sourani's definition, these families should have a strong FSOC. Seventeen families (24%), 13 in the high(P)/low(FM) range and 4 in the low(P)/high(FM) range, disagreed and were not in consensus, theoretically indicating a weak FSOC.

To further examine family sense of coherence and its relationship to FQOL, a comparison was done with the consensus pairings on family quality of life, developed in the same manner as the FSOC consensus pairings. When family consensus comparisons of FSOC and FQOL were done family by family, 48.6% of the families were in consensus on both variables and 51.4% of the families were not in consensus. Thus, over 50% of the families were not in agreement on FSOC and FQOL. However, 80% of the patients who scored high on the FSOC scale also had high FQOL scores.

Discussion

This chapter explored the family sense of coherence, a family resistance resource, and its relationship to family quality of life from a collective and a consensus family perspective. Family sense of coherence mean scores were found to be similar to values reported by Antonovsky and Sourani (1988). The results elicit two issues for discussion: (1) the implication of the strong relationship and the strong predictor nature of the FSOC to FQOL; and (2) the implication of determining the FSOC based on collective or consensus FSOC scores.

Relationship of Family Sense of Coherence to Family Quality of Life

The family sense of coherence was the variable most strongly correlated with family quality of life. In the regression analysis, the FSOC was the first predictor to enter in the stepwise procedure. In the final regression equation, the FSOC accounted for the largest portion of the variance. These findings indicate that the FSOC is clearly linked to the family's resiliency in the face of illness stress. The FSOC was found to be an important mediator in the impact of illness stress on the family, reducing the direct influence of illness stress on family quality of life by half.

The family sense of coherence was the only major variable whose overall variance did not change with the addition of illness stress, which attests to the hypothesis that the FSOC is a trait (Antonovsky, 1987). The fact that the FSOC remained constant in the face of serious illness diagnosis has significant health care management and policy implications for support programs designed to strengthen family functioning. It suggests the need for further study of chronic illness management and family outcomes with the inclusion of the resiliency dynamics of the family as critical components in practice and research in this area.

Family Consensus

Antonovsky and Sourani (1988) proposed that FSOC consensus is indicative of a strong FSOC and disagreement is indicative of a weak FSOC. They also argued that a strong FSOC is linked with a good adaptational outcome. In this study, the families demonstrated 75% consensus on the FSOC and 75% consensus on FQOL separately, but the case-by-case examination did not indicate that family consensus on the FSOC meant family consensus on FQOL. More importantly, low(P)/low(FM) consensus, indicative of a strong FSOC, did not usually indicate a high family rating on the family quality of life scale. Only 50% of the cases showed consensus on both family variables. Both a high(P)/high(FM) consensus rating and a high(P)/low(FM) rating were indicative of a higher level of family quality of life than family agreement per se. In this sample, family agreement on the FSOC and FQOL was more likely to be consistent with the patient ratings than with the family member ratings. Related to illness, patient congruence on the FSOC and FQOL scales was more important than family consensus in shaping family outcomes.

Implications of the Collective or Consensus Family Sense of Coherence

Antonovsky and Sourani (1988) explored whether the collective view (family mean scores) of the FSOC accurately reflects the family sense of coherence. Sagy and Antonovsky (see Chapter 11) have discussed whether one family member's high SOC score could raise the family's FSOC. Both studies determined that a high collective FSOC score is linked to a strong FSOC. The study discussed in this chapter supports the value of consensus pairings in determining whether the family as a whole agrees or disagrees on its ability to comprehend, manage, and give meaning to family life. Nevertheless, the strength of an individual patient's high FSOC score is more indicative of the strength of the overall family sense of coherence. These study results appear to be consistent with earlier research by Antonovsky and Sourani (1988) and Sagy and Antonovsky (see Chapter 11).

In determining the collective FSOC, it seems that after the onset of illness the patient FSOC controls the FSOC level and thus family resilience. Explanation of the influence of the higher patient FSOC level on the family FSOC in the early adjustment time to the diagnosis of a serious illness has important implications for family health management and intervention strategies of health care professionals. Intervention directed toward the family's ability to maintain a view that family life is manageable, meaningful, and comprehensible would affect family resiliency during illness.

Case-by-case analysis of illness stress, family variables, and family quality of life would provide a clearer picture of the dynamics in the family during illness and the implications for nursing and health care intervention. An examination of the aspects of illness stress that are affected by the family sense of coherence and other family variables is needed (Anderson, 1993b). Further study of the influence of the patient's perspective on the overall family sense of coherence and other family health outcomes during illness needs to be undertaken.

Conclusion

This study demonstrated a strong link between the family sense of coherence and family quality of life. The FSOC strongly predicted family quality of life, explaining over half of the variance in FQOL. The family sense of whether family members can manage, derive meaning from, and comprehend their family life during the early onset of illness was critical to their family quality of life. Determining whether health care providers can influence the family sense of coherence to enhance the family's ability to be resilient in the face of illness is essential to help families respond well to illness stress.

Note

1. The author would like to thank funding support that assisted in this research project: (1) National Center for Nursing Research (NIH), National Research Service Award (NRSA) Pre-Doctoral Fellowship, F31-NR06242, 1988–1992; (2) Bush Summer Leadership Fellowship, Bush Foundation, St. Paul MN, 1991; (3) University of Wisconsin–Eau Claire, Graduate School Grants, 1992; (4) University of Minnesota Graduate School and School of Nursing Grants. The author would also like to thank Dr. Joan Stehle Werner, Professor, School of Nursing, University of Wisconsin–Eau Claire, for her helpful comments on the first draft of this chapter and Dr. Patricia Short Tomlinson, Professor, School of Nursing, University of Minnesota, for her invaluable input on the original project as dissertation advisor.

References

Anderson, K. H. (1993a). *Illness severity rating scale.* Unpublished tool. Minneapolis, MN: University of Minnesota.

Anderson, K. H. (1993b). *Relative contribution of illness stress and family system variables on family quality of life during early chronic illness.* Unpublished dissertation. Minneapolis, MN: University of Minnesota.

Anderson, K. H., & Tomlinson, P. S. (1992). The family health system as an emerging paradigmatic view for nursing. *Image: Journal of Nursing Scholarship, 24*(1), 57–63.

Antonovsky, A. (1979). *Health, stress, and coping: New perspectives on mental and physical well-being.* San Francisco: Jossey-Bass.

Antonovsky, A. (1987). *Unraveling the mystery of health: How people manage stress and stay well.* San Francisco: Jossey-Bass.

Antonovsky, A., & Sourani, T. (1988). Family sense of coherence and family adaptation. *Journal of Marriage and the Family, 50*(1), 79–92.

Boss, P. (1987). Family stress. In M. Sussman & S. Steinmetz (Eds.), *Handbook of marriage and the family* (pp. 695–724). New York: Plenum Press.

Boss, P. (1988). *Family stress management.* Newbury Park, CA: Sage.

Boss, P., Caron, W., Horbal, J., & Mortimer, J. (1990, September). Predictors of depression in caregivers of dementia patients: Boundary ambiguity and mastery. *Family Process, 29*, 245–254.

Brown, R. (1992, October 6). *Family paradigm, meaning, and coping: Family adaptation to a child with mental retardation.* Paper presented at the Resiliency in Families Lecture Series, University of Wisconsin–Madison, Madison, WI.

Campbell, T. (1986). The family's impact on health: A critical review. *Family Systems Medicine, 4*(2&3), 135–328.

Carey, P. J., Oberst, M. T., McCubbin, M. A., & Hughes, S. H. (1991). Appraisal and caregiving burden in family members caring for patients receiving chemotherapy. *Oncology Nursing Forum, 18*(8), 1341–1347.

Chesler, M. A., & Barbarin, O. A. (1987). *Childhood cancer and the family: Meeting the challenge of stress and support.* New York: Brunner/Mazel.

Hill, R. (1958). Social stresses on the family: Generic features of families under stress. *Social Casework, 39,* 139–158.

Jassek, P. F., & Knafl, K. A. (1990). Quality of life in cardiovascular disease. *Seminars in Oncology Nursing, 6*(4), 298–302.

Knafl, K. A., & Deatrick, J. A. (1987). Conceptualizing family response to child's chronic illness or disability. *Family Relations, 36,* 300–304.

Larsen, A., & Olson, D. (1990). Capturing the complexity of family systems: Integrating family theory, family scores, and family analysis. In T. Draper & A. Marcos (Eds.), *Family variables: Conceptualization, measurement, and use.* Newbury Park, CA: Sage.

Lavee, Y., McCubbin, H., & Olson, D. (1987). The effect of stressful life events and transitions on family functioning and well-being. *Journal of Marriage and the Family, 49*(4), 857–873.

Lavee, Y., McCubbin, H., & Patterson, J. M. (1985). The double ABCX model of stress and adaptation: An empirical test by analysis of structural equation with latent variables. *Journal of Marriage and the Family, 47*(4), 811–825.

Lavee, Y., & Olson, D. H. (1989). *Family system types and adaptational outcomes.* Unpublished paper. St. Paul, MN: University of Minnesota, Department of Family Social Science.

Litman, T., & Venters, M. (1979). Research on health care and the family: A methodological overview. *Social Sciences and Medicine, 8,* 379–385.

Margalit, M., Leyser, Y., Avraham, Y., & Levy-Osin, M. (1988). Social-environmental characteristics (family climate) and sense of coherence in kibbutz families with disabled and non-disabled children. *European Journal of Special Needs Education, 3*(2), 87–98.

Massachusetts Medical Society. (1992, February 21). Mortality patterns – United States, 1989. *Mortality and Morbidity Weekly Review, 41*(7), 121–125.

McCubbin, H. I., Joy, C. B., Cauble, A. E., Comeau, J. K., Patterson, J. M., & Needle, R. H. (1980). Family stress and coping: A decade review. *Journal of Marriage and the Family,* 855–871.

McCubbin, H. I., & Patterson, J. M. (1983). The family stress process: The double ABCX model of adjustment and adaptation. In H. I. McCubbin, M. B. Sussman, & J. M. Patterson (Eds.), *Social stress and the family: Advances and developments in family stress theory and research.* New York: Haworth Press.

McCubbin, H. I., Patterson, J. M., Cauble, A. E., Comeau, J. K., Larsen, A. S., & Skinner, D. (1981). *Systematic assessment of family stress, resources, & coping: Tools for research, education, & clinical inter-*

vention. St. Paul, MN: University of Minnesota, Department of Family Social Science.

McCubbin, H. I., Patterson, J. M., & Wilson, L. R. (1983). *Family inventory of life events and changes (FILE)*. St. Paul: University of Minnesota.

McCubbin, M. A. (1993). Family stress theory and the development of nursing knowledge about family adaptation. In S. Feetham, S. Meister, J. Bell, & C. Gilliss (Eds.), *The nursing of families: Theory, research, education, and practice*. Newbury Park, CA: Sage.

McCubbin, M. A., & McCubbin, H. I. (1989). Theoretical orientations to family stress and coping. In C. R. Figley (Ed.), *Treating stress in families*. New York: Brunner/Mazel.

McCubbin, M. A., & McCubbin, H. I. (1991). Family assessment in health care. In H. I. McCubbin & A. I. Thompson (Eds.), *Family assessment inventories for research and practice* (2nd ed.). Madison, WI: University of Wisconsin-Madison.

Olson, D. H., & Barnes, H. (1982). Quality of life. In D. H. Olson, H. I. McCubbin, H. Barnes, A. Larsen, M. Muxen, & M. Wilson (Eds.), *Family inventories*. St. Paul, MN: University of Minnesota, Department of Family Social Science.

Olson, D. H., McCubbin, H. I., Barnes, H., Larsen, A., Muxen, H., & Wilson, M. (1983). *Families: What makes them work?* Beverly Hills, CA: Sage.

Olson, D. H., Portner, C. S., & Lavee, Y. (1985). *Family adaptation and cohesion evaluation scales (FACES III)*. Minneapolis, MN: University of Minnesota, Department of Family Social Science,.

Packa, D. R. (1989). Quality of life of cardiac patients: A review. *Journal of Cardiovascular Nursing, 3*(2), 1–11.

Patterson, J. M. (1988). Families experiencing stress: I. The Family Adjustment and Adaptation Model. II. Applying the FAAR Model to health-related issues for intervention and research. *Family Systems Medicine, 6*(2), 202–237.

Patterson, J. M., & Garwick, A. W. (See Chapter 4). *Theoretical linkages: Family meanings and sense of coherence.*

Ransom, D. C., Fisher, L., Phillips, S., Kokes, R. F., & Weiss, R. (1990). The logic of measurement in family research. In T. Draper & A. Marcos (Eds.), *Family variables: Conceptualization, measurement, and use*. Newbury Park, CA: Sage.

Reiss, A., Duncan, O., Hole P., & North, C. (1961). *Occupations and social status*. Glencoe, IL: The Free Press.

Reiss, D., & Klein, D. (1987). Paradigm and pathogenesis: A family-centered approach to problems of etiology and treatment of psychiatric disorders. In T. Jacob (Ed.), *Family interaction and psychopathology: Theories, methods, and findings*. New York: Plenum.

Rolland, J. (1990). Anticipatory loss: A family systems developmental framework. *Family Process, 29*(3), 229–244.

Sagy, S., & Antonovsky, A. (See Chapter 11). *The family sense of coherence and the retirement transition.*

Schwenk, T. L., & Hughes, C. C. (1983). The family as patient in family medicine. Rhetoric or reality? *Social Science and Medicine, 12*, 1–17.

Tomlinson, P., Kirschbaum, M., Anderson, K. H., & Fitzgerald, M. (1987, November). Family stress in a high technology environment. Paper presented at the National Conference on Family Relations, Atlanta, GA.

Turk, D. C., & Kerns, R. D. (1985). The family in health and illness. In D. C. Turk & R. D. Kern (Eds.), *The family in health and illness: A lifespan perspective.* New York: John Wiley & Sons.

Udelman, H., & Udelman, D. (1980). The family and chronic illness. *Arizona Medicine, 37,* 491–494.

Woods, N. F., Haberman, M., & Packard, N. (1987). *Demands of the illness inventory.* Seattle: University of Washington.

Chapter 10

Single Mothers of Children With Disabilities

The Role of Sense of Coherence in Managing Multiple Challenges

Alison Gottlieb

Recent years have seen a dramatic increase in families headed by single mothers. Lack of financial security has resulted in an increased proportion of these mothers who either rely on welfare or try to work full-time. As a consequence, single mothers often suffer from poverty, role strain, social isolation, and social stigma. During these same years, the philosophical and policy trends of deinstitutionalization and normalization encouraged families to raise children with developmental disabilities at home. The long-term care of such children often includes increased financial costs, caregiving burden, and restrictions on life-style and career opportunities. The combined result of these two trends is the increasing phenomenon of single mothers faced with providing for their families without the daily help of a spouse while coping with the special challenges of caring for a child with disabilities.

Research has emphasized stress and coping resources in single-mother families and families of children with disabilities. Most of the studies of single-mother families and, until recently, the literature on families of children with disabilities, have viewed the "problems" pathogenically, with the assumption that these stressors will result in less adaptive outcomes for the children and their families.

There has been little research directly focused on single mothers of children with disabilities. In fact, studies of single-mother families have excluded children with disabilities so as not to confound their findings (Polit, 1980). When families experiencing both types of stressors were included, early studies reported more stress and time demands for single mothers of children with mental retardation (Beckman, 1983; Holyroyd, 1974); more recent studies found no child-related differences, although single mothers reported greater stress for poverty-related issues (Schilling, Kirkham, Snow, & Schinke, 1986). McCubbin (1989) reported that single mothers experienced less financial well-being, but more flexible family functioning. In a study by Salisbury (1990), single mothers actually reported less stress than did married mothers.

Studies have reported fewer social supports and more social isolation for single mothers of children with mental retardation. In some studies, single mothers have reported fewer opportunities to work outside the home, yet a study by Breslau, Salkever, and Baruch (1982) reported that employment was not affected by the child's severity of disability. These mixed findings suggest a greater need to understand the factors that allow successful adaptation for single mothers of children with disabilities.

Rather than viewing the challenges and issues of single mothers caring for a child with disabilities pathogenically, the research for this chapter began with the assumption that many single mothers *were* successfully raising their children with disabilities and investigated *how* they did this, thus taking the salutogenic approach inspired by Antonovsky (1979). Antonovsky has proposed that differences in adaptations to life stressors over which one may have little control may be related to "a salutary factor": one's "orientation to life" or "sense of coherence" (SOC). According to Antonovsky (1993), this construct (the degree to which one views life as comprehensible, manageable, and meaningful) may be a prerequisite for successful coping.

The study reported in this chapter investigated associations between the sense of coherence and other factors in order to explore the following questions:

1. To what extent are various stressors associated with a lower SOC?
2. What internal and external coping resources are associated with the SOC?
3. What is the relationship between the SOC and life-situation adaptations for single mothers of children with disabilities?

It was hoped that a close look at these associations would lead to descriptions of families who seemed to be adapting most successfully and to service and policy recommendations targeted at families who may be at greater risk. It should be noted that, because the data used for this study were cross-sectional, the causal direction of any association between the sense of coherence and stressors, resources, and outcomes can only be speculated.

Method

Families

The findings in this study were based on survey data collected from 152 single mothers (27 never married, 18 separated, 99 divorced, and 8 widowed) of school-age children (ages 3 to 18) with a variety of developmental disabilities. The mothers ranged in age from 22 to 63, with a mean age of 39, were mostly Euro-American (92%), and had been single an average of six years. Their median education level was 14 years, and 60% were working or in school, most full-time. Median family income, however, was low, between $10,000 and $15,000.

By requirement, all of the target children were living at home. Most of the children had more than one disability, but primary disabilities included: 52 behavioral [autism or attention deficit disorder (ADD)], 78 cognitive (mental retardation or developmental delay), and 22 physical (muscular dystrophy or cerebral palsy) or sensory (vision or hearing impaired) disabilities. Two-thirds of the children were boys and the average child's age was ten and a half years.

Procedures

With the help of respite and family service agencies in Massachusetts, single mothers of children with developmental disabilities were invited to participate. Mothers who volunteered completed a mailed, self-report questionnaire. In addition, in-depth interviews were conducted with 11 of the mothers. Data collection was completed between September, 1991 and May, 1992. For their efforts, mothers received a token thank-you gift, selected findings, and the "advice" offered by each of the mothers.

Measures

The measures used in this study were taken from a detailed two-part survey exploring the lives of single mothers of children with disabilities. The survey included descriptive information, standardized questionnaires, and scales created specifically for this study.

The survey included the 13-item short form of the Orientation to Life Questionnaire (Antonovsky, 1987) that measures an individual's sense of coherence. A high score on this construct indicates a global, pervasive, and enduring sense of confidence that life events are meaningful, manageable, and understandable. The mean SOC score for these single mothers was 59.9, which, while lower than that reported for many samples, is comparable to mean SOC scores for other families faced with stressful life situations, such as kibbutz parents of children with disabilities and adults with cerebral palsy (cited in Antonovsky, 1992).

Other sections of the questionnaire addressed family stressors, resources, and outcomes (adaptations). The measures used for each of these domains are described briefly.

Stressors. Factors associated with a child with disabilities that are often considered stressors included age, gender, type of disability(ies), the degree of functional limitation, and the extent, if any, of the child's problem behaviors. This last was measured with the Problem Behaviors Scale (Bruininks, Hill, Weatherman, & Woodcock, 1986), which assesses the frequency of internalized, externalized, or asocial behaviors that may present challenges to family members. Problem behaviors include harming oneself or others, destroying property, withdrawal, repetitive habits, and socially offensive behaviors.

Since single-mother families often experience a variety of challenges, it was necessary to obtain an indicator of general life experiences that might be perceived as stressful. Family stressors included the frequency of potentially stressful recent life events (a weighted scale adapted from Abidin, 1983), and the percentage of a mother's social network she perceived as "not helpful."

Resources. Child resources included whether a child attended camp, the number of other recreational programs he/she attended, and the amount of respite or child care the family used. The level of a father's involvement, in terms of financial support, visitation, and instrumental help, was also considered a resource, as were government financial supports (Aid to Families with Dependant Children, Supplemental Security Income) and family income. Mothers' personal resources included education, religiosity, counseling, support groups, leisure activities, and volunteer work.

A measure of the size of a mother's emotional support network was based on the number of different individuals who provided emotional or instrumental support. The types of support most helpful to mothers, such as family members, informal supports (friends, neighbors, support groups), and formal supports (teachers, social workers, advocates), were also assessed with the Family Support Scale (Dunst, Trivette, & Deal, 1988).

Using a coping measure created for this study, mothers rated how often they used each of eight strategies to cope with stressful events associated with caring for their child. Items included: looking for the positive, taking one step at a time, discussing feelings with or seeking help from family or friends, using one's religious community, letting one's feelings out, and laughing about things.

Family environment was measured with the Family Adaptability and Cohesion Evaluation Scales (FACES II) by Olson, Bell, and Portner (1982). This scale assesses the degree of emotional cohesiveness and adaptability within a family, with higher scores indicating greater adaptability or cohesion.

Perceptions. A mother's perceptions about her ability to meet her family's and child's needs and her degree of parenting satisfaction were viewed as critical because, along with resources, positive perceptions often buffer the effects of stress (McCubbin & McCubbin, 1992). Mothers rated their levels of overall parenting satisfaction. They indicated how frequently they experienced difficulty meeting their child's social, educational, and daily caregiving needs based on a seven-item scale, with higher scores indicating greater perceived Need Difficulty. Mothers also rated their perception of financial security with a seven-item Financial Concern scale, where higher scores indicated greater concern.

Outcomes/Adaptations. Four outcome measures were used in this study. A Parenting Stress index (adapted from Pearlin & Schooler, 1978) asked mothers to rate how frustrated, tense, worried, upset, unhappy, emotionally worn out, and unsure of themselves they felt about parenting their child with disabilities.

The Center for Epidemiologic Studies Depression Scale (CES-D) (Radloff, 1977) measured depressive symptomatology, with higher scores corresponding to greater depression. The mean depression score for this group of women was 18.4, indicating that the majority of single mothers had depression scores higher than 15, the critical cut-off for "risk of depression."

Mothers' perceptions of their physical health problems were measured with six questions compiled from earlier studies (Veroff, Douvan, & Kulka, 1981; Campbell, Converse, & Rodgers, 1976).

Lastly, maternal well-being was measured with the Psychological Well-Being Scale from the Rand Mental Health Survey (Davies, Sherbourne, Peterson, & Ware, 1988), where higher scores indicate greater well-being. Mean well-being scores were 45.3, as compared to 59.2 for the standardization sample.

Mothers also responded to open-ended questions addressing their current worries and future hopes and were asked to offer advice to other mothers in their situations. In addition to the quantitative data, these comments often provided windows into how a mother's SOC may be challenged by her life situations as well as how she copes with these challenges.

Results

As was previously reported, the mean SOC score for these mothers was 59.9 with a standard deviation of 14.0. To examine the relationship between the sense of coherence and other variables, the sample of single mothers was divided into three groups based on SOC quartiles: the lowest quartile included scores ranging from 20 to 50 ($n = 36$), the middle two quartiles included scores ranging from 51 to 70 ($n = 76$), and the top quartile included scores ranging from 71 to 88 ($n = 40$). One-way analysis of variance was used to analyze differences between mothers with low, moderate, and high SOC scores.

Table 1 indicates that, for the most part, outlook on life did not distinguish single mothers on the basis of factors usually thought of as stressors. The only *child*-related stressor related to the SOC was behavior as measured on the Problem Behaviors Scale. While there appeared to be a negative linear relation between the SOC and problem behaviors, mothers with both moderate and low SOC scores reported more serious problem behaviors than did mothers with higher SOC scores.[1] The only *family* stressor associated with the SOC was Life Events (recent, potentially stressful family experiences). Once again, mothers with low to moderate SOC scores reported many more frequent stressful life events than did mothers with higher scores.

The sense of coherence *was* associated with many internal and external resources (see Table 2). A mother's education and family income were both linearly related to the SOC. Mothers with a high SOC had significantly higher incomes than did mothers with a low SOC, whereas mothers with a low SOC had considerably less education than other mothers. In terms of mothers' coping, religiosity was not related to the SOC, but mothers with low SOC scores used significantly fewer coping strategies than did other mothers.

Table 1
Associations Between Stressors and Sense of Coherence (SOC)

| | Low SOC | | Moderate SOC | | High SOC | | |
	Mean	SD	Mean	SD	Mean	SD	Sig.
Child behaviors	−16.9	(12.6)	−13.1	(12.6)	−7.4	(9.6)	**ab
Severity of disability	7.8	(3.1)	8.2	(2.7)	8.9	(2.7)	ns
Number of disabilities	2.2	(1.0)	2.6	(1.2)	2.6	(1.3)	ns
Child age	10.6	(4.9)	10.2	(4.0)	11.1	(3.9)	ns
Life events	17.4	(9.3)	16.5	(10.1)	10.9	(8.8)	**ab
Percent non-helpful support	27.1	(23.5)	24.9	(20.9)	19.4	(20.7)	ns

Significance levels: * < .05; ** < .01; *** < .001.
   a: high SOC significantly different from low SOC.
   b: high SOC significantly different from moderate SOC.
   c: moderate SOC significantly different from low SOC.

Looking at family functioning styles, mothers with a weak SOC described their families as quite rigid, as opposed to adaptable. Moreover, the SOC was directly associated with family cohesion. Mothers with higher SOC scores also described their families as more cohesive than other families. Lastly, mothers with low SOC scores were least likely to report having an intimate partner.

When external supports were investigated, no child (such as camp, recreational programs, or child care) or family (such as government supports or counseling) services were associated with the sense of coherence. Social supports, however, *were* related to the SOC. Mothers with high SOC scores had larger support networks than did either of the other two groups. Moreover, there were interesting differences between the function and structure of their support networks. While the SOC was positively related to instrumental support, no group differences were found. Mothers with low SOC scores, however, had significantly fewer helpful supports overall, and fewer people who provided emotional support. They also had fewer informal supports (such as friends, coworkers, or support-group associates) than did mothers with higher SOC scores.

Table 2
Associations Between Resources and SOC

	Low SOC		Moderate SOC		High SOC		
	Mean	SD	Mean	SD	Mean	SD	Sig.
Internal:							
Education	12.8	(3.0)	14.2	(2.4)	14.8	(2.5)	**ac
Income	13,890	(10,470)	18,500	(14,530)	22,240	(15,730)	*a
Religiosity	2.4	(1.0)	2.6	(0.9)	2.7	(0.9)	ns
Coping	11.6	(3.6)	13.9	(3.9)	15.6	(3.6)	***ac
Family adaptability	40.0	(7.0)	44.7	(7.7)	46.6	(6.4)	***ac
Family cohesion	51.5	(11.1)	57.8	(9.2)	62.6	(7.2)	***abc
Intimate partner?	$n = 4$	(11%)	$n = 27$	(36%)	$n = 14$	(35%)	*
External:							
Social support network							
Size	6.3	(3.3)	7.9	(3.8)	9.0	(3.4)	**a
Instrumental help	5.1	(3.4)	6.8	(3.4)	6.8	(3.6)	ns
Emotional help	6.9	(3.9)	9.6	(4.0)	10.5	(3.9)	***ac
Family support	2.4	(2.2)	2.5	(2.5)	3.1	(2.5)	ns
Formal support	5.6	(2.6)	5.9	(3.2)	6.1	(3.0)	ns
Informal/non-family	4.6	(3.4)	6.0	(4.2)	7.2	(4.8)	*a
Father involvement	3.8	(4.8)	4.0	(4.6)	7.2	(4.8)	ns

Significance levels: * < .05; ** < .01; *** < .001.
    a: high SOC significantly different from low SOC.
    b: high SOC significantly different from moderate SOC.
    c: moderate SOC significantly different from low SOC.

Table 3
Associations Between Perceptions and SOC

	Low SOC		Moderate SOC		High SOC		
	Mean	SD	Mean	SD	Mean	SD	Sig.
Parenting satisfaction	5.1	(1.3)	5.8	(1.2)	6.1	(0.9)	***ac
Need difficulty	8.6	(4.4)	7.1	(3.4)	4.9	(3.2)	***ab
Financial concern	11.7	(3.6)	9.3	(4.6)	8.3	(4.5)	**ac

Significance levels: * < .05; ** < .01; *** < .001.
    a: high SOC significantly different from low SOC.
    b: high SOC significantly different from moderate SOC.
    c: moderate SOC significantly different from low SOC.

Mothers' perceptions relating to their child with disabilities and financial situations were associated with the sense of coherence. As Table 3 indicates, mothers with low SOC scores experienced less parenting satisfaction and more financial concern than did mothers with moderate or high scores. On the other hand, mothers with both low and moderate SOC scores were more concerned that they could not meet their child's social, emotional, and other special needs.

The sense of coherence was highly related to all four measures of maternal adaptation used in this study, as can be seen in Table 4. Moreover, for each of these measures, mothers with low SOC scores had less adaptive outcomes than did moderate SOC mothers, who, in turn, had significantly less adaptive outcomes than did high SOC mothers. In general, mothers who had a more positive outlook on life, as indicated by higher SOC scores, were less depressed, had fewer health problems, and experienced more parenting satisfaction and greater well-being than other mothers. These findings confirm Antonovsky's salutogenic model, which posits an association between a strong sense of coherence and greater usage of resources and more adaptive outcomes.

Table 4
Associations Between Adaptations and SOC

	Low SOC		Moderate SOC		High SOC		
	Mean	SD	Mean	SD	Mean	SD	Sig.
Depression	29.3	(7.8)	18.7	(10.8)	8.2	(5.6)	***abc
Parenting stress	22.3	(3.2)	18.5	(3.9)	13.9	(4.0)	***abc
Health problems	13.4	(3.5)	11.3	(3.3)	6.2	(2.4)	***abc
Well-being	35.3	(10.6)	43.6	(11.2)	57.5	(11.0)	***abc

Significance levels: $* < .05$; $** < .01$; $*** < .001$.
    a: high SOC significantly different from low SOC.
    b: high SOC significantly different from moderate SOC.
    c: moderate SOC significantly different from low SOC.

Discussion

In this sample, mothers with a strong sense of coherence were less likely to have a child with behavior problems or to have experienced many recent stressful life changes within their families. Because this is a cross-sectional study, the direction of causality cannot be determined. It is not known whether a mother's SOC can affect her perception of her child's behavior or her ability to manage challenging behaviors (such that high SOC mothers less often view their child's behaviors as problems) or whether a mother's sense of coherence is eroded by the constant challenges of a child with autism, ADD, or other behavioral problems.

Likewise, while it appears that mothers with high SOC scores are experiencing more stable family lives, this study cannot determine whether a strong SOC buffers families, to some extent, from constant changes (many related to jobs or income), or whether situational changes, often beyond these mothers' control, wear down a mother's ability to view life as manageable, meaningful, and comprehensible. As Antonovsky has suggested (1993), both consistency and overload-underload balance are needed to strengthen an individual's belief that life is comprehensible and manageable.

Fewer of the mothers of children with challenging behaviors were working, and several commented that they had been forced to leave jobs because school or day-care providers could not manage their child. Since a strong SOC was associated with positive outcomes for single mothers caring for a child with disabilities, it is evident that policies and services should aim to strengthen or at least maintain a mother's SOC by providing the supports needed to manage a child with challenging behaviors.

In terms of resources, income and education were both positively associated with the SOC. It seems plausible that women with a strong sense of coherence would view higher education both as a route to economic independence and as a way to strengthen the meaningfulness of their lives. A number of women were currently in educational programs, and many indicated that further education was a goal. Higher incomes were, in part, related to education and employment, but were also related to receiving child support. While not statistically significant, mothers with a high SOC reported more child support and visitation from their child's father. Once again, the association between low SOC scores and lower incomes may reflect the erosion of the SOC among women who are constantly struggling to maintain adequate family budgets without any support from their child's father.

In general, the single mothers in this study had families that could be described as "rigid" as opposed to "adaptable" and "separated" as opposed to "cohesive," with respect to family functioning (Olson, Bell, & Portner, 1982). Studies of adaptations of single-mother families have often reported that more flexible, adaptable family patterns are associated with better outcomes (Polit, 1980;

Weiss, 1979). Moreover, a number of researchers have reported that families who are close-knit and regularly do things together adapt more easily to the challenges of a family member with a chronic disability (Curran, 1983; McCubbin, 1988; Shonkoff, Hauser-Cram, Krauss, & Upshur, 1990).

Clearly, the strong positive associations between the sense of coherence and both adaptability and cohesion support these findings. Mothers who had high SOC scores had more cohesive, adaptable family units, while mothers with low scores reported families who did not tend to share feelings or do things together and who did not share in decision making. A portion of these associations may reflect caring for a child with serious behavioral problems who may require "set" as opposed to flexible routines and may challenge a family's willingness and ability to do things together. While the direction of the relation cannot be determined, these findings suggest that family climates characterized by rigid or unclear rules and by a lack of family unity leave mothers feeling that life is difficult to manage and not very meaningful.

There was a positive association between the sense of coherence and the frequency and variety of coping strategies single mothers employed when faced with difficulties caring for their child with disabilities. This supports Antonovsky's view (1993, p. 118) that "the availability of a wide repertoire of coping strategies ... and flexibility in choice at any given time are crucial. ... What the person with a strong SOC does is to select the particular coping strategy that seems most appropriate to deal with the stressor being confronted."

Mothers with high SOC scores reported larger, more helpful support networks than did mothers with low scores. While mothers with a strong SOC viewed formal and family supports as slightly more helpful than did mothers with a weak SOC, informal supports significantly distinguished the two groups. Informal supports may include friends, church community, support groups, coworkers, and neighbors. While family and professionals may feel compelled to assist families confronting stress, informal supports are often associations which must be initiated and nurtured by personal effort.

Mothers with low SOC scores listed fewer sources of instrumental and emotional support. While the availability of people to help with caregiving or to talk with when life situations feel overwhelming depend, in part, on finances and social circumstances, they also involve being able to reach out for help, to initiate, and to reciprocate. Greater nurturing may lead to a stronger SOC, but it also seems likely that women with a strong SOC, when faced with challenges beyond their control, may be more likely to seek out or be receptive to physical help for their child or emotional support for themselves. A number of women, in their advice to other mothers, indicated the importance of seeking support, as the following quote reflects:

> Don't try to face all your problems alone. There's always someone who can help, even if it's only to listen. Keep knocking on doors or calling the calls till you get the answers and help you need. Most of the time, it's there, but it doesn't come looking for you.

A mother's perceptions about parenting and her ability to meet her child's and family's needs were both associated with her sense of coherence. Mothers with a low SOC also derived less satisfaction from being the parent of a child with disabilities. Once again, while the constant worry or demands associated with caregiving could affect both one's outlook on life and on parenting, it is equally possible that a mother's ability to view life as meaningful and manageable allows her to view parenting a child who is not "typical" as satisfying, despite or even because of the challenges. Mothers' descriptions of their children's positive qualities often reflected this positive perspective:

> She is beautiful, lovable, and so fragile that it brings out the best in all of us.

> His eagerness to learn, to get his thoughts across. His enthusiasm to sign "I love you" if you have captured his heart ...

Mothers with low SOC scores also experienced the most financial concern. Many of these mothers were in the lowest income category, but many mothers with moderate or high SOC scores also had very low incomes (as is indicated by the large variability in incomes for these groups). To a large degree, financial concern is a function of actual income, but it is also a function of financial stability and a sense of balance in life. If she cannot view life as comprehensible or manageable, a mother may feel financially insecure, even if her income is moderate.

Mothers with a high SOC expressed the least amount of difficulty meeting their child's needs. For this Need Difficulty scale, most of the variability was loaded on two areas: emotional and social needs. This would suggest either that mothers with a positive outlook on life were able to arrange recreational activities and a social life for their child with disabilities, or that these mothers had children who presented fewer social and/or emotional challenges.

While cause cannot be determined, these findings suggest that providing single mothers with adequate and dependable financial supports would assist a family's ability to function effectively. Including children with disabilities (even with serious problem behaviors) in community recreational programs and camps, and assisting with transportation and other supports so that single mothers feel they can meet their children's social needs, would also enhance family well-being.

The sense of coherence was directly related to each of the four measures of family outcome used in this study. While each of the three groups differed from the others, group differences were most dramatic for mothers with high SOC scores. Mothers with a strong sense of coherence were the only group to have mean CES-D scores below the critical cut-off for depression (Radloff, 1977). They were the only group to have well-being scores comparable to those reported in other studies (Veit & Ware, 1983; Barnett & Marshall, 1989). Their reported health difficulties were almost half those of mothers with moderate SOC scores, and less than half those with low scores. There were also dramatic differences between the three groups in terms of Parenting Stress. Thus, for this sample, mothers with a moderate SOC were experiencing significant physical and emotional strains, while those with a weak SOC appeared extremely fragile, based on their potential for physical and psychological well-being.

While, once again, causal implications must be viewed cautiously in this cross-sectional study, there is a clear connection between the sense of coherence of single mothers raising a child with disabilities and their experienced physical and psychological health. While each of the mothers was currently caring for her child at home, her long-term capacity to continue to provide this care may be jeopardized when her sense of coherence is low or eroding.

This study of single mothers of children with disabilities suggests the need for both systems changes and individualized, targeted services. In order to strengthen their sense of the "comprehensibility" of life, these families need to experience consistency. This could be achieved by drawing stable and adequate incomes from a variety of potential sources including dependable child-support payments, paid employment, Supplemental Security Income, and/or government-funded "family allowances" or cash assistance. Working single mothers will require job flexibility and affordable, appropriate child care. Yet in very few cases is employment, by itself, adequate. This study revealed that mothers working up to 20 hours a week experienced fewer physical health problems and less depression or parenting stress than did mothers who were not employed at all or mothers working more than 20 hours. (The SOC also followed this pattern but was not statistically significant.) It appears that for many single-mother families, work, accompanied by other dependable income sources and family health coverage,[2] may lead to the most successful outcomes.

Working part-time would also address the "overload-underload balance," which Antonovsky (1993) has suggested is needed for a person to view life as manageable. Much of the time, a single mother must face alone the constant worries and time-consuming activities associated with her child. Disproportionate time spent caring for her child or working may not leave enough time for herself or other family members. Many mothers emphasized the need for time apart from their children:

> Find time for yourself. Do things just for you—parenting a special needs child takes so much more giving of yourself—it's important to have ways to give some back—family, significant other, friends, your own interests.

> Take care of yourself because your child needs you.

> Maintain your own, separate sense of identity from your child. It is all too easy to become totally immersed in the role/identity of mother of a special needs child. Protect and guard those interests/activities that make up the core of who you really are.

Single-mother families need comprehensive supports that allow them to maintain balance in their lives. These might include flexible respite (including weekends, short vacations, or weekly time periods to allow mothers to pursue educational or recreational outlets), summer camp, recreational and day-care programs for the child with disabilities, transportation when needed, and opportunities for the mothers to attend appropriate support groups. A case manager or advocate who could help families coordinate these services and supports would also ease the feeling of overload or powerlessness experienced by many of these women.

Lastly, for these single mothers to feel that life is meaningful despite or because of their single status and child with disabilities, they need to feel more in control of their lives and the decisions that affect their child with disabilities. Advocacy, volunteer work, and support groups could help mothers find meaning in their parenting experience. Employment or education could also help mothers feel socially valued and perceive themselves as full participants in society, apart from their role as mother of a child with special needs. Again, both systems changes (government entitlements and enforced child support) and individualized services (an advocate or support group to assist mothers in defining their needs and priorities and navigating the systems) would help these mothers feel empowered. This study lends support to the salutogenic model and the importance of a strong orientation to life for single mothers raising a child with disabilities. It also suggests the need for longitudinal research to determine to what extent a strong sense of coherence may reinforce healthy family adaptations, and to what extent a build-up of stressors may erode a mother's SOC. This population would also be an appropriate target for efforts to enhance the sense of coherence through programs or support groups aimed at developing coping strategies, self-advocacy, or stress reduction.

Notes

1. It must be kept in mind that "moderate" SOC mothers often had scores lower than average scores for individuals facing fewer stressors.

2. A specific question on health insurance was not included in the survey instrument. In the in-depth interviews, however, health insurance was a major concern for each of the nine mothers not working full-time. Many other mothers mentioned health insurance as a concern in the open-ended section of the survey.

References

Abidin, R. R. (1983). *Parenting stress index*. Charlottesville, VA: Pediatric Psychology Press.

Antonovsky, A. (1979). *Health, stress, and coping*. San Francisco, CA: Jossey-Bass.

Antonovsky, A. (1987). *Unraveling the mystery of health: How people manage stress and stay well*. San Francisco, CA: Jossey-Bass.

Antonovsky, A. (1992, February). *The sense of coherence newsletter*. Tel Aviv, Israel: Ben-Gurion University of the Negev.

Antonovsky, A. (1993). The implications of salutogenesis: An outsider's view. In A. Turnbull, J. Patterson, S. Behr, D. Murphy, J. Marquis, & M. Blue-Banning (Eds.), *Cognitive coping, families, and disability*. Baltimore, MD: Paul H. Brookes.

Barnett, R. C., & Marshall, N. (1989). *Multiple roles, spillover effects, and psychological distress*. (Working Paper No. 200). Wellesley, MA: Wellesley College Center for Research on Women.

Beckman, P. J. (1983). Influences of selected child characteristics on stress in families of handicapped infants. *American Journal on Mental Retardation, 88*(2), 150–156.

Breslau, N., Salkever, D., & Baruch, K. S. (1982). Women's labor force activity and responsibilities for disabled dependents: A study of families with disabled children. *Journal of Health and Social Behavior, 23,* 169–183.

Bruininks, R. H., Hill, B. K., Weatherman, R. F., & Woodcock, R. W. (1986). *Technical summary for the inventory for client and agency planning: ICAP.* Cambridge, MA: DLM Teaching Resources.

Campbell, A., Converse, P. E., & Rodgers, W. L. (1976). *The quality of American life.* New York: The Russell Sage Foundation.

Curran, D. (1983). *Traits of a healthy family.* Minneapolis, MN: Winston.

Davies, A. R., Sherbourne, C. D., Peterson, J. R., & Ware, J. E. (1988). *Scoring manual: Adult health status and patient satisfaction measures used in Rand's health insurance experiment.* Prepared for the U. S. Department of Health and Human Services. Santa Monica, CA: RAND.

Dunst, C. J., Trivette, C. M., & Deal, A. G. (1988). *Enabling and empowering families: Principles and guidelines for practice.* Cambridge, MA: Brookline Books.

Holyroyd, J. (1974). The questionnaire on resources and stress: An instrument to measure family responses to a handicapped family member. *Journal of Community Psychology, 2,* 92–94.

McCubbin, M. (1988). Family stress, resources, and family types: Chronic illness in children. *Family Relations, 37,* 203–210.

McCubbin, M. (1989). Family stress and family strengths: A comparison of single- and two-parent families with handicapped children. *Research in Nursing and Health, 12*(2), 101–110.

McCubbin, M. A., & McCubbin, H. I. (1992). Family coping with health crisis: The resiliency model of family stress, adjustment, and adaptation. In C. Danielson, B. Hamel-Bissell, & P. Winstead-Fry (Eds.), *Families, health, and illness.* St. Louis, MO: Mosby.

Olson, D. H., Bell, R., & Portner, J. (1982). *FACES II.* St. Paul, MN: Family Social Science, University of Minnesota.

Pearlin, L. I., & Schooler, C. (1978). The structure of coping. *Journal of Health and Social Behavior, 19,* 2–21.

Polit, D. F. (1980). *The one-parent/one-child family: Social and psychological consequences.* Unpublished paper. Cambridge, MA: Institute in Woman and Families.

Radloff, L. S. (1977). The CES-D scale: A self-report depression scale for research in the general population. *Applied Psychological Measurement, 1*(3), 385–401.

Salisbury, C. (1990). Characteristics of users and nonusers of respite care. *Mental Retardation, 28*(5), 291–298.

Schilling, R. F., Kirkham, M. A., Snow, W. H., & Schinke, S. P. (1986). Single mothers with handicapped children: Different from their married counterparts? *Family Relations, 35,* 69–77.

Shonkoff, J. P., Hauser-Cram, P., Krauss, M. K., & Upshur, C. C. (1990). *The early intervention collaborative study: Final report of phase one.* Worcester, MA: University of Massachusetts Medical School.

Veit, C. T., & Ware, J. E. (1983). The structure of psychological distress and well-being in general populations. *Journal of Consulting and Clinical Psychology, 51*(5), 730–742.

Veroff, J., Douvan, E., & Kulka, R. A. (1981). *The inner American, a self-portrait from 1957 to 1975.* New York: Basic Books.

Weiss, R. S. (1979). *Going it alone.* New York: Basic Books.

III. Coherence and Aging

Chapter 11

The Family Sense of Coherence and the Retirement Transition[1]

Shifra Sagy and Aaron Antonovsky

"Stress is not an individual affair, but must be viewed in terms of the social context in which it occurs," wrote Levine and Scotch (1970, p. 287). Most theories of stress reactions and coping, however, have focused on the individual, while the larger social context is usually ignored (Pearlin, 1989). The purpose of this study is to focus on the *family* as a social system in which the individual experiences stressors and engages in coping. The subjects in this study had just experienced a major life transition, retirement. At this stage of the family life cycle, the nuclear family usually consists of the marital dyad. The theoretical approach, however, can be applied to families of any size. Our main question is comparative: Do characteristics of the individual or those of the larger social system in which the stress process occurs contribute more to the understanding of stress consequences?

The Sense of Coherence Model

The framework of the study is Antonovsky's theoretical "salutogenic" model (1979, 1987) and its central construct, the sense of coherence (SOC). Stressors, he argued, are ubiquitous in human existence; heterostasis is normative; the evidence of illness is far from rare. It is at least of equal importance to ask about the origins of health, of successful coping with stressors, as it is to ask the origins of pathology. The proposed answer to the salutogenic question was called the SOC, a global orientation which sees the world as more or less comprehensible, manageable, and meaningful (Antonovsky, 1987, p. 19). The sense of coherence, according to the model, is a determinant variable affecting health consequences and other aspects of well-being.

The stressor in this study is the retirement of a member of the family. The retirement process is a developmental transition (Levinson, 1980), usually described as a complex stressor which upsets one's balance and demands (Atchley, 1971), and hence is potentially pathogenic. The salutogenic model, however, would suggest focusing on the individuals for whom retirement is a eustressor, with positive consequences. This leads to the hypothesis that coping with the retirement transition would relate to the strength of one's SOC.

A systematic orientation, however, leads to the view that a developmental transition of one family member is a stressor for the whole family unit. Retirement is not only a transition point in the retiree's life but a stage in the family life cycle. The challenge for change is directed not only at the retiree's way of life, but to the family system as well. The changes are manifold: in role patterns, relations between spouses, patterns of common activities, money issues, and so forth. The literature on retirement rarely deals with the family. The SOC model would suggest that in a family, one of whose members is retiring, the family SOC would be decisive in successful coping and hence in shaping health status outcome.

What Is the Family
Sense of Coherence?

In the formulation of the SOC construct, reference was made to the SOC as applicable to the group as well as the individual (Antonovsky, 1987, pp. 170–179). But the concept itself as it appears in the model is built on the level of the individual. Although the assumption of the existence of family "personality" is accepted in family research, its meaning is inadequately elaborated (Walker, 1985). The question of operationalization remains wide open. Structural-behavioral characteristics have been the focus of research. The family SOC refers, however, to a *cognitive map*, a family perception, a family world view.

Few researchers have used this kind of category to characterize families. A prominent example is Reiss's (1981) idea of "shared constructs": The adaptation of a family to stressors is shaped by the family construction of the world it lives in, or "how the family views the world" (Oliveri & Reiss, 1984, p. 36). Reiss's model operationalizes the family cognitive construction in terms of observed behavior patterns. However, the assumption of a direct and unidimensional relation between cognitive construction and real behavior is not simple and clear-cut (Fishbein & Ajzen, 1975; Freeman & Romney, 1986; Godin, 1987). Reiss's technique is applied in a laboratory situation, using the observation of a family interaction in solving an intrafamily problem.

Another way to consider the issue of the family SOC is found in Antonovsky and Sourani (1988). The reference there, however, is to the extent to which each spouse sees *family life* as coherent. Another attempt to apply the SOC concept to study on the family level is found in Lavee, McCubbin, and Patterson's (1985) Double ABCX Model. In this model, the family SOC is seen as one of the mediating coping factors between family stressors and adaptation. Their definition of the family SOC, like Antonovsky and Sourani's, focuses on the narrow limits of family functioning.

In brief, we suggest that family research is still in a stage that does not enable a satisfactory operational translation of a complex collective concept like the family SOC. Actually, there are two dichotomous techniques which reflect two different theoretical approaches: the holistic approach, which is external and "objective," such as Reiss's work (1981), and the internal and subjective reductionist approach, such as McCubbin and Patterson's (1983). These two approaches may well represent a continuum of possible solutions of the issue. In this study, we have adopted a solution which is somewhere on this continuum. In order to inquire into the cognitive map of a *collective*, we have assumed that the cognitive representations of the individuals involved, as they are expressed by self-reports, should not be ignored. Such an interactive approach appears in only a few studies of systems. Two of the prominent are Miller's (1965) analysis of living systems and Miller and Miller's (1980) analysis of families. Both emphasize the need to relate to the interrelationships of subsystems in order to understand the whole system.

The methodological solution to the problem of studying the family SOC adopted here was to obtain self-reports of the SOC of individual family members, and then to build a collective measure on the basis of the *interrelations* of individual perceptions. We examined four alternative models as possible collective measures. Each model is derived from a different perspective and uses a different technique.

(1) The *aggregation* model sees the collective as an averaged sum of its individuals. This approach is in contrast to "general systems theory," which sees the whole as greater than the sum of its parts (Bertalanffy, 1968). Though it is the most frequently used measure of "family characteristics" (Fisher, Kokes, Ransom, Phillips, & Rudo, 1985), we found no theoretical justification for its use. The operational measurement for this model is the *mean* of the individual SOC scores as the unit score.

(2) The *pathogenic* model is based on a family systems approach. It emphasizes the interactional context in order to understand pathogenic behavior. It sees the family perception as expressed by the weakest member (Jacob, 1987; Minuchin, Roseman, & Baker, 1978). The coping of the whole family is characterized by the *lowest* SOC score among family members. This measure, though it seems an individual one, actually takes into account the entire family by "choosing" the score of only one member according to the *relative* scores. This kind of measure is rare in family research (Klein & Hill, 1979).

(3) The *salutogenic* model is based on a family systems approach too, but in the opposite direction. In this case, the family mapping is expressed by its "strongest" member. The operational measure is the *highest* SOC score. This approach to the evaluation of families is also rare in family research (Fleck, Quinlan, Jalali, & Resentech, 1988).

(4) The *consensus* model is based on the assumption that agreement among family members improves its coping and resistance ability (Booth & Welch, 1978). Antonovsky and Sourani (1988) suggested that lack of consensus among family members may be in itself an indication of a weak family SOC. The operational measurement here is the *absolute gap* among the family members' SOC scores.

The four alternative models are examined by a "results-centered method" (Greenwald & Pratkanis, 1988). This approach is proposed at a stage when there is as yet no sound basis for choosing among alternative operationalizations of a construct. The choice is made on the basis of which measure is most strongly related to the "dependent" variable, adaptation.

Adjustment to Retirement

Much research has been done in recent decades in order to find predictors or variables which are correlated with different measures of adaptability to retirement (for reviews, see Larson, 1978; Stull, 1988). Most studies used individual variables as predictors of successful coping. None, to the best of our knowledge, has considered the family context as a determinant factor in the retiree's adaptability. The few studies which related to the retiree's spouse tended to compare predictors of well-being for men versus women (see Atchley & Miller, 1983; Stull, 1988). We found no study in the retirement literature which considers *family* characteristics as predictors of adaptability.

Two variables were used in this study as indicators of successful coping of the retiree: subjective health status and life satisfaction. These criteria are in common use in research as indicators of adaptation to stressors (Lazarus & Folkman, 1984). In sum, the present study deals with three central issues: (a) How can a collective (in this case, the family) concept, representing its world-view perception (SOC), be measured? (b) Is the *family* SOC a good predictor of the individual retiree's adaptation to the retirement transition? (c) What are the differential weights of individual and family characteristics to the understanding of the retiree's adaptation?

Method

Sample

The original sample of retirees consisted of 805 (432 men and 373 women) respondents with whom interviews were successfully completed. They constituted 69.2% of the 1,163 persons whose names were made available to us by three major Israeli national pension funds as scheduled for "on-time" retirement, that is, around ages 60 and 65 for women and men, respectively. From the 805 respondents in the first year of the study (1986), a subsample meeting two criteria was selected: (a) The occupation of the retiree was classified as "white-collar" (Israel Central Bureau of Statistics, 1983); and (b) the retiree had been married for more than 10 years to his or her present spouse.

These criteria were set in keeping with the purpose of a more or less homogeneous sample and to ensure that the marriage was stable. Of the 464 retirees (288 men and 176 women) who met the criteria and hence were scheduled for interview in 1987, 286 couple-interviews were completed (62% of the subsample). The husband was the retiree in 182 of the couples, the wife in 104. Of the 464 couples, in 22% of the cases one of the spouses refused to be interviewed; in 5% one of the spouses had died or was too ill to be interviewed; in 3% the retirees had returned to work; the other 8% were not interviewed for various reasons (not at home, spoke inadequate Hebrew, etc.)

T tests on gender and education between retirees who were interviewed and those who were not indicate no significant difference between the groups. Most of the respondents (86% of the retirees and 70% of the spouses) had had more than nine years of education. This is congruent, in the Israeli context, with the selection of white-collar retirees only. Most of the respondents were of European origin (79% of the retirees and 77% of the spouses).

Though the white-collar respondents in the original sample constituted 72% of the entire sample, it must be kept in mind that the present subsample is not representative of all Israeli retirees. Further, these are all "on-time" retirees and do not include those who retired early, most often for health reasons.

In 1988 (two years after retirement), 214 of the 286 couples (75%) were re-interviewed. Refusal by one of the spouses (15%), death or illness (5%) and miscellaneous reasons (5%) accounted for the dropout from the subsample. The dropouts did not differ from those re-interviewed on sociodemographic variables.

Data Collection

Retirees were interviewed by interviewers who visited the family home. Simultaneously, in another room, retiree spouses self-completed the questionnaire. Budgetary limitations made doubling interviewed time prohibitive. Each person signed an informed consent form. The interviews were conducted in two "waves"—spring-summer and winter—according to the retirement schedules of pension funds.

Measures

The dependent variables were subjective health status and life satisfaction. The former was measured by three different scales. High scores represented positive well-being.

Revised Symptom Score (RSS). This score was adapted for the present study from the much more elaborate Quality of Well-Being Scale (Bush, 1987). The respondent was requested to indicate whether, on the day before the interview, or during the previous week, she or he suffered from any of a list of 20 symptom groups. The request was then made to indicate which of the checked symptoms "was the most undesirable to you." Three questions relating to functioning and physical mobility followed. Standard weights for the major symptom and the mobility rating are combined to provide an RSS score.

Multidimensional Health Scale (MHS). This score consists of five multiple choice items referring to pain, functional limitation, the seriousness of any existing medical conditions, the need for therapeutic intervention, and the distance one is from "a perfect state of health." This measure has been used in Israel previously (Antonovsky, 1979). In the present study, Cronbach's Alpha was .85.

Scale of Psychological Distress (SPD). This is a six-item psychosomatic symptom scale, referring to the frequency of occurrence of the symptoms in the past year, which was developed in Hebrew (Ben-Sira, 1982). It has been used in a number of studies, with satisfactory psychometric properties.

Life Satisfaction (LS). This measure was derived from a nine-point "ladder" question referring to satisfaction in "thinking of your life as a whole." This single-item question has been used in many studies and found to be an adequate measure in terms of construct validity and distribution in answers (Andrews & Withey, 1976).

Sense of Coherence (SOC). The SOC is measured by a series of 29 semantic differential items on a seven-point scale, with anchoring phrases at each end. High scores indicate a strong SOC. An account of the development of the SOC scale and its psychometric properties, showing it to be a reliable and reasonably valid scale, appears in Antonovsky (1987, chap. 4). Cronbach's Alpha was .88.

Family Sense of Coherence (SOC). This was determined by four measuring techniques: (a) the *lower* SOC score of the two scores of the spouses; (b) the *higher* SOC score of the two scores of the spouses; (c) the *mean* of the spouses' SOC scores; and (d) the absolute *gap* between the spouses' SOC scores.

Results

Table 1 displays score means and standard deviations of the variables at the first stage of the study (one year after retirement). Data are presented for retirees and spouses separately. Subsample retirees have somewhat higher scores, especially on the SOC, than their spouses. The latter are a more heterogeneous group than the retirees. Further, there is a higher proportion of males among the retirees. Data on the second year of the study, which show the same patterns, are omitted here.

Table 1
Means and Standard Deviations of Individual Variables (1987)

Variable	Whole Sample			Retirees			Spouses		
	n	Mean	SD	n	Mean	SD	n	Mean	SD
SOC	572	151.02	21.89	286	154.50	20.62	286	147.53	22.58
RSS	572	.77	.11	286	.77	.10	286	.76	.11
MHS	563	16.08	3.91	282	16.51	3.87	281	15.64	3.91
SPD	569	20.84	3.07	284	21.20	2.95	285	20.49	3.15
LS	570	6.48	1.67	286	6.59	1.67	284	6.42	1.58

Note. SOC = Sense of Coherence; RSS = Revised Sympton Score; MHS = Multidimensional Health Scale; SPD = Scale of Psychological Distress; LS = Life Satisfaction.

Table 2 displays the four family measures of the SOC, the means and standard deviations of each, and the correlations among them at stage one. The results in stage two were similar.

Table 2
Means and Standard Deviations of Family Sense of Coherence (SOC)
Scores and Pearson Correlations

SOC	n of Couples	Mean	SD	High	Mean	Gap
Low score	279[a]	141.25	21.31	.68	.93	− .37
High score	279[a]	160.18	18.09		.90	.21
Mean	286	151.02	18.17			− .23
Gap	286	18.47	16.02			—

Note. All correlations are significant at p ≤ .001.
[a] Couples in which the "high" and the "low" scores were identical were excluded from the analysis in these two measures, since they do not belong to any of the four groups.

The first issue to be considered is that of the "best predictor." The correlations among the four alternative measures of the family SOC provide an initial indication of the appropriate decision.

The high correlations between the mean score and the low and the high scores are expected, since the former is built from the two others. However, the high correlation (.68) between the high and the low scores indicates that actually three of the four alternative measures (the high score, the low score, and the mean) would have very similar correlations with the retiree's adaptation scores. That is, the decision among these three alternative family scores would not be clear or unequivocal. The correlations between the gap score, however, and the other three family measures are relatively low and their directions different (positive correlation with the high score and negative with the low and mean scores). The choice of the "best" family score then, would not be among the four measures, but between two patterns: the *level* of the family SOC score (as expressed in the high, low, and mean scores) versus the *structure* of the family SOC score (as expressed in the gap score).

Table 3 shows the correlations between the individual retiree's SOC and the four family SOC scores with the retiree's adaptation scores. All three measures of the level type (high, low, and mean) are significantly correlated with all four measures of well-being. The low family score has a consistently lower correlation with adaptation, and the high score correlations tend to be stronger than the mean score correlations. The differences, however, are quite small. On the other hand, none of the gap score correlations are significant.

Table 3
Pearson Correlations Between Retiree's SOC,
Family SOC Scores, and Retiree's Adaptations Scores

Retiree Adaptation Scores	Retiree		Family SOC			
	n	SOC	High	Low	Mean	Gap[a]
Revised Sympton Score	286	.19	.24	.14	.20	.08
Multidimensional Health Scale	282	.31	.29	.21	.27	.05
Scale of Psychological Distress	284	.36	.37	.24	.33	.10
Life Satisfaction	286	.42	.39	.38	.42	−.08

Note. All except the "gap" correlations are significant at $p \leq .001$.
[a] A positive correlation indicates that the greater the gap between the SOC scores of the spouses, the higher the adaptation score of the retiree.

Thus the question of the best family SOC predictor is clearly best answered by a measure of the *level* type and not of the structure type. The decision among the three level measures, however, is equivocal. Compelled to make a choice among the three, we would opt for the high (salutogenic) measure, which has the strongest correlation with three of the four adaptation scores. This pattern is repeated in 1988 data.

We now turn to the comparative question: the predictive power of the individual retiree SOC versus that of the family SOC. As Table 3 shows, no clear difference in predicting the retiree's adaptation is found when the three level type family measures are compared with that of the individual retiree's SOC. These results led us to analyze the data by taking into consideration the congruence of the family SOC in a way different from that of the gap measure. Both retirees and their spouses in the first stage of the study were divided into "high" and "low" SOC scores using the median of each group. No significant differences were found in the congruent families (where both spouses had either an above or below median score) between the power of the individual SOC versus the family SOC scores in predicting the retiree's adaptation (data not presented). An interesting pattern, however, emerges among the incongruent families. The high family score is clearly the most powerful predictor to retiree adaptation. In other words, when one member of the family has a high and the other a low SOC score, it is the score of the former which is decisive. True, the retiree SOC and the mean and gap family scores are also positively correlated with the adaptation measures, though not always significantly, but it is the high score which stands out (Table 4, Part A).

The predictive power of the high family score is seen even more clearly when the incongruent families are subdivided. In the group of retirees with high and spouses with low SOC scores, by definition, the retiree and high family SOC-adaptation correlations are identical. All are positive and three significant. This is also the case for the mean score. The low and gap scores show no pattern (Table 4, Part B). In the group of retirees with low and spouses with high SOC scores, the high family score is most strongly correlated with well-being, whereas the retiree's SOC score is useless as a predictor. Again, the mean and gap scores are positively correlated with well-being, but less clearly than the high score (Table 4, Part C).

In sum, *among incongruent families*, a high family SOC score is the best predictor of retiree adaptation, one which is better than the retiree's own score. Though the numbers are small, the data (not given here) show that this result is obtained whether the retiree is male or female.

Table 4
Pearson Correlations Between Retiree Adaptation
Scores and Retiree and Family SOC Scores
Among Incongruent Families (1987)

Retiree Adaptation Scores	Retiree		Family SOC			
	n	SOC	High	Low	Mean	Gap
Part A: All incongruent families						
Revised Symptom Score	91	.12	.36***	−.12	.13	.28***
Multidimensional Health Scale	88	.32***	.39***	−.01	.24*	.21*
Scale of Psychological Distress	90	.20*	.28**	−.10	.09	.26**
Life Satisfaction	91	.18	.24**	.15	.28**	.04
Part B: Retiree high/spouse low						
Revised Symptom Score	47	.47***	.47***	−.03	.20	.28*
Multidimensional Health Scale	46	.33**	.33**	.14	.27*	.05
Scale of Psychological Distress	47	.18	.18	.10	.17	.01
Life Satisfaction	47	.15	.15	.24*	.27*	−.14
Part C: Retiree low/spouse high						
Revised Symptom Score	44	−.19	.26*	−.21	.05	.29*
Multidimensional Health Scale	42	.10	.34**	.08	.30*	.15
Scale of Psychological Distress	43	−.13	.25*	−.11	.12	.26*
Life Satisfaction	44	.13	.30*	.14	.33*	.14

$*p \leq .05.$ $**p \leq .01.$ $***p \leq .001.$

Note that the gap score in this group of incongruent families is positively correlated with the adaptation scores of the retiree (Table 4, Parts A and C). The positive correlations, however, mean that as the SOC gap between the spouses grows, the retiree is better adapted. This finding is in contrast to the consensus hypothesis of the gap score (the family SOC is stronger as the gap narrows). However, it does fit the finding of the high family score as the best predictor of the retiree's adaptation in incongruent families.

The data in Tables 3 and 4 are from the first stage of the study, one year after retirement. Examining the correlations between the four adaptation measures and the retiree's SOC as well as each of the four family SOC scores (Table 3, using stage two data), very much the same results are obtained. That is to say, for the sample as a whole, two years after retirement: (a) the gap family SOC score is unrelated to the retiree's adaptation; (b) the other three family scores are strongly related to it, with the salutogenic, high score most strongly so; and (c) even the high score is no more strongly related to retiree adaptation than is his or her own SOC score (data not presented).

What happens, however, when the data are considered by the four family congruence subtypes? In the interest of parsimony, and following our "results-centered" procedure, only retiree and "high family SOC" (the salutogenic measure) correlations with the adaptation measures are presented (see Table 5). In order for the comparison to be as careful as possible, we used only the data for the couples who had been interviewed in both years, though this reduced the n to 214.

Table 5
Pearson Correlations Between Retiree Adaptation Scores and Retiree and Salutogenic Family SOC Scores by Congruence Subtype Families (1987 and 1988)

Retiree Adaptation Scores	n	Retiree SOC 1987	Retiree SOC 1988	Salutogenic Family SOC 1987	Salutogenic Family SOC 1988
Part A: Both spouses high	74				
Revised Symptom Score		.22	.07	.21	.13
Multidimensional Health Scale		.22	.27*	.21	.28*
Scale of Psychological Distress		.21	.24*	.21	.28*
Life Satisfaction		.26*	.63***	.32**	.61***
Part B: Both spouses low	72				
Revised Symptom Score		.13	.21	.15	.29*
Multidimensional Health Scale		.09	.54***	.11	.48***
Scale of Psychological Distress		.26*	.63***	.24*	.63
Life Satisfaction		.47***	.49***	.34**	.50***
Part C: Retiree high/spouse low	39				
Revised Symptom Score		.44**	.25	.44**	.25
Multidimensional Health Scale		.25	.25	.25	.25
Scale of Psychological Distress		.25	.18	.25	.18
Life Satisfaction		.08	.48**	.08	.48**
Part D: Retiree low/spouse high	29				
Revised Symptom Score		− .32	.27	.28	.24
Multidimensional Health Scale		− .06	.05	.32	.23
Scale of Psychological Distress		− .17	.39*	.29	.34
Life Satisfaction		.05	.25	.30	.35

$*p \leq .05.$ $**p \leq .01.$ $***p \leq .001.$

In the two congruent groups, and in the retiree high/spouse low group, the answer to our central question—Is the family SOC score more strongly related to retiree adaptation than is the retiree's own score?—is still negative. The group of most interest is the retiree low/spouse high SOC subtype. At first glance, it would seem that the fascinating 1987 finding, that the high family SOC score in this subtype was a better predictor of retiree adaptation than the retiree's own SOC, is not replicated. This is not, however, because of an attenuation of the family SOC as a predictor of retiree adaptation. The family SOC-adaptation correlations in 1988 are quite similar to those in 1987. What does happen is that the retiree SOC-adaptation correlations, negative in 1987 (nonsignificantly), become as positive as those with the family measure.

In other words, two years after retirement the salutogenic family measure remains a predictor of retiree adaptation in this subtype, but it is no longer a better predictor than the retiree score because the latter is now positively correlated with well-being.

The attempt to understand this change led us to consider the dynamics of the SOC scores in this second year of dynamic transition. As can be seen in Table 6, the 1987–1988 SOC score patterns are quite different in the different subtypes.

Table 6
Mean SOC Scores in 1987 and 1988 by Family Subtype

	Retiree	Spouse	n
Both spouses high			
1987	171.31	168.49	74
1988	163.90***	157.77***	74
Both spouses low			
1987	136.89	128.89	72
1988	137.80	135.35**	72
Retiree high/spouse low			
1987	167.85	130.90	39
1988	155.21**	131.88	39
Retiree low/spouse high			
1987	142.29	161.15	29
1988	144.77	148.23**	29

Note. The n's, which refer to couples, add up to 214. These are the couples who were interviewed in both years, so that the comparisons are exact.
T test value between 1987 and 1988 SOC scores is significant: **$p \le .01$. ***$p \le .001$.

High/high: There is a strong, significant, and similar decline in the SOC scores of both spouses in the second year after retirement.

Low/low: While retiree scores do not change, spouse scores show a significant increase.

Retiree high/spouse low: Retiree scores show a strong significant decline but spouse scores remain stable.

Retiree low/spouse high: Retiree scores do not change, but spouse scores show a significant decrease.

Discussion

The SOC of the individual has been shown (Antonovsky, 1987; Antonovsky, Adler, Sagy, & Visel, 1990) to be related to successful coping with stressors, contributing to health and well-being. The present study, whose data confirm this finding, was designed to apply the concept to the level of the family. Our specific empirical concern was to advance understanding of adaptation to the complex stressor of the life cycle developmental transition of retirement. The study tested the hypothesis that the family SOC is related to adaptation of the retiree. Further, we asked the comparative question of the relative contribution of the individual characteristics and of the larger social system to adaptation.

In the attempt to translate a dispositional orientation from the individual to the collective level, the philosophical examination of the existence of a collective character cannot be ignored. Can one speak of a collective dispositional orientation, of a social system that perceives, thinks, has a world view? This issue has been confronted over the course of many centuries. Our approach followed that of Miller's remark (1965, p. 370) that "the culture of a society is an abstraction like the personality of a human organism." To say that an individual perceives is an abstraction formulated by an observer which is inferred from the behavior, verbal or otherwise, of that individual. The cognitive map of a family, its SOC, is precisely such an abstraction.

In a different, narrow, and restricted way, this work tried to deal with the question by means of an empirical examination, using a results-centered method, to compare four alternative models.

The data did not allow an unequivocal decision as to which one of the four models is the best predictor to retiree adaptation, though there is a hint that the salutogenic measure may be a bit better. They do suggest a clear division between the two types of measurement: the level versus the structure type. Only the level type was found to be a good predictor of adaptation. But what meaning can be given to this finding?

At the level type, in contrast to the structure type, the emphasis is on the level of the individual characteristics as the elements which "build" the family concept. Moreover, despite the fact that each measure of the level type derives from a different theoretical approach, they all have a similar predictive value. This raises the question of the existence of a collective-familial measure as a different measure or a different concept, apart from its individual components. The familial character, it seems, is only a causal and inconsistent result of *one* of the three individual measures. Or, in other words, it is enough to know the disposition of one of the family members (or, in the case of the aggregation measure, the separate score of each member) in order to arrive at a family score.

This finding may be explained, first, in methodological terms. The similar correlations of the three level type measures between the SOC and adaptation scores stem from the very high correlations of the two individual spouse SOC scores (.68 in the first stage and .73 in the second stage). However, if the extent of any similarity between spouses is crucial in family measures, we would expect that the gap measure, which actually measures the extent of consensus between the spouses, would also predict adaptation. This, however, is not the case. Moreover, similarity between spouses has not always been found to be a frequent familial characteristic (Gruen, Folkman, & Lazarus, 1987). The finding of this study, in a selected sample of older spouses married for many years, cannot be seen as definitive. Conceivably, the different measures, applied to other samples, might produce different results.

This indeterminate finding led us to a more detailed analysis, using spouse similarity as a differentiating factor among families. Among the incongruent families in stage one, the *high* family score was found to be the best family score predictor of adaptation. This measure, it will be recalled, is derived from a salutogenic approach, which considers the family as expressed by its strongest member. The finding, however, was supported only in part in stage two: The family SOC-retiree adaptation correlations remain positive, but the retiree SOC, unrelated to adaptation in stage one, becomes positively related in stage two.

These data may well not be robust and the change may be due to chance. It may be that our sample numbers are simply too small. An alternative substantive explanation, however, is at least plausible. It will be recalled that in this retiree low/spouse high group, retiree SOC scores increased very slightly in the second year of retirement, while spouse scores declined considerably. It may be that, in the acute transitional year after retirement, requiring extensive readjustment, a strong spouse SOC becomes a decisive buffer variable when the SOC of the retiree is weak. The spouse, however, pays a price and, in the more "normal" second year, her or his diminished strength, while still relevant to well-being, no longer is decisive.

The fact that measures of the family SOC do predict the well-being of the retiree, and that there is some suggestive evidence that one of these measures may be a particularly powerful predictor, leads to a consideration of the theoretical meaning of the findings. First, it can be inferred that one may speak of a family collective orientation which is not identical with the orientation of its individual members. One cannot, however, ignore the prob-lematics of such an analysis. A collective orientation is an abstract concept which cannot be examined or observed as clearly as an individual orientation (Steinglass, 1987). The family as perceiver, thinker, or possessor of a cognitive orientation is, in the last analysis, a concept only in the mind of an observer. In this sense, the family SOC is not a direct representation of a concrete reality but an abstraction of it, which may be heuristic to the researcher. The question, "Which family members express the family orientation?" is one possible concrete way to get at the abstract experience of family existence. In this study, with its limited tools, this way did seem to make a meaningful contribution in explaining adaptation in the subgroup of incongruent families.

The translation of an individual concept to the family level was here derived from a systems approach. However, empirical application of systems principles in family research has been found to be very complex and to date has produced no adequate measures (Jahoda, 1989). The limited results of this study hint at a concrete possibility of a combination of a reductionist approach with a holistic one. This combination, we suggest, can lead to obtaining meaningful information in the study of family concepts. A family collective characterization is not independent of its individual elements, but it is also not a simple aggregation of these elements. Mapping relations among the parts may provide a key to understanding the collective orientation.

The second theoretical inference to be drawn from the results of the study relates to the strength of the salutogenic approach. Both among the congruent families at the two stages of the study, and even more clearly among the incongruent families, having a strong family SOC consistently predicted adaptation. The meaning of this finding might be explained by the use of concepts familiar to family research, such as social support and power. That is, if there is an individual member of the family with a strong SOC, she or he provides the support or applies the orchestration resources needed to cope successfully with stressors. This approach can be enriched by using family systems concepts. A systems approach would define the *whole* family unit as having a strong or weak sense of coherence as an expression of the cognitive mapping of the family.

Another important meaning of the findings is that the system explanation allows the characterization of the whole system by one of its *subsystems*. The pathogenic orientation, which is well known in family therapy, defines the whole unit as ill by identifying the illness of one member. Our findings, however, support a *salutogenic* orientation, an approach rarely found in family research or clinical work. It suggests that we would do well to heed Antonovsky's (1979, 1987) call to study salutary rather than only risk factors.

Is this salutogenic finding determined by the specific stage in the family life cycle studied? The question of generalization to other life stages cannot be answered by our study. It may be that the high proportion of congruent families (65%) in our sample characterizes this later stage of family life more than other stages. The gerontological literature indicates changes in this stage toward more similarity between males and females, more equality in role allocation, and even a tendency toward androgyny in behavior (Blieszner, 1988).

We now turn to the comparative question of the individual and family contributions to coping with stressors. The specifics of this study (the particular sample, the results-centered method) undoubtedly limit the possibilities of an answer. Moreover, the high intercorrelations of SOC scores between the spouses do not enable a clear-cut decision. For the sample as a whole, both individual and family orientations seem to be of equal power in explaining adaptation. Occam's razor principle of parsimony would, then, suggest that, at least in measurement, if not in explanation, we make do with individual scores. The results among the incongruent families, however, though only partially supported in replication, do suggest that knowing the family orientation would provide a better understanding of adaptation than only knowing the orientation of the individual.

The study is limited by the fact that the sample consisted of Israeli, white-collar, on-time retirees and their spouses. The generalizability of the findings to other segments of the population, such as blue-collar workers, should be further investigated.

Finally, we would note that our study poses two linked heretical challenges to the dominant orientation in family therapy. The common approach to family therapy considers the whole system as the source of dysfunction or illness of one of its members. The basic unit for change is, then, the whole family. This emphasis on the whole leads to an inclination to disregard the parts, the individuals. In this study, the whole family was characterized by data obtained from individuals. The findings indicate that, at least in the cognitive map of incongruent families, there is salience to one member. Moreover, that member is the one with a strong SOC. It may, then, be wise to combine the holistic and individual approaches in therapeutic thought, rather than regarding them as polar contrasts. Both the family and the individual may become the units for change (Slipp, 1989). Moreover, this approach would contribute to a more salutogenic view of family therapy, one which would search for sources of strength and health, rather than of weakness and pathology.

Note

1. Originally published in *Journal of Marriage and the Family, 54,* 983–993. © 1992 by the National Council on Family Relations, 3989 Central Ave. NE, Suite 550, Minneapolis, MN 55421. Reprinted by permission. The larger study within whose frame this work was done, "Retirement, Coping, and Health: A Longitudinal Study," is supported by grant HUD-25 R01 AGO5206 from the United States National Institute on Aging. This article is based on Sagy's unpublished doctoral dissertation, The Family Sense of Coherence and Adjustment to Stressors: The Retirement Transition (1991), Faculty of Health Sciences, Ben-Gurion University of the Negev, Beersheba, Israel. Correspondence concerning this article should be addressed to Shifra Sagy.

References

Andrews, F. M., & Withey, S. B. (1976). *Social indicators of well-being.* New York: Plenum.

Antonovsky, A. (1979). *Health, stress, and coping.* San Francisco: Jossey-Bass.

Antonovsky, A. (1987). *Unraveling the mystery of health.* San Francisco: Jossey-Bass.

Antonovsky, A., Adler, I., Sagy, S., & Visel, R. (1990). Attitudes toward retirement in an Israeli cohort. *International Journal of Aging and Human Development, 31,* 57–77.

Antonovsky, A., & Sourani, T. (1988). Family sense of coherence and family adaptation. *Journal of Marriage and the Family, 50,* 79-92.

Atchley, R. C. (1971). Retirement and leisure participation: A continuity of crisis. *The Gerontologist, 11,* 13–27.

Atchley, R. C., & Miller, S. J. (1983). Types of elderly couples. In T. H. Brubaker (Ed.), *Family relationship later in life.* Beverly Hills, CA: Sage.

Bateson, G. (1972). *Steps to an ecology of mind.* New York: Ballantine.

Ben-Sira, Z. (1982). The scale of psychological distress (SPD). *Research Communications in Psychology, Psychiatry, and Behavior, 7,* 329–346.

Bertalanffy, L. von. (1968). *Organismic psychology and systems theory.* Worcester: Clark University Press.

Blieszner, R. (1988). Individual development and intimate relationships in middle and late adulthood. In R. M. Milardo (Ed.), *Families and social networks* (pp. 147–165). Newbury Park, CA: Sage.

Booth, A., & Welch, S. (1978). Spousal consensus and its correlates: A reassessment. *Journal of Marriage and the Family, 40,* 23–31.

Bush, J. W. (1987). General health policy model: The quality of well-being (QWB) scale. In N. K. Wenger, M. E. Mattson, C. D. Furberg, & J. Elison (Eds.), *Assessment of quality life in clinical trials of cardiovascular therapies* (pp. 189–199). New York: Le Jacq.

Fishbein, M., & Ajzen, I. (1975). *Belief, attitude, intention, and behavior.* Reading, MA: Addison-Wesley.

Fisher, L., Kokes, R., Ransom, D., Phillips, S., & Rudo, P. (1985). Alternative strategies for creating a "relational" family data. *Family Process, 24,* 213–224.

Fleck, S., Quinlan, P., Jalali, B., & Resentech, R. (1988). Family assessment. *Social Psychiatry and Psychiatric Epidemiology, 23,* 137–144.

Freeman, L., & Romney, K. (1986). Words, deeds, and social structure. *Human Organization, 9,* 109–134.

Godin, G. (1987). Importance of the emotional aspect of attitude to the prediction of intention. *Psychological Reports, 61,* 719–723.

Greenwald, A. G., & Pratkanis, A. R. (1988). On the use of "theory" and the usefulness of theory. *Psychological Review, 95,* 575–579.

Gruen, R. J., Folkman, S., & Lazarus, R. S. (1987). Dyadic response patterns in married couples, depressive symptoms, and somatic dysfunction. *Journal of Family Psychology, 1,* 168–186

Israel Central Bureau of Statistics. (1983). *Key for coding occupations.* Jerusalem: Central Bureau of Statistics.

Jacob, T. (1987). Family interaction and psychopathology: An historical review. In T. Jacob (Ed.), *Family interaction and psychopathology: Theories, methods, and findings* (pp. 1–21). New York: Plenum.

Jahoda, M. (1989). Why a non-reductionist social psychology is almost too difficult to be tackled but too fascinating to be left alone. *British Journal of Social Psychology, 28,* 71–78.

Klein, D. M., & Hill, R. (1979). Determinants of family problem-solving effectiveness. In W. R. Burr, R. Hill, F. I. Nye, & I. L. Reiss (Eds.), *Contemporary theories about the family* (Vol. 1, pp. 493–548). New York: Free Press.

Larson, R. (1978). Thirty years of research on subjective well-being of older Americans. *Journal of Gerontology, 33,* 109–125.

Lavee, Y., McCubbin, H. I., & Patterson, J. M. (1985). The double ABCX model of family stress and adaptation: An empirical test by analysis of structural equations with latent variables. *Journal of Marriage and the Family, 48,* 811–825.

Lazarus, R. S., & Folkman, S. (1984). Coping and adaptation. In W. D. Gentry (Ed.), *Handbook of behavioral medicine* (pp. 282–325). New York: Guilford Press.

Levine, S., & Scotch, N. A. (1970). Perspectives on stress research. In S. Levine & N. A. Scotch (Eds.), *Social stress* (pp. 279-291). Chicago: Aldine.

Levinson, D. J. (1980). Toward a conception of the adult life course. In N. J. Smelser & E. H. Erikson (Eds.), *Themes of work and love in adulthood* (pp. 265–290). Cambridge: Harvard University Press.

McCubbin, H. I., & Patterson, J. M. (1983). The family stress process: The double ABCX model of adjustment and adaptation. In H. I. McCubbin, M. B. Sussman, & J. M. Patterson (Eds.), *Social stress and the family: Advances and development in family stress theory and research* (pp. 7–37). New York: Haworth.

Miller, J. G. (1965). Living systems: Basic concepts. *Behavioral Sciences, 10,* 193–237.

Miller, J. G., & Miller, J. L. (1980). The family as a system. In C. K. Hofling & J. M. Lewis (Eds.), *The family: Evaluation and treatment* (pp. 141–184). New York: Brunner/Mazel.

Minuchin, S., Roseman, B. L., & Baker, L. (1978). *Psychosomatic families.* Cambridge: Harvard University Press.

Oliveri, M. E., & Reiss, D. (1984). Family concepts and their measurement: Things are seldom what they seem. *Family Process, 23,* 33–48.

Pearlin, L. I. (1989). The sociological study of stress. *Journal of Health and Social Behavior, 30,* 241–256.

Reiss, D. (1981). *The family construction of reality.* Cambridge: Harvard University Press.

Slipp, S. (1989). A differing viewpoint for integrating psychodynamic and systems approaches. *Journal of Marital and Family Therapy, 15,* 13–16.

Steinglass, P. (1987). A systems view of family interaction and psychopathology. In T. Jacob (Ed.), *Family interaction and psychopathology: Theories, methods, and findings* (pp. 25–65). New York: Plenum.

Stull, D. E. (1988). A dyadic approach to predicting well-being in later life. *Research on Aging, 10,* 81–101.

Walker, A. J. (1985). Reconceptualizing family stress. *Journal of Marriage and the Family, 47,* 827–837.

Chapter 12

Salutogenesis, Successful Aging, and the Advancement of Theory on Family Caregiving[1]

Jeffrey D. Brooks

The families of older Americans are often mentioned in family caregiving literature as the best and last opportunity for older people to avoid institutionalization (Doty, 1986). This issue alone makes family caregiving a significant issue, but the topic is even more significant because research on the consequences of caregiving for the caregiver has resulted in some investigators describing caregivers as "hidden patients" (Schultz, Visintainer, & Williamson, 1990, p. 188). These authors based this assessment on studies that used measures of self-reported health, utilization of health services, and immune function. The purpose of this chapter is to suggest that salutogenic theory provides a framework that could help guide research on ways to postpone or possibly avoid becoming dependent and also to propose that salutogenic theory is useful as a framework for conducting theory-driven research about caregiving.

The first section of this chapter reviews the results of "A Salutogenic Theory of Successful Aging" (Brooks, 1991, 1992), which was derived directly from Antonovsky's salutogenic theory (1979, 1987). Applied to the study of aging, the salutogenic model has the potential to explain variations in the quality of life in later life, and the continued development of salutogenic theory could produce insights on ways to prevent the elderly from becoming dependent. The second section of this chapter provides an overview of the field of caregiving for the elderly, describing why it is appropriate to apply salutogenic theory to the topic of caregiver stress. The goal is to demonstrate that salutogenic theory has the potential to stimulate progress in the field of caregiver research.

A Salutogenic Theory
of Successful Aging

The starting point in proposing a salutogenic theory of successful aging came from two suggestions made by officials at the National Institute of Aging (NIA). Riley and Bond (1983) suggested that investigators should place physical health high on the research agenda. This writer interprets the call for more research on health to mean that the definition of successful aging should be expanded to include physical health. The need for a broader definition of successful aging stems from the fact that social gerontologists have historically concentrated on psychological adjustment as the sole criterion of successful aging. Physical health has only been considered for its ability to predict psychological adjustment (Markides, Laing, & Jackson, 1990). Social activity levels also gained some popularity as criteria of successful aging and as predictors of psychological adjustment. Drawing on the NIA proposals, previous work (Brooks, 1991) on successful aging led to the conclusion that psychological adjustment, social activity, and physical health are all important dimensions of successful aging.

Enlarging the definition of successful aging in this way means that the overarching theory must be broad enough to predict health, but social gerontology currently lacks such a theory (Brooks, 1991). Since the principal objective in salutogenic theory is to explain who stays healthy under stress, Antonovsky's (1979, 1987) theory was adopted for this study in an attempt to fill the existing research gap.

The second suggestion made by Riley and Bond was that studies need to examine the influence of social psychological processes on the overall quality of life in old age. Riley and Bond contended that this is a very important topic, proving that psychosocial processes do influence the quality of life in old age would also demonstrate that the goal of aging successfully can be met. Psychosocial variables are a fundamental part of salutogenic theory, increasing the suitability of its application to the study of aging. As a life-course approach, salutogenic theory has the potential to help point the way for people to "live lives of vitality till very close to the end of their biologically allotted span" (Antonovsky, 1987, p. 14). The phrase "lives of vitality" implies that a person would be psychologically and physically healthy and capable of functioning in social roles. Stated differently, the theory offers a system for exploring ways to avoid the physical and social dependence that sometimes occurs in old age.

Perhaps the most promising aspect of examining salutogenic theory is that the core concept in the theory appears to correspond with psychological traits that many social gerontologists have alluded to as being important determinants of the quality of life in old age. With these points in mind, an initial test of a salutogenic theory of successful aging was proposed, allowing theory-driven research of a fundamental problem in social gerontology. The general question is: Why do variations in successful aging occur? A more specific question asks: Does the core concept from salutogenic theory predict variations in successful aging?

Salutogenic Theory and the Quality of Life in Old Age

Antonovsky (1979) proposed salutogenic theory as a novel addition to stress theory. Salutogenic theory follows other stress research in that it accounts for health problems by treating them as limitations in adaptation. It is a distinctly different approach, however, striving to shift the focus of research from pathology to healthy adaptation and improvements in health. In Antonovsky's terms, the salutogenic orientation can be used to predict someone's location on the "health ease/dis-ease continuum" (1979). Antonovsky maintained that it is important for studies of health to see the subject in a broad context, going beyond the physiological level of disease to include the dimensions of psychological adjustment and overall functioning (1979, p. 67). He defined overall functioning as the extent to which the individual is a functioning member of the community (Antonovsky, 1979, p. 55).

The rationale for proposing a salutogenic stress theory is based, in part, on previous research on the health consequences of encounters with stressful life events. Stressors such as those covered in the Social Readjustment Rating Scale (Holmes & Rahe, 1967) have attained a wide acceptance. However, their notoriety occurs in spite of the fact that stress research typically yields modest results, reflecting the failure of researchers to acknowledge that different people react differently to a given event (Chiriboga, 1989).

The idea that individuals react differently to events is at the very core of salutogenic theory. Antonovsky built upon a point initially identified as a vital issue by Selye (1974), who drew what he felt to be the most important moral to be learned from stress research: It is not what we face, but how we face it (1980, p. 143). It is important to point out that Antonovsky (1979) formulated the salutogenic orientation to have a broader emphasis than other stress theorists used when examining the cognitive processes commonly called coping.

Coping is often defined as a reaction, or how a person evaluates costs and probability of success in reacting to stressful situations. Attempting to deal with questions such as "Am I in trouble?" and "What can I do about it?" has been called reactive coping (Coyne & Lazarus, 1980, p. 153). Antonovsky espoused a more general view of coping, proposing that turning attention away from reactive coping would allow researchers to include more successful patterns of coping. Personality traits such as rationality, flexibility, and farsightedness influence how a person adapts (Antonovsky, 1979, p. 112). In salutogenic theory, a researcher's question was no longer "What keeps one from getting sicker?" but "What facilitates one's becoming healthier?" (1984, p. 117). As applied in this study, the question was "What facilitates successful aging?"

Antonovsky called the factors that facilitate continued healthy adjustment generalized resistance resources (GRRs). These GRRs are useful predictors of quality of life and refer to any characteristic of the person, group, or environment that can facilitate effective management of stress or tension (Antonovsky, 1979, p. 99). In addition to GRRs, Antonovsky proposed a sense of coherence (SOC) variable, calling the SOC the core concept of salutogenic theory.

The Sense of Coherence as a Key to Successful Aging

A strong sense of coherence is both common to all other GRRs and central to the processes linking GRRs to health. In general terms, coherence is a stable and enduring dispositional trait or general orientation to one's world. The more formal definition of the SOC is as follows:

> a global orientation that expresses the extent to which one has a pervasive, enduring though dynamic feeling of confidence that (1) the stimuli deriving from one's internal and external environments in the course of living are structured, predictable, and explicable; (2) the resources are available to meet the demands posed by these stimuli; and (3) these demands are challenges, worthy of investment and engagement (Antonovsky, 1987, p. 19).

Antonovsky devoted most of his effort to developing the coherence concept, including both a description of the origins of the SOC and the construction of an operational measure. A person's sense of coherence comes from his or her life experiences and the resources that make up these experiences. Briefly put, resources such as social support, money, religious faith, work role autonomy, and cultural stability provide continuing life experiences with three characteristics: consistency, an underload-overload balance, and participation in socially valued decision making (Antonovsky & Sourani, 1988). Coherence can be further defined as consisting of three dimensions that Antonovsky called manageability, meaningfulness, and comprehensibility. Manageability involves the extent to which one perceives that the resources at one's disposal are adequate to meet the demands imposed. Meaningfulness refers to the extent to which one feels that life makes sense emotionally. This aspect incorporates the idea that challenges can be welcome rather than perceived as a threat. Comprehensibility refers to the extent to which one perceives stimuli as making cognitive sense. A person with this trait feels that information is orderly, consistent, structured, and clear, rather than chaotic, disordered, or inexplicable (Antonovsky, 1987, p. 17).

Antonovsky's (1979) efforts to establish a firm foundation for the coherence concept included an extensive literature review of the similarities between the dimensions of coherence and existing research. He compared his core concept to Bandura's (1977) work on self-efficacy and to Rotter's (1966) locus of control (LOC). These comparisons were particularly significant because Lachman (1986) reported that the preponderance of evidence upheld the hypothesis that efficacy and control do not change dramatically during old age. Lachman's summary supported the idea that coherence remains stable in later life.

Antonovsky's initial test of the reliability of the SOC scale also provided the opportunity to conduct a preliminary test of the central hypothesis of the salutogenic model. Wherever people were located on the health continuum, he proposed, salutogenic theory would predict that the stronger their SOC, the more likely they would be to maintain that location or to improve it (Antonovsky, 1984, p. 120). The hypothesis that the SOC and positive health are related has been clearly supported (Antonovsky, 1983).

Other applications included studies of the psychological adjustment of elderly retirees in Israel (Antonovsky, 1985; Antonovsky, Sagy, Adler, & Visel, 1990; Sagy, Antonovsky, & Adler, 1990). A prospective study of older veterans who were patients at the St. Louis Department of Veterans Affairs Medical Center (age 55 and older) provided some of the strongest support for Antonovsky's core hypothesis (Coe, Romeis, Tang, & Wolinsky, 1990). In Coe's study, correlations between coherence (taken as a baseline measure) and a variety of measures of health status (taken six months later) were all significant (see Chapter 14 for a report on the five-year follow-up study).

Additional support for the SOC can be found in research on similar concepts, which shows that cognitive processes are important to the quality of life in old age. Schunk and Carbonari (1984), in a summary of recent research, illustrated that aging individuals can postpone or prevent many health problems by exerting a measure of control over their lives. Rodin (1986), Kuhl (1986), Lachman (1986), Lawton (1988, 1989), Piper and Langer (1986), and Costa and McCrae (1989) all provided evidence that cognitive processes such as the sense of coherence can help explain variations in the quality of life of the elderly.

The technique for an initial test of the theory as an approach to successful aging consisted of showing that the SOC predicts three dimensions of quality of life that are elements of successful aging. The specific dimensions of quality of life examined in this study were life satisfaction (Adams, 1969), social health (Donald, Ware, Brook, & Davies-Avery, 1978), and overall physical health (Bergner et al., 1979). Thus, the general proposition was actually three related propositions, collectively indicating that a strong sense of coherence is predictive of successful aging. Other GRRs (education, finances, and health history) were included but were treated as background variables.

Methods: The Sample and Measures

The data set was generated by mailing 300 questionnaires to males that had recently participated in an activity known as the Senior Games. The Senior Games include billiards, bowling, golf, swimming, tennis, track and field events, and a card tournament. The card tournament attracts the majority of the participants.

Since eligibility requirements for the Games include a minimum age of 55, all of the respondents in this study were 55 years of age or over. The study also targeted only the male participants. All the respondents lived in central Indiana, with the majority from Lafayette, the largest city in the region. It is an economic center because it has a large industrial base, is home to a large university, and qualifies as the only Standard Metropolitan Statistical Area in the region.

Data collection took place in April and May of 1991. The Total Design Method (Dillman, 1978) was the guide for procedures used in constructing the questionnaire and other matters related to collecting the data. Dillman's method proved quite effective in generating a satisfactory response rate. The overall response rate was 71%. The elimination of incomplete questionnaires and surveys returned by females reduced the data set to 199 subjects. Budget limitations precluded attempts to enhance the response rate (by conducting additional mailings) or to ascertain information about those who failed to respond. The data received was generally complete; only the income question had recurring missing cases, and these were very few (1.5% of total).

There was a strong background for measuring most of the concepts in this study, so the questionnaire consisted largely of previously developed scales. For detailed reports about most of the measures, the interested reader can see the following: Kane and Kane (1981), McDowell and Newell (1987), Mangen and Peterson (1982, 1984), and Streiner and Norman (1989).

The multidimensional assessment of successful aging was composed of previously developed measures for psychological, social, and physical aspects of the quality of life. The psychological dimension of the quality of life was measured using the 18-item version (Adams, 1969) of the Life Satisfaction Index (LSI) (developed by Neugarten, Havighurst, & Tobin, 1961). The Social Health Scale (SHS) (Donald et al., 1978) measures social circumstances on two dimensions: the number of social resources a person has available; and the frequency with which he or she is in contact with friends, relatives, and organizations.

A series of 73 questions from the short form of the Sickness Impact Profile (SIP) (developed by Bergner et al., 1979) made up the physical dimension of the dependent variable. The SIP measures health status by directly asking the respondent about the impact that any and all health problems have on normal functioning (Gilson et al., 1975). Additional questions about health history were included but served only as background variables, in conjunction with a series of sociodemographic questions concerning age, marital status, educational attainment, income, and occupation.

The operational measure of the independent variable, the sense of coherence, consisted of a series of 13 questions with a seven-point response range for each question (Antonovsky, 1983, 1987). Several studies have demonstrated the validity and reliability of the coherence scale (Antonovsky, 1993).

Overview of the Data and Results

As a whole, the group was well educated. One third of the respondents had attended college for four years (12%) or had graduate training (21%). Twenty-eight percent had completed high school and 27% had some type of additional education after high school. The respondents' reported incomes corresponded to their high levels of education. Twenty-one percent reported earning more than $50,000 annually, and 26% earned between $30,000 and $50,000. The modal response (37%) was for the category from $15,000 to $29,999. These incomes were surprising, considering that 80% of the respondents reported that they were retired.

Table 1
General Information on Major Variables

Variable	Range	Mean	Mode	Std. Dev.	Var.
Age	55 – 88	69.5	66		6.8
Occupation (Duncan's SES)	10 – 96	54.3	84	24.02	.44
Income	1 – 5[a]	3.5	3	1.007	.29
Education	2 – 7[b]	5	4	1.37	.27
Life Satisfaction	4 – 36	28.3	34.0	6.2	.219
Sickness Impact*	0 – 51.7	5.840	0.0	8.37	1.43
Social Health	13 – 47	30.9	38.0	7.9	.256
Sense of Coherence	21 – 91	70.6	79	10.7	.152

Note. The variability on the Social Health Scale was actually far greater than indicated in Table 1. Some of the responses to questions about memberships in organizations, number of acquaintances, and how many close friends a person felt they could confide in were extensive. Extreme responses to open-ended questions were assigned a maximum value of eight (8).

[a] 1 = less than $5,000
2 = $5,000–14,999
3 = $15,000–29,999
4 = $30,000–49,999
5 = more than $50,000

[b] 2 = 6–8 years
3 = 9–11 years
4 = 12 years
5 = some college or other schooling
6 = 4 years of college
7 = post-graduate work

*Reflects score with weights assigned.

Table 1 contains the ranges, means, and standard deviations for the major variables. Overall, the measures for the independent variables and dimensions of dependent variable exhibited adequate reliability. Cronbach's Alpha for the SOC scale was .82. This is consistent with other reports of the short form of the SOC questionnaire. The Social Health Scale (SHS), of the scales used, obtained the lowest score for Cronbach's Alpha (.70). A test of the reliability of the Life Satisfaction Index (LSI) produced an Alpha of .80, and the Sickness Impact Profile (SIP) also possessed a high reliability (Cronbach's Alpha = .92).

Testing the Hypotheses

The correlations presented in Table 2 provide a starting point for evaluating the hypothesis of this study. All correlations in the table greater than .14 are significant at .01 unless otherwise indicated. The correlations between the SOC and the dimensions of successful aging are all in the predicted direction. A most promising point is the strength of the correlation ($r = -.50$) between the SOC and the physical health measure.

Table 2
Correlation Coefficients

Variable	Inc	Educ	Occup	Age	Past Health	SIP	LSI	SHS	SOC
Income	1.0	.49	.51	−.31	−.10	−.26	.19	−.03	.26
Education	.49	1.0	.66	−.15*	.07	−.13	.13	.01	.15*
Occupation	.51	.66	1.0	−.19	−.04	−.08	.20	.06	.15*
Age	−.31	−.15*	−.19	1.0	−.04	.23	−.05	.14*	.006
Past Health	−.11	.07	−.04	−.04	1.0	−.38	.19	.12	.21
Sickness Impact	−.26	−.13	−.08	.23	−.38	1.0	−.42	−.12	−.50
Life Satisfaction	.20	.13	.20	−.05	.19	−.42	1.0	.34	.44
Social Health	−.03	.01	.06	.14*	.12	−.12	.34	1.0	.27
Sense of Coherence	.26	.17*	.15*	.00	.22	−.50	.44	.27	1.0

Note. All correlations > .14 are significant at .01 unless otherwise indicated.
*$p \leq .05$.

Further analysis with partial correlations indicates the relationship between the SOC variable and the dimensions of successful aging remains significant when a variety of controls are brought into the analysis. As can be seen in Table 3, correlations between the SOC and dependent variables remain statistically significant in spite of using various first-, second-, third-, and fourth-order partial correlations for the background variables of age, socioeconomic status, and measure of past health.

The next step of the analysis was to include all of the variables having significant correlations with independent or dependent variables in a regression analysis. The results of multiple regression analysis provide additional support for the proposition that the

Table 3
Partial Correlation Analysis

Independent Variable	Life Satisfaction	Social Health	Sickness Impact Profile
Sense of Coherence	.38*	.26*	– .46*

Note. Controlling for: Age, Income, Education, Occupation, and Past Health.
*$p \leq .01$.

SOC is a positive influence on successful aging. As can be seen in Table 4, the SOC accounts for a modest but statistically significant amount of the variation in each of the measures. It was hoped that the variables would have greater predictive capacity. However, if one considers all of the possible influences on the process of growing old, it is not surprising that the R square is not larger.

Table 4
Regression Results

Dependent Variable	Multiple R	R Square	Adj. R Sq.
Sickness Impact*	.612	.375	.365

*Variables entered in the equation, in the order in which they were entered in the stepwise multiple regression: SOC, Past Health, Age.

Dependent Variable	Multiple R	R Square	Adj. R Sq.
Social Health*	.315	.099	.089

*Variables entered in the equation, in the order in which they were entered in the stepwise multiple regression: SOC, Age.

Dependent Variable	Multiple R	R Square	Adj. R Sq.
Life Satisfaction*	.467	.218	.210

*Variables entered in the equation, in the order in which they were entered in the stepwise multiple regression: SOC, Occupation.

Summary of the Results

The hypotheses of the initial test of the theory were supported. The sense of coherence is correlated with the dimensions of successful aging. The most impressive characteristic in the results is the strength of the relationship of the SOC with physical health as measured by the Sickness Impact Profile. These relationships remain statistically significant when further tested with statistical controls in partial correlation analysis and when subjected to regression analysis.

These findings indicate that the SOC is one of the psychosocial variables that deserves the attention of social gerontologists interested in explaining variations in the quality of life. They also suggest that salutogenic theory merits attention as a theoretical orientation for predicting the quality of life in later life. Furthermore, and at the very least, the findings from this study suggest that the effort and expense of conducting a longitudinal study of a salutogenic theory of successful aging are justified.

Some words of caution are needed here. The nature of the data does not provide any way to answer questions about causal links between coherence and successful aging. Also, the data were not taken from a representative sample of men and did not include any information from women. Therefore, a tentative interpretation of these results would indicate that the cognitive processes tapped by the SOC are factors that enhance the opportunities for an individual to maintain a high quality of life into old age.

The first part of this chapter reviewed results showing that salutogenic theory provides a promising approach for explaining variations in the quality of life of older people. The discussion now turns to demonstrating the considerable promise that salutogenic theory also exhibits for the related topic of helping families care for their ill or frail older members.

Significance of Caregiving
for the Elderly: An Overview

Stone and Kemper (1989) estimated that there were more than 3.5 million noninstitutionalized elders that needed assistance in the activities of daily living or in the instrumental activities of daily living, and another 0.9 million that were in nursing care facilities. They also estimated that there were 4.4 million spouses and children who were active as primary caregivers, and another 9.9 million potential caregivers (Stone, 1991; Stone & Kemper, 1989). These numbers would be even larger if other family members (such as siblings), friends, or other people known to be sources of informal caregiving were included. Demographic projections (Doty, 1986) suggest that the numbers of elderly in need of assistance will increase until early in the next century.

Zarit (1989) described a family's potential for providing care as being of pivotal importance in the long-term care of disabled elders. Chiriboga, Weiler, and Nielson suggested that family members were not only major sources of help, they were often the preferred sources of care (1990, p. 124). Family members are often called informal caregivers, but this phrase is not meant to imply that their duties are not important. As was indicated previously, the care recipient receives assistance for things they are unable to do for themselves. A caregiver contributes companionship and other forms of personal assistance. Caregivers may also contribute to material well-being by directly providing valued resources or doing things that help to conserve the care recipient's financial resources.

Caregiving as a Stressor

Caregiving for a disabled older family member also has drawbacks. After reviewing literature on the prolonged or cumulative consequences of exposure to the stress of caregiving, Schultz et al. (1990) concluded that providing care for a disabled person creates varying levels of psychiatric and physical morbidity, financial problems, and familial strain for informal caregivers. Extensive evidence exists regarding the emotional strains of caring for a disabled family member (Scharlach, Sobel, & Roberts, 1991).

Other studies have shown caregiving burdens can cause strains in interpersonal relations (Cicirelli, 1981; Kahana & Kinney, 1991; Kinney & Stephens, 1989). Possible results for the caregiver include economic strain, limitations of outside activities and relationships, and increased interpersonal conflict. Employed caregivers are often unable to devote themselves fully to their jobs (Pearlin, 1989, p. 248), and work disruption can be a factor in caregiver strain (Scharlach et al., 1991).

The growing concern about caregiving and caregiver burdens has become a political issue. Some corporations consider the problem of employees' caregiving strains so important that they have set up various assistance programs to help maintain worker productivity and control corporate costs (Stone & Kemper, 1989; Gorey, Rice, & Brice, 1992). Social workers and clinicians have begun to concentrate on the goal of alleviating interpersonal strains in caregivers (Kahana & Kinney, 1991).

Caregiving burden is seen not only as a consequence of the current caregiving situation but also as a predictor of future behavior (Montgomery, 1989, p. 205). In other words, caregiving strains may have consequences for the care recipient. Increased burdens may reduce the willingness and ability of a caregiver to provide care, thereby increasing the elderly care recipient's risk of institutional placement (Scharlach et al., 1991). Caregiving stressors can be factors in the utilization of formal social and health care services (Schultz et al., 1990, p. 181) and may also contribute to elder abuse.

Critical Views of the Field: Opportunities for Salutogenic Theory

The field of caregiver research has been repeatedly criticized for a lack of theoretical development. As one author noted, much of the research on family caregiving and associated burdens has been conducted with little theoretical guidance (Montgomery, 1989). Therefore, the development of useful theoretical frameworks is one of the most important issues for the field to address.

George (1990) contended that there was a repetitive theme and lackluster quality in much of the literature on caregiving, and she decided that the topic had been exhausted by gerontologists' work of the preceding 15 years. Part of the reason for her dissatisfaction was that studies of caregiving consistently failed to develop any specific theoretical foundation. Kahana and Kinney (1991) also recognized the failure of researchers in family caregiving research to develop a strong emphasis on theory. Without a theoretical framework, the field of caregiving studies would not be in a position to help family members cope with the consequences of their roles as caregiver. Enhanced theoretical development, according to Kahana and Kinney, would create closer ties between theory and practice (Kahana & Kinney, 1991, p. 123).

While researchers may fail to fully or explicitly develop theoretical aspects of their work, many do follow the basic elements of stress theory. Many investigators of the effects of caregiving have conceptualized caregiver burden as a type of stress or strain and used the terms *caregiver burden* and *caregiver stress* interchangeably (Montgomery, 1989, p. 209). There are also many research projects that follow the central tenet of stress research: physical morbidity results from encounters with stressful situations. The need for a theoretical model has been recognized by Schultz et al., who suggested that an appropriate model would include measures of stressors, assessments of how those stressors are perceived by the caregivers, and a repertoire of health outcomes (1990, p. 190).

While the burdens or stressful aspects of caregiving, as well as the outcomes, are well documented, the model proposed by Schultz et al. fails to adequately develop the role of a caregiver's perceptions of a situation. Studies of both general stress [see Holmes & Rahe, 1967, on stressful life events (SLE)] and the more specific topic of caregiver stress enjoy a consistency of findings about stressors having a deleterious impact on well-being. The fact is, however, that the relationships observed between stressors (caregiving burdens) and a caregiver's well-being are generally modest. As Chiriboga et al. (1990) noted, there are many cases that show no signs of strain and no deleterious consequences of the burden of caregiving. The field of caregiver stress has failed to investigate a hypothesis that, as other stress literature has suggested, is important: different individuals react differently to stress (Chiriboga, 1989).

Assessments of how caregivers' characteristics influence stress outcomes often include only sociodemographic variables (see Stone & Kemper, 1987; Montgomery, 1989; Pearlin, Mullan, Semple, & Skaff, 1990). Borrowing from work in general stress studies, Coe et al. (1992) helped to create a more complete picture of caregiving by exploring the relationship between a person's sense of coherence and his or her perceptions of caregiver burden. From the results of this study, the SOC appears to be useful in trying to operationalize the factor that is currently missing in the model proposed by Schultz et al. (1990).

Another extremely important aspect absent from the model proposed by Schultz et al. (1990) concerns the extent to which the influence of stressors on caregivers' mental and physical health is buffered by resources. As stated by Kahana and Kinney, "the resources available to caregivers can help to offset the negative consequences to a caregiver's health and well-being that sometimes result from caregiving stresses" (1991, pp. 126–127). More general theories of stress, such as the environmental fit theory (Kahana & Kahana, 1984), emphasize potential resources. Kahana and Kinney theorized that a fit or match between the demands presented by the stress and the available resources would prevent a negative effect on a person's well-being. Conversely, a mismatch between a person's resources and demands increases the likelihood that there will be distress or other negative outcomes.

Pearlin (1989) advised researchers to look beyond the primary stressors associated with caregiver burden; a wider view of the whole constellation of stressors would be necessary to success-fully explain why people differ in stress adaptations. Family stress theorists (McCubbin & Patterson, 1983) have also maintained that it is important for the "pile-up" of stressful events to be considered in trying to explain the different outcomes of encoun-ters with stress. Chiriboga et al. (1990) produced one study of caregiver burden that did include measures of stress encountered outside those activities specific to caregiving. They found that stress from other areas of the caregiver's life explains more of the variation in caregiver well-being than does the stress directly related to caregiving. As Chiriboga et al. (1990) noted, assess-ments of overall stress are rarely included in caregiving research, so their results should be replicated.

The idea that a person's overall stress exposure influences his or her well-being clearly indicates that more diverse measures of stress need to be included in caregiver research and suggests that the results from general studies of stress and coping would be valu-able to the study of caregiver stress. Adding resources to the Schultz et al. (1990) proposal makes it a more complete model of the basic elements identified as important in the family stress theories pro-posed by Antonovsky and Sourani (1988) and McCubbin and Patterson (1983). The additions to the framework developed by Schultz et al. (1990) can easily be translated into variables of gener-alized resistance resources and generalized resistance deficits, which are integral parts of Antonovsky's salutogenic model. In other words, the findings from general studies suggest that a caregiver's SOC and the availability of other GRRs for dealing with the total pile-up of stressors can be predictors of who copes effectively with stress and who experiences strain.

Thinking Salutogenically:
Developing the Salutogenic Imagination

The points in the discussion thus far have focused on ways salutogenic theory could help stimulate the traditional topics in caregiver research. While these points may be very significant in their own right, they are not truly examples of what Antonovsky called thinking salutogenically: "It is of equal importance to seek to explain the origins of health—of successful coping with stressors—as it is to explain the origins of pathology" (Antonovsky & Sourani, 1988, p. 80).

A discussion of a few more critical assessments of the field shows that thinking salutogenically, or developing the salutogenic imagination, would be welcomed by at least some researchers on caregiving. Such a discussion would encourage them to try to break free of the pathogenic preoccupation, which has been, at the very least, overly pessimistic and almost completely focused on distress and its harmful consequences.

Citing an example of the pathogenic emphasis in the field of caregiving research, Montgomery observed that caregiving is often seen as being synonymous with "decrements" in selected dimensions of well-being. She noted that caregiver burdens are by definition viewed as negative, but she contended that not all the duties of caregiving are oppressive (Montgomery, 1989, p. 205). Montgomery is just one of several scholars who have criticized the field of caregiving research for being overly pessimistic. Matthews (1988) agreed, pointing out that the dominant tendency of using research samples composed almost exclusively of disadvantaged families causes an exaggeration in the negative outcomes of caregiving. She concluded that samples containing fewer disadvantaged families would reveal that many caregivers are able to cope effectively.

Matthews also argued that a favorite research sample includes caregivers for Alzheimer's patients, and this may cause overstated results and conclusions. Another study (Chiriboga et al., 1990) suggested that even caregivers of Alzheimer's patients do not inevitably become distressed. Chiriboga et al. found that 24% of the caregivers reported they were "only a little" or "not at all" troubled by the burdens they encountered. The study also reported that some individuals reacted to the conditions imposed with a sense of challenge and seemed to thrive in the situation (Chiriboga, 1989, p. 135).

It may well be that the negative image of caregiving in the literature is inevitable, since the topic is treated as a social problem. However, Kahana and Kinney (1991) and Montgomery (1989) have suggested that clinicians and researchers consistently impose a more negative assessment of burdens than do caregivers. Working with other associates, both Kahana and Kinney have suggested that the field has failed to develop an appreciation for the possibility that there are positive aspects of caregiving. Kahana and Young (1990) pointed out that there is a need for still more dimensions of caregiving to be acknowledged; for example, symmetry can exist in relationships, producing positive consequences for both care recipients and caregivers (1990, pp. 76–77). Similarly, Kinney and Stephens (1989) have documented that many caregivers feel that some aspects of their work are uplifting.

Exploring these views is consistent with Antonovsky's idea that we should devote some of our research efforts toward positive aspects and positive outcomes, enhancing our understanding of ways to promote these positive outcomes in others. Developing the salutogenic imagination involves using these ideas in future research: studying the experience of uplifts and symmetry of outcomes, selecting more representative samples, and investigating the possibility that the SOC can predict who experiences caregiving as uplifting rather than burdensome.

Practical Implications

Caregiving is a dynamic process. There are many cases of lengthy or progressive illnesses, and consequently, caregiving can become progressively more demanding. In these situations, caregivers or entire families may eventually become distressed. Recognizing this dynamic quality in caregiving increases our awareness of the complexity of building policies for the timing of intervention (Kahana & Kinney, 1991).

Observing that many families become exhausted before seeking assistance from more formal systems of health care, Kahana and Kinney have suggested that we need to develop general techniques to identify those caregivers and other family members who are likely to experience strains and stress when the health problems of an afflicted family member are chronic or progressive. In theory, these individuals and families are more likely to suffer the harmful consequences of stress; the caregivers can be seen as hidden patients.

Kahana and Kinney have provided an example of one way the sense of coherence concept might be useful in caregiver research. The SOC scale might be valuable as a screening device for identifying those who are the most vulnerable family caregivers. Based on the findings in the Coe et al. (1992) study, suggesting that caregiver burdens can be predicted using the SOC scale, it seems reasonable to propose that using the SOC as a screening device may prove helpful in determining who would experience burden. Family members of patients diagnosed with Alzheimer's or other debilitating diseases could be screened with the SOC scale, and those with low scores would be monitored more closely.

Further evidence that the coherence concept may have some additional practical value comes from another observation made by Kahana and Kinney. Both empirical studies and therapeutic perspectives have suggested that people with lesser degrees of perceived competence tend to manage difficult events less successfully. This led Kahana and Kinney to speculate that interventions should be based on the ability to identify a person's coping skills and that one goal of intervention should be to boost the competence and coping abilities of family members, maximizing their abilities to deal with stress (Kahana & Kinney, 1991, p. 132). The SOC scale might prove useful in determining whether the activation of social services has a uplifting effect on a caregiver's sense of coherence.

Conclusion

It is somewhat bewildering that the field of caregiver research has not developed beyond its current state; many of the troublesome topics have a large literature base in more general stress studies that appears to provide ready-made solutions. A similar assessment of the failure to utilize related research has been made about caregiver studies and what has come to be called social support theory (Kahana, Kahana, Johnson, Hammond, & Kercher, 1994).

This chapter is intended, in part, to show that researchers interested in family caregiving could borrow from salutogenic theory to advance their cause. Developing theory is critical to progress in the field, and innumerable sources of potential models remain untapped. The environmental fit model provides a potentially powerful framework (see Kahana & Kahana, 1984, or Kahana & Kinney, 1991), and the same argument may be made for the Double ABCX Model (see McCubbin & Patterson, 1983). Whether researchers use salutogenic theory or these alternatives is of course up to them.

While it has not been estimated how much those services provided by informal caregivers would cost if provided on a fee-for-service basis, it is clear that many older Americans cannot afford to pay for the services provided by informal caregivers. It is also apparent that government programs have their own budget limitations. Therefore, efforts to postpone or prevent elderly people from becoming disabled, and attempts to reduce the strains of their caregivers when disabilities do occur, will be valuable. The development of such practices will help elderly individuals and their caregivers and will conserve community resources.

Considering the general projections for growth in the older population (Siegel & Taeuber, 1986) and more specific projections about the numbers of elderly needing care (Doty, 1986), it is reasonable to expect the problems associated with the care of the elderly to increase. These projections take on a much more ominous quality if speculation on the future costs of formal health care services are included, given the current budget problems in national and local government. These population projections, and the economic trends of increasing health care costs, make research on caregiving and successful aging extremely important. It is hoped that the ideas expressed here will help bridge the gap that, as Kahana and Kinney (1991) have suggested, currently prevents the field of caregiver studies from achieving its full potential.

Note

1. The author wishes to thank Lisa, Robert, and Virginia Mangus and Jennifer Kinney for technical assistance in this project.

References

Adams, D. L. (1969). Analysis of a life satisfaction index. *Journal of Gerontology, 24,* 470–474.

Antonovsky, A. (1979). *Health, stress, and coping: New perspectives on mental and physical well-being.* San Francisco: Jossey-Bass.

Antonovsky, A. (1983). The sense of coherence: Development of a research instrument. *Newsletter and Research Reports, 1,* 1–11. W. S. Schwartz Research Center for Behavioral Medicine, Tel Aviv University.

Antonovsky, A. (1984). The sense of coherence as a determinant of health. In J. D. Matarazzo, S. M. Weiss, J. A. Herd, N. E. Miller, & S. Weiss (Eds.), *Behavioral health: A handbook of health enhancement and disease prevention* (pp. 114–130). New York: Wiley.

Antonovsky, A. (1985). The life cycle, mental health, and the sense of coherence. *Israel Journal of Psychiatry and Related Sciences, 22,* 273–280.

Antonovsky, A. (1987). *Unraveling the mystery of health.* San Francisco: Jossey-Bass.

Antonovsky, A. (1993). Using the sense of coherence scale. *Social Science and Medicine, 36,* 725–733.

Antonovsky, A., Sagy, S., Adler, I., & Visel, R. (1990). Attitudes toward retirement in an Israeli cohort. *International Journal of Aging and Human Development, 31*(1), 57–77.

Antonovsky, A., & Sourani, T. (1988). Family sense of coherence and family adaptation. *Journal of Marriage and the Family, 50,* 79–92.

Bandura, A. (1977). *Social learning theory.* Englewood Cliffs, NJ: Prentice Hall.

Bergner, M., Bobbitt, R. A., Kressel, S., Pollard, W. E., Gilson, B. S., & Morris, J. R. (1979). The sickness impact profile: Conceptual formulation and methodology for the development of a health status measure. In J. Elinson & A. E. Siegmann (Eds.), *Socio-medical health indicators* (pp. 9–25). New York: Baywood Publishers.

Brooks, J. D. (1991). *A salutogenic theory of successful aging.* Unpublished doctoral dissertation, Purdue University, West Lafayette, IN.

Brooks, J. D. (1992). *A salutogenic theory of successful aging: An exercise in psychosocial stress research.* Paper presented at the International Conference on Social Stress Research, Venice, Italy.

Chiriboga, D. A. (1989). The measurement of stress exposure in later life. In K. S. Markides & C. L. Cooper (Eds.), *Aging, stress, and health* (pp. 13–42). New York: John Wiley & Sons.

Chiriboga, D. A., Weiler, P. G., & Nielsen, K. (1990). The stress of caregivers. In D. E. Biegel & A. Blum (Eds.), *Aging and caregiving: Theory, research, and policy* (pp. 121–138). Newbury Park, CA: Sage.

Cicirelli, V. (1981). *Helping elderly parents: The role of adult children.* Boston: Auburn Press.

Coe, R. M., Miller, D. K., & Flaherty, J. (1992). Sense of coherence and perception of caregiver burden. *Behavior, Health, and Aging, 2,* 93–99.

Coe, R. M., Romeis, J. C., Tang, B., & Wolinsky, F. (1990). Correlates of a measure of coping in older veterans: A preliminary report. *Journal of Community Health, 15*(5), 287–269.

Costa, P. T., Jr., & McCrae, R. R. (1989). Personality, stress, and coping: Some lessons from a decade of research. In K. S. Markides & C. L. Cooper (Eds.), *Aging, stress, and health* (pp. 269–285). New York: John Wiley & Sons.

Coyne, J. C., & Lazarus, R. S. (1980). Cognitive style stress perception and coping. In I. L. Kutash & L. B. Schlesinger (Eds.), *Handbook on stress and anxiety* (pp. 144–158). San Francisco: Jossey-Bass.

Dillman, D. A. (1978). *Mail and telephone surveys: The total design method.* New York: Wiley.

Donald, C. A., Ware, J., Jr., Brook, R. H., & Davies-Avery, A. (1978). *Conceptualization and measurement of health for adults in the health insurance study: Vol. IV, Social health.* Santa Monica, CA: RAND.

Doty, P. (1986). Family care of the elderly: The role of public policy. *The Milbank Quarterly, 64,* 34–75.

George, L. K. (1990). Caregiver stress studies: There really is more to learn. *The Gerontologist, 30,* 580–581.

Gilson, B. S., Gilson, J., Bergner, M., Bobbitt, R. A., Kressel, S., Pollard, W. E., & Vesselago, M. (1975). The sickness impact profile: Development of an outcome measure of health care. *American Journal of Public Health, 65*(12), 1304–1310.

Gorey, K. M., Rice, R. W., & Brice, G. (1992). The prevalence of elder care responsibilities among the work force population. *Research on Aging, 14,* 399–418.

Holmes, T. H., & Rahe, R. H. (1967). The social readjustment rating scale. *Journal of Psychosomatic Research, 11,* 213–218.

Kahana, E., & Kahana, B. (1984). Stress reactions. In P. Lewinsohn & L. T. Elmsfor (Eds.), *Clinical geropsychology* (pp. 139–169). New York: Pergamon.

Kahana, E., Kahana, B., Johnson, J. R., Hammond, R., & Kercher, K. (1994). Developmental changes and family caregiving: Bridging concepts and research. In E. Kahana, D. Biegel, & M. Wykle (Eds.), *Family caregiving across the lifespan.* Newbury Park, CA: Sage.

Kahana, E., & Kinney, J. M. (1991). Understanding caregiving interventions in the context of the stress model. In R. Young & E. Ohlsen (Eds.), *Health, illness, and disability in later life: Practice issues and interventions* (pp. 122–142). Newbury Park, CA: Sage.

Kahana, E., & Young, R. (1990). Clarifying the caregiver paradigm. In D. E. Biegel & A. Blum (Eds.), *Aging and caregiving: Theory, research, and policy* (pp. 76–97). Newbury Park, CA: Sage.

Kane, R. A., & Kane, R. L. (1981). *Assessing the elderly: A practical guide to measurement.* Lexington, KY: Lexington Books.

Kinney, J. M. , & Stephens, M. P. (1989). Hassles and uplifts of giving care to a family member with dementia. *Psychology and Aging, 4,* 402–408.

Kuhl, J. (1986). Aging and models of control: The hidden costs of wisdom. In M. M. Baltes & P. B. Baltes (Eds.), *The psychology of control and aging* (pp. 1–34). Hillsdale, NJ: Lawrence Erlbaum Associates.

Lachman, M. E. (1986). Personal control in later life: Stability, change and cognitive correlates. In M. M. Baltes & P. B. Baltes (Eds.), *The psychology of control and aging* (pp. 207–236). Hillsdale, NJ: Lawrence Erlbaum Associates.

Lawton, M. P. (1988, February 20). *Environmental proactivity and affect in older people.* Paper presented at the Fifth Annual Symposium on Applied Social Psychology, The Claremont Colleges, Pomona, CA.

Lawton, M. P. (1989). Environmental proactivity in older people. In V. L. Bengston & K. W. Schaie (Eds.), *The course of later life* (pp. 15–24). New York: Springer.

Mangen, D., & Peterson, W. (1982). Research instruments in social gerontology, Vol. 2. In D. Mangen & W. Peterson (Eds.), *Clinical and social psychology.* Minneapolis, MN: University of Minnesota Press.

Mangen, D., & Peterson, W. (1984). Research instruments in social gerontology, Vol. 3, Health, program evaluation, and demography. In D. Mangen & W. Peterson (Eds.), *Clinical and social psychology.* Minneapolis, MN: University of Minnesota Press.

Markides, K. S., Laing, J., & Jackson, J. (1990). Race, ethnicity, and aging: Conceptual and methodological issues. In R. H. Binstock & L. K. George (Eds.), *Handbook of aging and the social sciences* (3rd ed., pp. 112–129). San Diego, CA: Academic Press.

Matthews, S. H. (1988). The burdens of parent care: A critical evaluation of recent findings. *Journal of Aging Studies, 2,* 157–165.

McCubbin, H. I., & Patterson, J. M. (1983). The family stress process: The double ABCX model of adjustment and adaptation. In H. I. McCubbin, M. B. Sussman, & J. M. Patterson (Eds.), *Social stress and the family: Advances and developments in family stress theory and research* (pp. 7–38). New York: Haworth Press.

McDowell, I., & Newell, C. (1987). *Measuring health: A guide to rating scales and questionnaires.* New York: Oxford University Press.

Montgomery, R. (1989). Investigating caregiver burden. In K. S. Markides & C. L. Cooper (Eds.), *Aging, stress, and health* (pp. 201–218). New York: John Wiley & Sons.

Neugarten, B. L., Havighurst, R., & Tobin, S., (1961). The measurement of life satisfaction. *Journal of Gerontology, 16,* 134–143.

Pearlin, L. I. (1989). The sociological study of stress. *Journal of Health and Social Behavior, 30,* 241–256.

Pearlin, L. I., Mullan, J. T., Semple, S. J., & Skaff, M. M. (1990). Caregiving and the stress process: An overview of concepts and their measures. *The Gerontologist, 30,* 583–591.

Piper, A. I., & Langer, E. J. (1986). Aging and mindful control. In M. M. Baltes & P. B. Baltes (Eds.), *The psychology of control and aging* (pp. 71–90). Hillsdale, NJ: Lawrence Erlbaum.

Riley, M. W., & Bond, K. (1983). Beyond ageism: Postponing the onset of disability. In M. W. Riley, B. Hess, & K. Bond (Eds.), *Aging in society: Selected reviews of recent research* (pp. 243–252). Hillsdale, NJ: Lawrence Erlbaum Associates.

Rodin, J. (1986). Health, control, and aging. In M. M. Baltes & P. B. Baltes (Eds.), *The psychology of control and aging* (pp. 139–168). Hillsdale, NJ: Lawrence Erlbaum.

Rotter, J. (1966). Generalized expectancies for internal versus external control of reinforcement. *Psychological Monographs, 80*(609), 1–28.

Sagy, S., Antonovsky, A., & Adler, I. (1990). Explaining life satisfaction in later life: The sense of coherence and activity theory. *Behavior, Health, and Aging, 1,* 11-25.

Scharlach, A., Sobel, E., & Roberts, R. E. L. (1991). Employment and caregiver strain: An integrative model. *The Gerontologist, 31,* 778–787.

Schultz, R., Visintainer, P., & Williamson, G. M. (1990). Psychiatric and physical morbidity effects of caregiving. *Journal of Gerontology, 45,* 181–191.

Schunk, D. H., & Carbonari, J. P. (1984). Self-efficacy models. In J. D. Matarazzo, S. M. Weiss, J. A. Herd, N. E. Miller, & S. Weiss (Eds.), *Behavioral health: A handbook of health enhancement and disease prevention* (pp. 230–247). New York: Wiley.

Selye, H. (1974). *Stress without distress.* Philadelphia: Lippincott.

Selye, H. (1980). The stress concept today. In I. L. Kutash & L. B. Schlesinger (Eds.), *Handbook on stress and anxiety* (pp. 127–143). San Francisco: Jossey-Bass.

Siegel, J. S., & Taeuber, C. M. (1986). Demographic perspectives on the long-lived society. *Daedalus, 115,* 77–117.

Stone, R. I. (1991). Defining family caregivers of the elderly: Implications for research and public policy. *The Gerontologist, 31,* 724–725.

Stone, R. I., & Kemper, P. (1989). Spouse and children of disabled elders: How large a constituency for long-term care reform? *Milbank Quarterly, 67,* 485–506.

Streiner D. L., & Norman, G. R. (1989). *Health measurement scales: A practical guide to their development and use.* New York: Oxford Press.

Zarit, S. H. (1989). Do we need another "stress and caregiving" study? *The Gerontologist, 29,* 147–148.

Chapter 13

The Correlates of Coherence in Caregivers to Demented and Nondemented Elderly in Belgium

An Interim Report[1]

Morton O. Wagenfeld, Franz Baro,
Timothy J. Gallagher, and Kristien Haepers

Over 40 years ago, Parsons and Fox (1952) raised some questions about the ability of the nuclear family to respond to illness in one of its members. Due to significant demographic changes (the "graying" of the population) in recent years, there has been a shift in emphasis. Considerable concern has been expressed about the ability of the family to care for the increasing proportion of elderly with chronic diseases and handicapping conditions. With respect to Belgium, in the beginning of the 1980s, 14.4 out of every 100 persons were 65 and older. This figure is projected to reach 16.9 by 2000 and no less than 21.3 in 2025 (Dooghe & Vanden Boer, 1987).

By definition, chronic disease and handicap represent long-term or lifetime problems in management for the patient and his or her family. The net result is an increased share of work or burden for the family. Faced with this increased burden, the nature of the family has changed. The widespread entrance of women into the work force, rising rates of separation and divorce, and increased geographic mobility have compromised the ability of the family to care for its sick elderly members. Yet many families continue to choose home care for elderly family members with chronic diseases or handicapping conditions. In Belgium, Breesch-Grommen (1988) has noted that interest in family care stems from financial, scientific, and ideological considerations. It is widely felt that the welfare state has reached the limit of its ability to provide entitlements. In addition, a substantial body of evidence from health psychology and social epidemiology points to the importance of family and other informal support systems in the maintenance of health and the recovery from disease. Finally, interest in family care stems from a rediscovery of the value of small-scale activities that emphasize solidarity and traditionalism.

Unquestionably, caring for a chronically ill elderly family member at home is a stressful experience. Significant research on the problem began about 30 years ago. Horowitz (1985) has provided an extensive review of the literature. Broadly speaking, caregiving encompasses five domains: emotional support, direct service provision, mediation with formal organizations and providers, financial help, and sharing a household (Horowitz, 1985). A variety of terms have been used to refer to the effects of caregiving on the caregiver: caregiver burden, caregiver strain, the costs of care, family inconvenience, caregiving consequences, personal strains, negative feelings, stress effects, and caregiving impact. This chapter will use "caregiver burden" because it is the term most commonly used. Specifically, it has been defined by George and Gwyther (1986, p. 253) as "... the physical, psychological or emotional, social, and financial problems that can be experienced by family members caring for impaired older adults."

More recently, concern with caregiving and its consequences has focused on dementing disorders, particularly Alzheimer's Disease (AD) (see Cohen & Eisdorfer, 1986; Mace & Rabins, 1981). While the focus on AD and other dementing disorders is necessary, it is important to recognize that there are other chronic diseases and that they, too, exact a toll on caregivers. There has been a paucity of research comparing the consequences of caring for elderly patients with dementing and nondementing disorders.

To care for an elderly person in the changing milieu of the family calls for an understanding of the effect of disease and handicap on the family and the ways in which the ability of the family to meet these challenges can be strengthened. Since 1988, a longitudinal study has been conducted to determine how families cope with a variety of chronic illnesses and handicapping conditions in an elderly member. The study was designed to assess the extent to which certain factors can mediate or alleviate the burden of care and prevent untoward physical or psychosocial consequences. An early version of the conceptual model used in the study has been described in Haepers, Baro, and Wagenfeld (1990).

The researchers were intrigued with the possible heuristic value of the sense of coherence (SOC) as a mediator or ameliorator of caregiver burden. In a study similar to the one reported here, Coe, Miller, and Flaherty (1992) examined 148 caregivers to elderly persons with a number of chronic conditions. They found that the SOC was inversely related to the perception of burden for all but one problem (urinary incontinence). This chapter will further examine the utility of the concept by exploring the correlates of the SOC and aspects of both the caregiving situation and the characteristics of the caregiver. In the last section, the discussion will extend beyond these exploratory, zero-order correlational findings and consider some additional, multivariate analyses.

The Nature of the Variables

Sense of Coherence

A Flemish (Dutch) version of the sense of coherence scale has been developed and validated (Pottie, 1990). Pottie found that the SOC scale displayed a high level of internal consistency (Cronbach's Alpha = .89). Antonovsky (see Chapter 2) reported international psychometric data on both the long and short forms of the SOC questionnaire. Mean values for the long version ranged from 117.0 to 152.6. The mean for the sample of Belgian caregivers discussed in this chapter was 138.16, with an SD of 21.96, falling near the middle of the reported distribution.

Patient Disability

Presumably, greater patient disability is associated with higher levels of caregiver burden. Since the patients suffered from a variety of disorders, no single measure of pathology could be employed. In addition, specific pathology, per se, was less likely to be significant with respect to caregiver burden. Rather, in concert with numerous researchers, a measure was used to find the degree to which the patient was unable to perform various activities of daily living, using a modification of two related scales, Activities of Daily Living (ADL) (Katz, Ford, Moskowitz, Jackson, & Jaffe, 1963) and Instrumental Activities of Daily Living (IADL) (Lawton & Brody, 1969). Examples of ADL would be toileting or feeding, while IADL would include activities such as driving a car or using the telephone. The scale's reliability was high (Cronbach's Alpha = .91). In an important sense, the measure underestimates the extent of disability and, indirectly, caregiver burden, in those cases with a dementing disorder. Indeed, twice as many caregivers to dementing versus nondementing patients (30% versus 15%) reported the maximum value of patient disability, indicating the measure to be more insensitive to the higher levels of burden in the dementing group. The scale does not measure cognitive loss or behavioral problems associated with dementing disorders. Pearlin, Mullan, Semple, and Skaff (1990) developed scales to measure these dimensions in their study of caregivers to persons with AD. These measures have been employed in this research but, obviously, cannot be used in comparing the two groups of caregivers.

Antonovsky regarded the sense of coherence as a dispositional orientation that can help prevent breakdown in a stressful situation. A somewhat different and conceptually rich approach has been developed by Pearlin and his associates (Pearlin & Aneshensel, 1986; Pearlin & Schooler, 1978; Pearlin et al., 1990). Briefly, this framework (which we will refer to as "Stress/Coping") sees at the heart of the stress process *stressors*, which are defined as:

> conditions, experiences, and activities that are problematic for people; that is, that threaten them, thwart their efforts, fatigue them, and defeat their dreams (Pearlin et al., 1990).

Pearlin has applied this model to a study of burden in a cohort of caregivers to patients with Alzheimer's Disease. The research reported in this chapter has used a number of the variables that he developed.

Stress/Coping Measures

According to Pearlin's model, the caregiving experience can involve both deprivations and gains. Deprivations are recorded in two dimensions: (1) a three-item scale measuring deprivation of intimate exchange ("How much have you lost the person that you used to know?"); and (2) a three-item scale measuring deprivation of goals and activities ("How much have you lost a chance to do some of the things that you planned?"). Cronbach's Alphas were .79 and .55, respectively. Caregiving can also represent an opportunity for personal growth and enhanced self-confidence. To measure this aspect, Pearlin et al. (1990) developed a four-item Personal Gain Scale (Cronbach's Alpha = .74).

Two of the most vexing consequences of caring for a person with a dementing disorder are dealing with the cognitive status and handling the problematic behavior of the patient. The Pearlin scales that measure these factors produced Cronbach's Alpha coefficients of .79 and .70, respectively.

It is important to address the role of self-concept in the consequences of caregiving strain. Is a strong self-concept protective in some way in the stress/coping process? Rather than looking at self-concept in a global sense, Pearlin measured several aspects of the self relative to caregiving: Caregiving Competence ("How much do you feel that all in all, you're a good caregiver?"), Role Captivity ("How much do you wish you could just run away?"), and Loss of Self ("How much have you lost a sense of who you are?"). Cronbach's Alphas were .68, .81, and .72, respectively, for the three dimensions.

Social Support/Family Conflict Measures

The literature confirming the relationship between social support and health is impressive (see Cohen & Syme, 1985; House & Kahn, 1985). Pearlin used three measures of family conflict to determine the quality of social support in caregiving situations: Issues of Seriousness and Safety of the AD Patient, Attitudes and Actions Toward the Patient, and Attitudes and Actions Toward the Caregiver. The first scale was oriented toward AD patients, while the latter two were phrased in a more general way. Attitudes and Actions Toward the Patient measures disagreement between the caregiver and members of the family around issues of spending enough time with the patient or doing a fair share of the work of caregiving. In contrast to attitudes toward the patient, Attitudes and Actions Toward the Caregiver relates to disagreement over a lack of appreciation for the caregiver's work or the tendering of unwanted advice. Parenthetically, Pearlin et al. (1990, p. 588) argued that conflicts directly involving the caregiver were most likely to arouse distress. Cronbach's Alphas were .68, .95, and .87, respectively. Pearlin also developed an eight-item scale of Perceived Adequacy of Expressive Support from friends and family ("There is really no one who understands what you are going through"). Cronbach's Alpha was .73.

Nottingham Health Profile

The Nottingham Health Profile (NHP) was developed in England as both a clinical and survey measure of perception of health status and change (Hunt, McEwan, & McKenna, 1986). It consists of two parts. The first (NHP) consists of 38 items divided into six subscales: Emotions, Energy, Social Isolation, Sleep, Pain, and Physical Mobility. Cronbach's Alphas for the profiles were .70, .68, .47, .74, .76, and .71, respectively.

The second part (NHP2) consists of ratings of the extent to which the caregiving experience has interfered with eight areas of life: work, home activities, social life, home life, sex life, interests and hobbies, and holidays. The item on sex life was deemed inappropriate for the respondents and was dropped; an item on economic impact was substituted. Results are reported as a single scale ("Caregiver Life Changes") and display an acceptable level of reliability (Cronbach's Alpha = .72).

Sample and Methods

The present study is based on data from the Belgian Family Coping Project. Respondents were drawn from the registry of the Christian Mutual Health Insurance Fund and affiliated organizations in Dendermonde, in the Flemish province of East Flanders. Coverage for illness in Belgium is via a series of sick funds. The Christian Mutual Health Fund covers approximately 75% of the population in the Dendermonde region. All cases of persons at least 60 years old with a dementing or nondementing chronic disorder and cared for outside of an institution were selected (n = 140). This method of selection avoids the potential bias commonly encountered in studies of caregiver burden where respondents are drawn from the membership of self-help groups. Caserta et al. (1987) found that caregivers who did not seek assistance for AD support groups tended to be younger, taking care of less impaired persons, and had other sources of support. The vast majority of caregiver studies rely either on membership in self-help groups or on hospital admissions.

The interviews were conducted over a four-month period ending in March of 1991. About half (53%) of the interviews were conducted by nurses from the White/Yellow Cross (similar to Visiting Nurses), and the remaining interviews were conducted by social workers. Interviews lasted about two hours. In many instances, the interviewers were professionally acquainted with the patients and caregivers. As a result, the response rate was quite high (90%).

The sample consists of primary caregivers to 126 elderly persons with either a dementing chronic disorder (n = 45), a nondementing chronic disorder (n = 71), or both (n = 10). Cases with a dual diagnosis were combined with the dementing disorders group (n = 55). Patients with dementing disorders were diagnosed as suffering from a variety of disorders including Alzheimer's Disease, multi-infarct dementia, and Korsakoff's Psychosis. Patients with nondementing disorders were more heterogeneous, including cases with heart disease, arthritis, cancer, diabetes, and Parkinson's Disease. In 106 (84%) of the cases, the caregiver was living with the patient at the time of the interview. Forty percent of the caregivers were spouses, 49% children, with the balance divided among other relationships. The majority of caregivers (71%) were female, and the average age was 60.2 years

Table 1
Summary Statistics of Caregiver and Patient Characteristics

	Dementing Patient (n = 55)	Nondementing Patient[a] (n = 71)
Caregiver		
Age	60.4 (12.5)	60.0 (13.1)
Female Sex (%)	70.0	72.0
Education (%)		
Grade School	43.6	49.3
High School	30.9	29.8
College	25.5	20.9
Family Income (Bfr)	45k (3.5k)	43k (3.4k)
Relation to Patient (%)		
Spouse	41.8	39.4
Adult Child	50.9	47.9
Sibling	1.8	1.4
Other Relation	5.5	11.3
Reside with Elder		
Patient (% yes)	87.3	81.7
Patient		
Age	78.4 (9.4)	79.4 (8.4)
Female Sex (%)	69.1	66.3
Education (%)		
Grade School	45.4	31.0
High School	32.9	42.0
College	21.7	27.0
Duration of Illness (yrs)	8.4 (9.2)	10.0 (9.4)

Note. SD in parentheses.

[a] None of the tests of difference were significant at the .05 level.

(SD = 12.82). Patients ranged in age from 60 to 99 years, with an average age of 80 years (SD = 8.83).

Duration of the disorder was measured by response to the question: "How long ago [in months] did you realize that something was wrong with your [relative]?" The patients were a truly chronic group. As noted in Table 1, the means and standard deviations, respectively, for the patients with dementing disorders were 8.4 and 9.2; for those with nondementing disorders they were 10.0 and 9.6. The between-group difference was not statistically significant.

An analysis of the distribution of missing data revealed that it was random and that less than one-third of 1% of caregiver responses were missing. Median scores for the sample were substituted for missing values. Comparing the computed t tests, correlations, and multiple regressions of the adjusted and unadjusted data, no differences were found.

Findings

Table 2 presents the scale means and standard deviations for a number of the variables used in the research. No significant difference was noted in the SOC for the two groups of caregivers. As expected, the level of disability of those with a dementing disorder was significantly greater (Table 2). In view of the thrust of the literature stressing the uniquely burdensome and debilitating nature of dementing disorders, it was surprising to find that there were virtually no significant differences between the groups on the several outcome variables. The only variables to show significant differences were Deprivation of Intimate Exchange, Loss of Self, and one of the Nottingham Health Profiles (Energy).

Since the two groups of caregivers differed significantly on only a few of the outcome variables, the protective effect of a strong SOC was evident. Table 3 presents the results of the correlational analysis of the SOC and the series of patient and caregiver variables. More than half of the associations are significant in the expected direction: A strong SOC appears to protect against most of the untoward consequences of caregiving. For caregivers to persons with a dementing disorder, the SOC is significantly associated in the expected direction with problematic patient behavior, but not patient memory problems. This is not surprising, since there is evidence (see Deimling & Bass, 1986; Haley, Brown, & Levine, 1987) that patient behavioral problems, rather than memory loss, are more stressful for caregivers.

The sense of coherence was relatively unrelated to patient disability and family/social support variables. Stronger associations were noted for caregiver burden/gain, caregiver life changes, and the Nottingham Health Profile sets. The failure to find any relation whatsoever for perceived gain in the caregiving situation was surprising. For the NHP, significant associations were found in four of the six profiles: emotions, energy, sleep, and social isolation. The

Table 2
Scale Means and Standard Deviations for Subgroups

Scale	Dementing Patient ($n = 55$)		Nondementing Patient ($n = 71$)	
SOC	137.0	(26.7)	139.0	(17.6)
ADL/IADL**	54.5	(6.5)	46.2	(11.9)
Family Conflict/Social Support				
Expressive Support	24.1	(4.5)	25.0	(4.1)
Patient Safety	4.5	(1.2)	4.7	(1.6)
Attitudes toward Patient	4.4	(1.2)	5.2	(2.8)
Attitudes toward Caregiver	4.9	(2.2)	4.7	(2.1)
Caregiver Burden/Gain				
Relational Deprivation				
Deprivation of Goals and Achievement	6.4	(2.4)	6.7	(2.4)
Deprivation of Intimate Exchange**	7.1	(2.9)	5.0	(2.1)
Gain	10.7	(2.9)	10.8	(3.1)
Loss of Self*	3.5	(1.8)	3.0	(1.3)
Role Captivity	5.6	(2.4)	5.4	(2.2)
Caregiver Competence	12.9	(2.3)	12.5	(2.1)
Role Overload	8.8	(3.0)	8.5	(3.4)
Caregiver Life Changes	3.4	(1.7)	3.1	(1.9)
Nottingham Health Profile				
Emotions	14.9	(20.1)	14.8	(17.8)
Energy**	15.9	(31.5)	29.1	(36.1)
Isolation	12.3	(16.9)	13.6	(20.2)
Sleep	25.3	(32.9)	21.1	(27.2)
Pain	11.1	(19.0)	14.3	(22.9)
Mobility	10.7	(13.7)	11.1	(17.3)

Note. SD in parentheses.
*$p < .05$. **$p < .01$.

Table 3
**Pearson Product Moment Correlation Coefficients
for Sense of Coherence with Patient Disability
and Selected Caregiving Outcomes**

Sense of Coherence by	Dementing Patient (n = 55)	Nondementing Patient (n = 71)
Patient Disability		
ADL	.25	.07
Memory	.19	—
Behavior	− .30*	—
Family/Social Support		
Expressive Behavior	.19	.22*
Patient Safety	− .23*	—
Attitudes toward Patient	− .23*	− .26*
Attitudes toward Caregiver	− .41**	− .26*
Caregiver Burden/Gain		
Relational Deprivation		
Deprivation of Goals and Achievement	− .38**	− .20*
Deprivation of Intimate Exchange	− .30**	− .27*
Gain	.02	.00
Loss of Self	− .46**	− .16
Role Captivity	− .48**	− .13
Caregiver Competence	.28**	.20
Role Overload	− .56**	− .22*
Caregiver Life Changes	− .34**	− .30**
Nottingham Health Profile		
Emotions	− .61**	− .48**
Energy	− .43**	− .26*
Sleep	− .37**	− .24*
Isolation	− .49**	− .35**
Pain	− .01	.13
Mobility	− .20	.16

*p < .05. **p < .01.

more physical profiles of pain and physical mobility were not significantly associated with the SOC.

However, a striking—and theoretically interesting—pattern is evident when we compare the two groups. With only two exceptions, the SOC/caregiver outcome correlations are consistently higher for the group of caregivers to patients with a dementing disorder. The magnitude of the between-group differences is also noteworthy, about 30–50% higher for the dementing group.

Discussion

Several recent papers have employed multivariate approaches to examine the utility of the sense of coherence. These will be mentioned briefly to provide a context for the discussion. Gallagher, Wagenfeld, Baro, and Haepers (in press) tested the relationship between the SOC, coping strategies, and role overload. The study found that those who care for persons with a dementing disorder differ in their response from those who care for a family member with a nondementing disorder. The sense of coherence was protective against role overload for the total sample and for caregivers to persons with a dementing disorder.

This difference between groups was also manifested in the SOC/coping strategies relationship. Caregivers with a strong SOC are more likely to cope in situationally appropriate ways: redefining the meaning of the situation, selecting realistic coping strategies, and avoiding potentially maladaptive or unhealthy behaviors. In the multiple regression solution, the SOC and taking medication were the only significant predictors of role overload (betas = −.48 and .23, respectively) for caregivers to a dementing patient, while certain coping strategies and ADL/IADL deficits remained in the model for caregivers to nondementing patients. The sense of coherence was not a significant predictor for role overload in the latter group.

The greater strength of the SOC/role overload relationship for caregivers to patients with a dementing disorder led us to speculate about the existence of a "threshold effect" of the SOC in protecting against role overload in the face of caring for patients with cognitive loss. In other words, the SOC seems to be more protective in situations of greater morbidity. To reprise a clichéd locker room exhortation: "When the going gets tough, the tough get going."

Another paper (Baro, Wagenfeld, Gallagher, & Haepers, 1992) examined the SOC in relation to caregiver life changes and each of the Nottingham Health Profiles. In the multiple regression analyses for caregivers to patients with a dementing disorder, the SOC emerged as the sole significant predictor for three of the six profiles: emotional reactions, energy, and sleep. Not surprisingly, the SOC and caregiver life changes were both significant for the social isolation profile. The same relationship, albeit at a lower level, was found for caregivers in the nondementing group. In this group, pain also emerged as a significant profile.

This chapter has presented bivariate correlational data from the first wave of a study of burden in caregivers to elderly persons with dementing and nondementing disorders. Several conclusions seem warranted. First, the strong associations between the SOC and the selected measures of caregiver burden, self-image, life changes, and perceived health change lend further support to Antonovsky's view that the sense of coherence is protective against breakdown in the face of stressful life situations. Second, the differential protective effect of the SOC has been further confirmed: The effect is greater for those caring for a family member suffering from a dementing disorder.

The sense of coherence was significantly associated with ten measures in both groups: Attitudes and Actions Toward the Patient and the Caregiver, Deprivation of Goals and Achievements and Intimate Exchange, Role Overload, Caregiver Life Changes, and four of the six Nottingham Health Profiles. In all but one case, the protective effect of the SOC was higher in the dementing group.

Attitudes and Actions Toward the Caregiver relates to disagreement over a lack of appreciation for the caregiver's work or the tendering of unwanted advice. As noted, Pearlin et al. (1990, p. 588) argued that conflicts directly involving the caregiver were most likely to arouse distress. The significant associations between the SOC and this variable for both groups is theoretically consistent.

The Loss of Intimate Exchange—not being able to confide in the patient, missing the person that you used to know well and who really knew you well—is centrally tied to the nature of a dementing disorder. The significant relationship in the non-dementing group suggests that this may be a common characteristic of all chronic illness. One could argue that a patient struggling with cancer or heart disease is not the same person that he or she was prior to the onset of the disorder.

Life changes associated with caregiving are a reality; they do happen. The mean number of life changes experienced by caregivers in each group did not differ significantly. In each instance, though, the SOC was protective. While the SOC's protective effect against perceived health changes extends only to the psychological or psychosocial profiles, we would point out the consistency and magnitude of the associations.

Why does the SOC work? Antonovsky (1990) has argued that persons with a strong SOC are more likely to engage in behaviors that promote health. Thus, someone with a strong SOC is more likely to: (1) adapt his or her responses to the demands of the specific situation rather than routinely responding in a rigid manner to all situations; and (2) select from the available coping responses those that are either neutral or health-promoting (such as choosing to exercise to reduce tension rather than drinking alcohol). This situationally appropriate response is more likely to lead to a neutralization or diminution of the tension that predisposes an individual to negative health outcomes. Antonovsky (1987, pp. 163–170) offers another possible explanation for the health-promoting effects of the SOC. He has argued that a person with a strong SOC will seek to create order out of chaos.

Finally, the situationally appropriate coping responses of a person with a strong SOC are likely to result in fewer behavior problems in the patient. As Zarit (1989, p. 147) has pointed out, "The caregiver who is coping in effective ways (such as being able to calm down a disruptive patient) will report fewer behavior problems, while the less effective coper will report more." How the caregiver interacts with the patient affects the magnitude of the stressor of patient behavior. The findings reported here continue to be consistent with our notion of the "threshold effect." Some interaction exists between aspects of the personality of the caregiver and the characteristics of the caregiving situation. We would argue that future research needs to look at this interactive effect.

The sense of coherence—as an exemplar of the salutogenic orientation—is a viable and potentially powerful concept in helping to understand some of the consequences of caregiving for a sick elderly family member. This is consonant with the conclusions voiced by Coe, Miller, and Flaherty (1992, p. 98) in commenting on their own study: "These data ... demonstrate the powerful association of the SOC with selected other attributes of subjects, especially health-related attributes and coping behaviors."

Note

1. Data are from a study ("Family Coping With Chronic Illness and Handicap in the Elderly") funded by a grant from the Belgian National Fund for Scientific Research (Franz Baro, MD, PhD, Principal Investigator). We would also like to acknowledge the assistance of a Faculty Research Fellowship and Grant (#87-006) from Western Michigan University to the Co-Principal Investigator, Morton O. Wagenfeld, PhD. We're pleased to acknowledge the insightful comments of Aaron Antonovsky and the assistance of Leonard Pearlin in sharing with us some prepublication versions of his scales.

References

Antonovsky, A. (1987). *Unraveling the mystery of health*. San Francisco: Jossey-Bass.

Antonovsky, A. (1990). A somewhat personal odyssey in studying the stress process. *Stress Medicine, 6*, 71–80.

Antonovsky, A. (See Chapter 2). *The structure and properties of the sense of coherence scale.*

Baro, F., Wagenfeld, M. O., Gallagher, T. J., & Haepers, K. (1992, September). *Psychosocial and health consequences of caregiving to the demented and nondemented chronically ill elderly.* Paper presented to the Eighth International Meeting and Conference of Alzheimer's Disease International, Brussels, Belgium.

Breesch-Grommen, R. (1988). De draagkracht van een gezin in een situatie vanthuisverzorging (Family strength in a home care situation). *Welzijnwerk kroniek, 115.*

Caserta, M. S., Lund, D. A., Wright, S. D., & Redburn, D. E. (1987). Caregivers to dementia patients: The utilization of community services. *The Gerontologist, 27*, 209–214.

Coe, R. M., Miller, D. K., & Flaherty, J. (1992). Sense of coherence and perception of caregiving burden. *Behavior, Health, and Aging, 2*(2), 93–99.

Cohen, D., & Eisdorfer, C. (1986). *The loss of self: A family resource for the care of Alzheimer's Disease and related disorders*. New York: W. W. Norton.

Cohen, S., & Syme, S. L. (Eds.). (1985). *Social support and health*. Orlando, FL: Academic Press.

Deimling, G. T., & Bass, D. M. (1986). Symptoms of mental impairment among elderly adults and their effects on family caregivers. *Journal of Gerontology, 41*(6), 778–784.

Dooghe, G., & Vanden Boer, L. (1987). *Care for the elderly in Belgium.* Working Document No. 37. Brussels: Centrum voor Bevolking en Gezinsstudies (Center for Population and Family Studies).

Gallagher, T. J., Wagenfeld, M. O., Baro, F., & Haepers, K. (in press). Sense of coherence, coping, and caregiver role overload. *Social Science and Medicine.*

George, L. K., & Gwyther, L. P. (1986). Caregiver well-being: A multidimensional examination of family caregivers of demented adults. *The Gerontologist, 30*, 253–259.

Haepers, K., Baro, F., & Wagenfeld, M. O. (1990, September). *Family coping with chronic illness and handicap in the elderly.* Paper presented to the 6th International Conference of Alzheimer's Disease International, Mexico City, Mexico. Available from M. O. Wagenfeld, Sociology Department, Western Michigan University, Kalamazoo, MI 49008.

Haley, W. E., Brown, S. L., & Levine, E. G. (1987). Family caregiver appraisals of patient behavioral disturbance in senile dementia. *Clinical Gerontologist, 6*(4), 25–34.

Horowitz, A. (1985). Family caregiving to the frail elderly. *Annual Review of Gerontology and Geriatrics, 5*, 194–206. New York: Springer Publishing Company.

House, J. S., & Kahn, R. L. (1985). Measures and concepts of social support. In S. Cohen & S. L. Syme (Eds.), *Social support and health* (pp. 83–108). Orlando, FL: Academic Press.

Hunt, S., McEwan, J., & McKenna, S. P. (1986). *Measuring health status.* London: Croon Helm.

Katz, S., Ford, R. W., Moskowitz, R. W., Jackson, B. A., & Jaffe, M. W. (1963). Studies of illness in the aged: The index of ADL, a standardized measure of biological and psychological function. *Journal of the American Medical Association, 186,* 914–919.

Lawton, M. P., & Brody, E. M. (1969). Assessment of older people: Self-maintaining and instrumental activities of daily living. *The Gerontologist, 9,* 179–186.

Mace, N. R., & Rabins, P. V. (1981). *The thirty-six hour day.* Baltimore, MD: Johns Hopkins University Press.

Parsons, T., & Fox, R. (1952). Illness, therapy, and the modern American family. *Journal of Social Issues, 8,* 31–44.

Pearlin, L. I., & Aneshensel, C. (1986). Coping and social supports: Their functions and applications. In L. H. Aiken & D. Mechanic (Eds.), *Applications of social science to clinical medicine and health* (pp. 417–437). New Brunswick, NJ: Rutgers University Press.

Pearlin, L. I., Mullan, J. T., Semple, S. J., & Skaff, M. M. (1990). Caregiving and the stress process: An overview of concepts and their measures. *The Gerontologist, 30*(5), 583–594.

Pearlin, L. I., & Schooler, C. (1978). The structure of coping. *Journal of Health and Social Behavior, 19,* 2–21.

Pottie, C. H. (1990). *Antonovsky's "sense of coherence" and the operationalization of this concept in a Flemish version questionnaire.* Unpublished master's thesis, Faculteit der Psychologie en Pedagogische Wetanschappen (Faculty of Psychology and Pedagogic Sciences), Katholieke Universiteit Leuven, Belgium.

Zarit, S. H. (1989). Do we need another "stress and caregiving" study? *The Gerontologist, 29*(2), 147–148.

Chapter 14

Sense of Coherence and Survival in the Chronically Ill Elderly

A Five-Year Follow-Up

Rodney M. Coe, James C. Romeis,
and Maria M. Hall

This chapter reports the results of a study to predict survival over five years for a sample of elderly men (age 55 and over) who were enrolled in a general or geriatric medicine outpatient service in a Department of Veterans Affairs (VA) medical center at the time of baseline measurements. The predictor variable to be investigated is the sense of coherence (SOC), a concept developed by Antonovsky (1979, 1987). The sense of coherence is a perception of the ability to cope with stressful stimuli in the environment and is defined as:

> ... a global orientation that expresses the extent to which one has a pervasive, enduring though dynamic feeling of confidence that (1) stimuli deriving from one's internal or external environment in the course of living are structured, predictable, and explicable; (2) the resources are available to one to meet the demands posed by these stimuli; and (3) the demands are worthy of investment and engagement (Antonovsky, 1987, p. 19).

Thus, the sense of coherence comprises a perception of the degree to which life events are comprehensible, manageable, and meaningful. It is a central concept in the theoretical framework of salutogenesis (Antonovsky, 1979, 1987), which attempts to explain how those with a strong sense of coherence cope more successfully with stress and are generally at the positive end of the health ease/dis-ease continuum. A weak SOC is associated with unsuccessful coping and the negative health end of the continuum. In short, the key to successful coping is understanding the nature and source of stress (comprehension) and effectively using resources (management) to deal with significant problems (meaningfulness).

Research with the sense of coherence has resulted in nearly fifty publications and even more dissertations, theses, and reports of works in progress (Antonovsky, see Chapter 2). Few of these, however, deal with the health concerns of the elderly. Among those few was a longitudinal study of transition to retirement in which the SOC, health status, and family contacts all contributed significantly to life satisfaction (Sagy, Antonovsky, & Adler, 1990; Sagy & Antonovsky, see Chapter 11). An earlier report from the baseline data of this investigation showed that the SOC was highly correlated with other measures of health status and was the strongest factor in a measure of subjective health (Coe, Romeis, Tang, & Wolinsky, 1990). Two studies of caregiver burden also revealed strong associations with the sense of coherence. Coe, Miller, and Flaherty (1992) reported significant inverse relationships between the SOC and perceived burden on caregivers to elderly persons who suffered from Alzheimer's Disease, were confused, needed assistance in walking, or had a recent fracture. Gallagher, Wagenfeld, Baro, and Haepers (1992) reported that a strong SOC was associated with lower perceived stress in caregivers to demented patients. For caregivers of patients with problems other than dementia, there was no statistically significant relationship between the SOC and caregiver stress. Finally, a strong SOC has been linked with moderate (or lower) use of alcohol in older adults compared to older persons who are heavy drinkers (Midanik, Soghikian, Ransom, & Polen, 1992).

Reports and studies of correlates of the SOC in non-elderly populations show a consistently strong association with measures of physical and mental health status. Short-term (six months) change in SOC scores has been shown to be correlated with changes in health status (Coe et al., 1990). However, this is the first study to examine the SOC as a predictor of survival in the longer term (five years).

Baseline Survey

Data for the original study, which form the baseline for this follow-up, were collected by means of a personal interview, anthropometry, and laboratory evaluation of male patients in two outpatient clinics in the same VA medical center. Subjects who were at least 55 years old and had at least one current chronic condition in need of treatment were selected from consecutive appointments to the clinics. The final sample was 377 patients (64% of those contacted for the study).

The personal interview asked for information on demographic and family characteristics, perceived health status, functional health status [Activities of Daily Living (ADL), Instrumental Activities of Daily Living (IADL)], nutritional status, morale, and utilization of health services, such as physician visits, hospitalization, and emergency room use. Anthropometric measures included midarm circumference, biceps, triceps, subscapular and suprailiac skinfolds, height, and weight. Laboratory evaluations included hematocrit, hemoglobin, total lymphocyte count, serum albumin, and serum total protein.

The sense of coherence can be measured by a 29-item semantic differential format that assesses perceptions of global experiences in terms of comprehensibility, manageability, and meaningfulness. There is also a 13-item short form of the SOC questionnaire. Acceptable levels of reliability and validity have been reported for both forms (Antonovsky, see Chapter 2). In this project, the long form of the questionnaire (which includes the 13 items of the short form) was mailed to each patient at baseline after his initial assessment. The return rate was 87% ($n = 240$). The long form of the SOC questionnaire was readministered by telephone at six months and the short form was completed by telephone at five years. Return rates were 94.6% and 81.6%, respectively.

Results From Baseline Study

At least three results from the analysis of baseline data are relevant to the follow-up study. First, it was determined that the short form of the SOC questionnaire (13 items) had the same scale statistics as the long form (29 items). The means and standard deviations were different, of course, but both were consistent with those measures reported for similar known groups (Antonovsky, see Chapter 2). Item means, inter-item correlations, and measures of internal consistency (Cronbach's Alpha) were not significantly different. This supports the decision to use the short form of the SOC questionnaire in the follow-up investigation.

Second, the sense of coherence was highly correlated with all measures of health status. Bivariate correlations ranged from .17 ($p < .01$) for ADL to .71 ($p < .001$) for mental health (morale). Further, in a factor analysis of all health status measures, the SOC had the strongest loading (.79) on the subjective health factor.

Third, a principal components factor analysis of the SOC scale itself produced one factor on which all 29 items loaded at .40 or more. This indicates that the constructs of comprehensibility, manageability, and meaningfulness are represented in each item and are not separable into three independent factors.

Methods

Data for this five-year follow-up were collected in telephone interviews that requested information on current residence, current health status [including perceived health, ADL (Katz, Ford, Mos-kowitz, Jackson, & Jaffe, 1963), IADL (Duke University Center for the Study of Aging and Human Development, 1978), number of falls, morale (Lawton, 1975), and utilization of physician, hospital, and ER services (in the past year)], life events over the five years, and the sense of coherence. Life events were coded as positive health, positive social, negative social, and negative health. For this follow-up, the 13-item short form of the SOC was used because it is as effective as the full form (Coe et al., 1990).

An effort was made to contact all 377 of the original sample. Contact was made with 313 subjects (83%), of which 194 (62%) were interviewed, 90 (28.7%) were deceased, 21 (6.7%) refused, and 8 (2.6%) were unable to answer questions in an interview. The rest (64) could not be contacted either by telephone or by mail.

Data analysis involved: (1) comparison of status (marital status, living arrangements, health, etc.) at follow-up (survivors who were interviewed compared with non-respondents who were not deceased according to VA records) on key variables measured at baseline to assess potential bias introduced by non-response; (2) comparison of survivors (who were interviewed) with deceased (after the study began) subjects on theoretically important variables measured at baseline; (3) logistic regression with survival status at follow-up as the dependent variable to assess the relative predictive power of the same variables examined in the bivariate analysis; and (4) an analysis of change in SOC scores. Theoretically important variables measured at baseline, relevant to this report, included demographic characteristics (age, marital status, household type, perceived income adequacy), mental health status (cognitive function, morale), physical health status (sensory health, perceived health status, ADL, IADL, disability days, bed disability days), health-promoting behavior (smoking status, alcohol consumption, exercise), utilization of services (physician visits, ER visits, hospital nights), life events over five years, and, of course, the sense of coherence.

Results

A comparison was made between interviewed survivors (n = 194) and non-respondent survivors (n = 93) on the variables noted above. Statistically significant differences were found for marital status (p < .03), living arrangements (p < .03), and perceived income adequacy (p < .03). Interviewed survivors were more likely than non-respondents to have been married at the time of baseline (74.4% vs. 57.6%) and thus less likely to have been widowed, divorced, or separated (20.5% vs. 34.8%). With respect to perceived income adequacy, more interviewees were at both extremes. They were more likely than non-respondents to report having a comfortable income (24.6% vs. 17.6%) and also not having "enough income to get by" (17.9% vs. 11.0%). Otherwise, there were no significant differences in measures of mental and physical health status, utilization of health services, or in perceived ability to cope with stress (SOC). It appears that any bias introduced by non-response would be minimal.

Table 1
Correlations of Sense of Coherence (SOC)
and Health Status Variables at Follow-up

Variable	SOC
Perceived health	− .458**
ADL[1]	.266**
IADL[1]	.419**
Disability days	− .446**
Bed disability days	− .356**
Falls	− .214**
Morale[1]	.760**
Nutritional risk index	− .452**

[1]Higher score = better health status.
*p < .01. **p < .001.

Sense of Coherence

Scores on the follow-up administration of the short form of the SOC questionnaire (n = 183) ranged from 57.0 to 91.0 (91 is the maximum score) with a mean of 69.10 (SD = 17.49). Table 1 shows the zero-order correlations of the SOC with other health status measures at follow-up. All were statistically significant, which is consistent with data from evaluations of baseline data (Coe et al., 1990). This further validates the use of the SOC scale as a measure of current health status and suggests that little non-response bias was introduced.

Table 2
Characteristics at Baseline of Survivors and Deceased

Characteristic	Survivors (n = 195)	Deceased (n = 90)
A. Demographic		
Age (% 65+)	49.2	58.9
Race (% white)	93.3	91.1
Marital status (% married)	74.4	60.0*
Living arrangements (% alone)	17.4	23.3*
Perceived income adequacy (% comfortable)	24.6	17.0
B. Health Status		
Minimental status examination (max = 30)	26.36	25.59
Morale (max = 7)	4.28	4.11
Sensory health status (max = 20)[1]	11.58	12.52**
Perceived health status (max = 4)[1]	2.70	2.94
ADL (max = 10)	9.93	9.97*
IADL (max = 14)	13.32	12.59**
Disability days (in 30 days)[1]	5.42	6.30
Bed disability days (in 30 days)[1]	1.24	1.51
C. Health-Promoting Behavior		
Smoking status (% no)	69.2	54.4*
Alcohol consumption (% moderate)	34.9	24.5
Exercise (% yes)	84.6	76.7
D. Utilization of Services		
Physician visits (last 12 months)	7.01	6.05
Emergency room visits (last 12 months)	1.74	1.96
Hospital nights (last 12 months)	23.1	22.8
E. Sense of Coherence		
SOC (max = 91)	61.60	60.52

[1]Lower number = better health.
*p < .05. **p < .01.

Characteristics of Survivors and Deceased Subjects

Table 2 displays the results of comparisons between survivors and deceased subjects on variables measured at baseline. Survivors were more likely than deceased subjects to have been married, thus less likely to live alone. There were no differences between the groups on measures of mental functioning, but survivors were more healthy on measures of sensory health (vision, hearing, taste, touch, and smell) and IADL.

The deceased were slightly more functional on ADL measures, but the differences were very small and most subjects in both groups functioned independently on all dimensions. Among measures of health-promoting behavior, only cigarette smoking significantly differentiated the two groups (lower prevalence of smoking was associated with survival). No differences were observed on any measure of utilization of services. Similarly, there were no differences between the groups on mean SOC scores.

Logistic Regression

These same variables were then entered as a block in a logistic regression process to predict survival after five years. Collectively, these variables correctly classified 78.13% of the cases (95% of survivors, 30% of deceased). Table 3 shows that only two of the factors considered contributed significantly and uniquely to predicting survival. Better functional health as measured by IADL (RR = 1.45) and being more likely to live with spouse and children (RR = .33) emerged as contributing independently. The importance of better functional health status is apparent. Living with spouse and children is interpreted as better than with spouse alone (indicating older age) or alone. Among the factors which did not emerge as significant predictors of survival in this study was the sense of coherence (beta = −.01, SE = .01, $p > .30$)

Table 3
Significant Factors Predicting Survival

Variable	Beta	SE	Sig.	Adjusted Relative Risk
IADL	.369	.182	.04	1.45
Household type	− 1.095	.472	.02	.33

Change in Sense of Coherence Scores

The sense of coherence questionnaire was administered at three points—baseline (T_0), six months later (T_1), and at five years follow-up (T_2). The baseline (long form) measure was obtained by personal interview. Follow-up measures, T_1 (long form) and T_2 (short form only) were obtained by telephone interview. Mean scores for the full scale and short form of the SOC questionnaire for the three time periods are shown in Table 4. There was no discernible change from T_0 to T_1 on either form of the SOC and only a slight, statistically nonsignificant improvement in scores on the short form from T_1 to T_2. This trend is found also in change from baseline to long-term follow-up (T_0–T_2). Mean change was 8.68 (SD = 15.4) with a range from −50 (decline) to +54 (improvement). About 80.4% had scores that improved over the five-year period (n = 138).

Table 4
Change in SOC Scores

SOC Scale	T_0	T_1	T_2	P
Full scale (29 items)	139.60 (36.4)	140.99 (35.5)	—	N.S.
Short form (13 items)	61.93 (17.8)	62.44 (17.2)	69.10 (17.5)	N.S.

As expected, SOC scores are consistent as good predictors of future SOC scores. Correlations for the short form were .770 (T_0–T_1), .597 (T_0–T_2), and .565 (T_1–T_2). The strength of the association declines over time.

The association of the sense of coherence with measures of health status is also found in changes in both variables. Data in Table 5 show that declines in morale and perceived health status over the six-month period from T_0 to T_1 are statistically significantly related to declines in SOC scores over the five-year period from T_0 to T_2. The association with IADL shows a similar trend but does not reach statistical significance.

Finally, change in SOC scores from baseline to follow-up was examined in relationship to significant life events occurring during the five-year period and reported by subjects in response to an open-ended question. Events were classified as positive or negative and health-related or social in nature. For example, the death of a spouse is a negative social event. Recovering from surgery is a positive health event. Data in Table 6 show a trend of association between improved SOC scores and positive life events, but the differences are not statistically significant.

Table 5
Change in Health Status (T_0-T_1) and SOC (T_0-T_2)

Health Status Indicator (T_0-T_1)	n	Change in SOC (T_0-T_2)		P
		Improve	Decline	
Decline in mental health (morale)	124	23.4%	46.7%	.041
Decline in perceived health status	128	17.3	36.7	.008
Decline in IADL	126	1.0	6.7	.075

Table 6
Change in SOC Scores and Life Events (%)

SOC	Life Event				
	Positive Health Event	Positive Social Event	Neutral Event	Negative Social Event	Negative Health Event
Improve	83.3	91.7	75.0	79.6	69.7
Decline	16.7	8.3	25.0	23.1	30.3
n	6	12	4	26	33

$X^2_{(1)}$ = 0.57 (NS).

Discussion

Data from this five-year follow-up of a sample of clinic patients did not support the hypothesis that a strong sense of coherence was associated with long-term survival, despite the significant correlations with other measures of health status. In fact, in this analysis, survival was significantly related to only two factors: functional health as measured by IADL, and integration in a support system as measured by marital status. These findings are similar to those of Narain et al. (1988) and Cohen et al. (1992), who reported measures of functional health as predictors of mortality.

Perhaps it should not be too surprising that SOC scores are not significantly related to survival over a five-year period. Measures of perception, such as the sense of coherence, are often sensitive to situational events at the time of measurement, although perceived health status has been reported as a predictor of mortality under certain conditions (Idler & Kasl, 1991). Since a causative relationship has not been established, it is not clear whether changes in health status, which are related to survival, precede or follow changes in the sense of coherence. In addition, changes in SOC scores in this sample were modest. It was reported above that from baseline to follow-up the mean SOC score improved by only 8.68 points (zero equals no change). While the range of discrepancy was wide (−50 to +54), the outliers represent only four cases that gained or lost more than 35 points. This finding provides some support for the assertion that the sense of coherence in normal adults is a very stable characteristic (Antonovsky, 1987).

The implications of this study are more positive from a policy perspective. That is, the two significant predictors of survival in this community-dwelling population suggest that efforts should be directed toward maintaining functional health and the integration of the individual in a support group. In an era when the appropriateness of providing long-term care services in an acute-care inpatient setting is being questioned, these findings promote the use of out-of-hospital services from both formal and informal sources. While these policy implications may be most relevant to the Department of Veterans Affairs (this was a sample of VA patients), the general principle of emphasizing out-of-hospital ambulatory and home-based services for long-term care is gaining momentum for the general population (Brickner, Lechich, Lipsman, & Scharer, 1987).

The finding that the sense of coherence did not have a direct effect on survival over five years does not mean that perception of ability to cope with stress is not an important factor. It is likely that the sense of coherence has an indirect effect on survival because the sense of coherence is significantly (and consistently) related to functional health status in a cross-sectional perspective and, in this study, functional health did predict survival. Furthermore, the sense of coherence can be used as a screening instrument for assessing current ability to cope with stress and indicating when timely intervention is needed.

References

Antonovsky, A. (1979). *Health, stress, and coping.* San Francisco: Jossey-Bass.

Antonovsky, A. (1987). *Unraveling the mystery of health.* San Francisco: Jossey-Bass.

Antonovsky, A. (See Chapter 2). *The structure and properties of the sense of coherence scale.*

Brickner, P. W., Lechich, A. J., Lipsman, R., & Scharer, L. K. (1987). *Long-term health care.* New York: Basic Books.

Coe, R. M., Miller, D. K., & Flaherty, J. (1992). Sense of coherence and perception of caregiving burden. *Behavior, Health, and Aging, 2,* 93–99.

Coe, R. M., Romeis, J. C., Tang, B., & Wolinsky, F. D. (1990). Correlates of a measure of coping in older veterans: A preliminary report. *Journal of Community Health, 15,* 287–296.

Cohen, H. J., Saltz, C. C., Samsa, G., McVey, L., Davis, D., & Feussner, J. R. (1992). Predictors of two-year post-hospitalization mortality among elderly veterans in a study evaluating a geriatric consultation team. *Journal of the American Geriatrics Society, 40,* 1231–1235.

Duke University Center for the Study of Aging and Human Development. (1978). *Multidimensional functional assessment: The OARS methodology.* Durham, NC: Duke University.

Gallagher, T. J., Wagenfeld, M. O., Baro, F., & Haepers, K. (1992). *Sense of coherence and caregiver role overload.* Paper presented at the North Central Sociological Association, Fort Wayne, IN.

Idler, E. L., & Kasl, S. (1991). Health perceptions and survival: Do global evaluations of health status really predict mortality? *Journal of Gerontology, 46,* 555–565.

Katz, S., Ford, A. B., Moskowitz, R. W., Jackson, B. A., & Jaffe, M. W. (1963). Studies in illness in the aged: The index of ADL: A standardized measure of biological and psychosocial function. *Journal of the American Medical Association, 185,* 914–919.

Lawton, M. P. (1975). The Philadelphia Geriatric Center morale scale: A revision. *Journal of Gerontology, 30,* 85–89.

Midanik, L. T., Soghikian, K., Ransom, L. J., & Polen, M. R. (1992). Alcohol problems and sense of coherence among older adults. *Social Science and Medicine, 34,* 43–48.

Narain, P., Rubenstein, L. Z., Wieland, G. D., Rosbrook, B., Strome, L. S., Pietruszka, F., & Morley, J. E. (1988). Predictors of immediate and six-month outcomes in hospitalized elderly patients and the importance of functional status. *Journal of the American Geriatric Society, 36,* 775–783.

Sagy, S., & Antonovsky, A. (See Chapter 11). *The family sense of coherence and the retirement transition.*

Sagy, S., Antonovsky, A., & Adler, I. (1990). Explaining life satisfaction in later life: The sense of coherence model and activity theory. *Behavior, Health, and Aging, 1,* 11–25.

IV. Coherence and Immunology

Chapter 15

The Role of Sense of Coherence in Mediating the Effects of Mental Imagery on Immune Function, Cancer Outcome, and Quality of Life[1]

Janice Post-White

The two purposes of this chapter are: (1) to introduce a model that attempts to explain how the sense of coherence (SOC) may mediate the psychoneuroimmune effects of a mental imagery/ support group intervention in individuals with cancer; and (2) to explore the concept of the sense of coherence as a dynamic (versus stable) disposition. The relationships within the model are discussed in the context of results from a longitudinal, experimental study that tested the effects of mental imagery (within a support group setting) on hope, the SOC, cellular immune function, disease state, and quality of life in individuals receiving chemotherapy for cancer. This chapter focuses on the direct relationships to the sense of coherence. Details of other relationships and differences between experimental and control groups are reported elsewhere (Post-White, 1991).

Theoretical Framework: Sense of Coherence and Psychoneuroimmunology

In his salutogenic model of health, Antonovsky (1979, 1984, 1987) asserted that stressors lead to a stress response through tension.

He proposed that a strong sense of coherence can reduce tension, thus modulating the psychological, neurological, hormonal, and immune systems and resulting in reduced stress responses and improved health. This chapter explores *how* the sense of coherence may mediate these interactions.

The Effects of Stress on Immune Function

Stress is thought to play a role in immune regulation by altering brain and plasma levels of certain neurotransmitters, neuropeptides, and hormones (Shavit, 1991). The limbic system of the brain, which mediates aspects of affective and cognitive behavior, directly regulates the autonomic outflow of the central nervous system that influences immune function (Camara & Danao, 1989). The classic adrenal stress response involves the release of corticotropin releasing factor from the hypothalamus, the release of adrenocorticotropic hormones from the anterior pituitary, and the release of glucocorticoids from the adrenal cortex (Blalock, Harbour-McMenamin, & Smith, 1985; Keller, Schleifer, & Demetrikopoulos, 1991). The release of these neurohormones results in suppression of cellular immune function.

The way in which an individual copes with stressors is important in determining immune function. Poor coping skills were found to decrease natural killer (NK) cell activity in highly stressed undergraduates (Locke & Kraus, 1981), whereas good coping skills and a positive attitude increased NK and neutrophil function (Locke et al., 1984). Social support was also an important factor in buffering response to stressors, contributing to increased NK function (Levy, Herberman, Lippman, & d'Angelo, 1987). The negative emotional states that result from the psychological response to stressors may explain how psychosocial events produce immuno-suppression (Kiecolt-Glaser & Glaser, 1991) and contribute to the increased incidence of infections, autoimmune disease, and cancer.

Practicing Mental Imagery to Reduce Tension

The way in which an individual with cancer interprets and responds to the demands of having cancer determines his or her psychological tension state (Sims, 1987). High psychological tension activates the sympathetic branch of the autonomic nervous system, causing anxiety (Spielberger, 1966), depression, hopelessness, helplessness (Sims, 1987), and glucocorticosteroid release (Fisher, 1991). Imagery and relaxation techniques are behavioral interventions that may reduce psychological tension, offer a sense of participation, and aid in coping with cancer as a stressor (Post-White & Johnson, 1991). Reducing psychological tension and the accompanying stress response can improve quality of life and counteract the effects of stress by reducing sympathetic nervous system activity (Benson, 1975; Olness & Gardner, 1988). Theoretically, the psychological response to imagery may reduce hypothalamic-pituitary-adrenal axis stimulation, resulting in improved immune function and an increased sense of well-being.

The Role of Sense of Coherence as Mediator

This study examined the role of the sense of coherence in mediating the psychologic and immunologic responses to cancer and its treatment. The intervention, which included learning relaxation and imagery techniques within a support group setting, was designed to assist individuals in identifying and mobilizing resources to help them cope with the diagnosis and treatment of cancer, to provide a social network in which to explore the meaning of cancer in their lives, and to reduce psychological tension resulting from stressors associated with having cancer.

Hope was measured with the sense of coherence to determine the relationship and similarities between the variables. Hope is an emotion in human experience that entails finding meaning in a situation, perceiving a possible solution, envisioning a future goal, and participating to achieve that goal (Lynch, 1965; Stotland, 1969). Hope is a situational, learned response that motivates the individual to achieve realistic, important goals (Mowrer, 1969). In this study, hope was interpreted as a measure of positive attitude in response to intervention and as a motivator to participate in restoring health.

It was proposed that the combined imagery/relaxation/support group intervention would strengthen the sense of coherence of individuals in the experimental group by helping them make sense of the event (comprehensibility), find meaning in the situation (meaningfulness), and mobilize resources to cope (manageability). The person with a strong SOC who practiced the relaxation/imagery techniques would feel more hopeful and thus be able to reduce psychological tension and prevent the transformation of tension into a stress response. Because stress can activate the sympathetic nervous system and suppress immune function, it was hypothesized that avoiding or redefining stressors would reduce tension, activate the immune system, and move the individual toward the health-ease end of the health continuum.

Design and Methods

Thirty-eight outpatients with solid tumors who were receiving che-motherapy were randomly assigned to an experimental or control group. Experimental group patients (n = 22) met as a support group every two weeks for one month and then monthly for a total of four months. They were taught mental imagery techniques for relaxation, symptom management, and participation in getting well, and they were given audiotapes to practice with at home. Control group patients (n = 16) were a time-matched control. All patients completed questionnaires on hope (Nowotny, 1989), the SOC (Antonovsky, 1987, 13-item), and quality of life (QOL) (Padilla et al., 1983) before the study and once a month for four months. At the same time, peripheral blood was drawn to assess circulating ß(beta)-endorphins, natural killer (NK) and lymphokine activated killer (LAK) cell function, and monocyte cytotoxicity.[2] Disease state was quantified on a six-point scale ranging from absence of disease to death; it was assessed before and immediately after the exper-imental intervention, and again 6 and 12 months afterwards. The quality of imagery for experimental group subjects was measured with the Image-CA (Achterberg & Lawlis, 1984), and frequency of practice was documented in a journal.

The age of the participants ranged from 31 to 70 years (Mean = 54.7). The majority of subjects were female (63%), white (95%), and married (55%). Thirteen (34%) had college degrees at the graduate or undergraduate level. Most subjects had either breast (55%) or colorectal (26%) cancer, with two-thirds (66%) having stage III or IV disease at entry into the study. Half of the participants (50%) were being treated for primary disease and half for recurrence.

Repeated measures analysis of variance (ANOVA) was used to test the effects of the imagery/support group intervention and is reported elsewhere (Post-White, 1991). Relationships hypothesized in the model were examined with Pearson product moment correlation (two-tailed, a = .05) and simultaneous regression [structural equation modeling (SAS), a = .05]. Simultaneous regression is specifically designed to deal with a large number of variables with multiple interactions in which variables are used more than once (Judge, Griffiths, Hill, Lutkepohl, & Lee, 1990).

Results Specific to Sense of Coherence

According to Antonovsky's salutogenic theory (1979) and the proposed study model, participants who had a high sense of coherence and reduced psychological tension (presumably in response to the imagery/support group intervention) were expected to show an overall improvement in immune function and disease state. For discussion, the analyses reported here are divided into: (1) the effects of the intervention on the SOC; (2) the relationship between the SOC and immune function; (3) the relationship of the SOC to other variables; and (4) individual change in SOC scores over time.

Effects of Imagery/Relaxation/ Support Group on Sense of Coherence

There was no difference in the SOC scores between the experimental and control groups with ANOVA; as a group, mean scores remained steady (63–66.5 for the 13-item scale) over time (Figure 1). Within

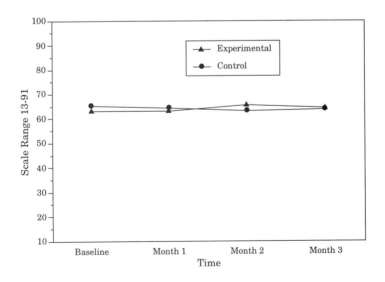

Figure 1
SOC: Experimental vs Control Group

Note. Due to dropout at Time 5, data was analyzed over three months instead of four.

the experimental group, however, the ability of the participants to perceive their body as strong, believe that the chemotherapy was helpful, and image their immune system fighting their cancer (measured with Image-CA) was correlated with a higher sense of coherence ($r = .23$, $p < .05$) and with more hopefulness ($r = .31$, $p < .05$). The quality or quantity of imagery was not a determinant of the SOC or hope in the regression model.

Figure 2
Simultaneous Regression Model

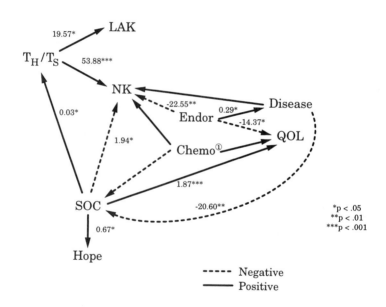

①Time since chemotherapy; not a measured variable.
Model $r^2 = .31$.

Relationship Between Sense of Coherence and Immune Function

In this model, the sense of coherence was a predictor of increased NK function and T_H/T_S ratios (Figure 2). Higher T_H/T_S ratios also explained increases in NK and LAK function. Natural killer cells increased their activity with further time from the last course of chemotherapy, with greater disease, and in response to lower ß-endorphin levels. Variables in the model explain only 10% of the variance of NK and LAK cell function and 18% of T_H/T_S ratios, suggesting that factors other than those measured in the model also contributed to immune function of the individuals in this study.

Relationship of Sense of Coherence to Other Variables

The sense of coherence correlated with and directly predicted an increase in quality of life (QOL) ($r = .67, p < .001$) and resulted in a more hopeful attitude ($r = .64, p < .001$). Seventy-seven percent of the variance of QOL was explained by the SOC, time since chemotherapy, disease state, and ß-endorphin levels. The beta value of 1.87 for the SOC suggests that for every 1-point increase in the sense of coherence (scale range 7–91), quality of life improves 1.87 points (range 0–100). The only variables in the model that determined SOC scores were a better disease state and more recent time since the last course of chemotherapy, which accounted for 28% of the variance. Fatigue and nausea and vomiting (N/V) were subscales of the QOL questionnaire that correlated negatively with the SOC (both $r = -.31, p < .001$) and with hope (fatigue: $r = -.41$, $p < .001$; N/V: $r = -.34, p < .001$).

Demographic factors that influenced the SOC, assessed with ANOVA independent from the regression model, were the stage of the disease (the less disease, the higher the SOC), the age of the participant (50- to 61-year-old subjects had the highest mean SOC scores), and years of education (over 14 years corresponded with increased SOC scores). Factors that did not influence the SOC included gender, marital status, employment status, diagnosis, private versus government health care, and frequency of imagery practice.

Individual Change in Sense of Coherence Over Time

Even though the *mean* SOC score for the control and experimental groups remained stable over time (Figure 1), SOC scores within some individuals fluctuated over the four months, with both increases and decreases measured. Ten of the participants' SOC scores increased (Mean = 15.3 points) and ten scores decreased (Mean = 11.1 points) more than five points from baseline to the fourth month. Changes of 5% or less were not considered as a change over baseline. Approximately one-fourth of both the experimental and control group participants' SOC scores increased (Table 1). A greater percentage of the experimental group (versus control group) participants experienced decreases in SOC scores.

Table 1
Individual Change in Sense of Coherence over Time

	SOC Increase > 5% n (% of group)	SOC Decrease > 5% n (% of group)	SOC ± 5% n (% of group)
Experimental group participants	6 (27)	7 (32)	9 (41)
Control group participants	4 (25)	3 (19)	9 (56)

Note. Table 1 represents the changes in SOC of individuals over a four-month time period. SOC change (increase or decrease) of greater than 5% is considered a change in SOC scores over time.

Discussion

It was hypothesized that the sense of coherence would mediate the effects of an imagery/relaxation/support group intervention on immune function, cancer outcome, and quality of life. Comparison between experimental and control group effects on individual variables is reported elsewhere (Post-White, 1991). Despite the lack of change in the SOC over time as a group (with ANOVA), the sense of coherence was related to quality of imagery and disease state and predicted immune function and quality of life. Explanations for the difference in analyses include a lack of statistical power with ANOVA and individual (versus group) changes, suggesting factors other than the intervention were also responsible for changes in participants' SOC scores and outcomes.

Results of the correlation and regression analyses support the SOC as an important variable influencing immune function and disease state in this sample of individuals with cancer. The increase in NK cell function, T_H/T_S ratios, and subsequent activation of LAK function (important for controlling malignant tumor cells) indicate that the SOC can activate immune cells to fight cancer. This activation could potentially help to control tumor replication. Despite convincing evidence in the literature, however, the relationship between immune function and the control of disease was not significant in this study. Possible explanations include the suppression of immune function by chemotherapy (and reduced chemotherapy administration with advanced disease) or insufficient time (four months) to produce a measurable response. Further study of patients not currently receiving chemotherapy is required to verify the association between the SOC and immune function and to retest the relationship between immune function and disease state.

Conversely, disease state was a significant component in determining the sense of coherence; greater disease predicted a lower SOC score. This relationship may in part be due to the negative relationship between the SOC and fatigue, nausea, and vomiting. Although these symptoms may result from chemotherapy, they also are observed in advanced stages of the disease. Tishelman, Taube, and Sachs (1991) measured a similar response in patients with cancer; reports of increased symptom distress were associated with lower scores on the 13-item SOC scale. In their study, the symptom distress scale included nausea, vomiting, and fatigue, as well as pain, breathing, coughing, mobility, bowel function, insomnia, mood, outlook, appearance, and concentration. As the disease progresses and physical discomfort increases, the individual may find it harder to make sense of the cancer and suffering and may feel that the cancer and its consequences are not as manageable as once perceived. Similarly, the negative relationship between chemotherapy and the sense of coherence may indicate that the hopefulness and sense of manageability that accompanies chemotherapy treatment dissipates the further one gets from treatment and the greater the disease.

Even though the SOC did not directly influence disease state, a stronger SOC did result in better quality of life and a more hopeful state. The strength of this relationship with QOL suggests that a high sense of coherence is important to one's perception of a quality life and that similar factors contribute to both the SOC and QOL. Quality of life, however, may be more responsive to current symptoms and side effects; the greater the amount of time that had passed since chemotherapy, the greater the QOL. This observation is reasonable considering the multiple physical side effects experienced with chemotherapy. The reversed effects of chemotherapy timing on SOC scores may indicate that the sense of coherence is a more stable characteristic comprised of psychological as well as physical components.

The role of ß-endorphins in the model was hypothesized to increase in response to feelings of general well-being, a positive attitude, and a more hopeful state. The literature contains conflicting evidence for the role of ß-endorphins in mediating the effects of the central nervous system on the immune system. Opioid peptides, such as ß-endorphins, have been shown to have an immunoenhancing effect (Plotnikoff et al., 1987) and an immunosuppressive effect (Weber & Pert, 1989), depending on their concentration *in vitro* and on the immunocompetence of the donor (Shavit, 1991). Although ß-endorphins enhance NK activity *in vitro*, the effects of stress on ß-endorphins and the role of opioids on NK cells *in vivo* are unknown. The results of the regression model provide support for ß-endorphins as a responder to stress (released with adrenocorticotropic hormone from the anterior pituitary) that may suppress NK cell activity and result in greater disease and poorer quality of life.

Additional analyses were completed to determine whether the SOC is a dynamic disposition that changes with the individual's physical and psychological state, as suggested in the results of the regression model. Indications that the SOC changes over time (at least temporarily) are provided by the significant relationships between the SOC and symptoms of fatigue, nausea, and vomiting, quality of imagery, stage of the disease, and age. The results of the analysis of individual data (indicating an increase or decrease in the SOC scores of 20 participants in the experimental and control groups) do not identify the factors that result in the change in the SOC over the four months. Within the experimental group, the participants that had stronger images also had higher SOC scores, but this relationship does not explain why four of the control group participants had increases of greater than 5% of their SOC scores. Observations of the individual data indicate that the significant factors, such as time since chemotherapy, disease state, and symptoms, may contribute to changes in SOC scores. However, the factors appear to be individualized to the participant, with some participants' SOC scores responsive to disease state and others' scores not responsive. Multiple factors comprise one's sense of coherence, including life experiences, past coping, and resources, and it is likely that changes in the SOC will be stimulated by exposure to and perception of different events. How one perceives the circumstances, makes sense of the event, and finds meaning in the situation may be very individualized and may not be amenable to group analysis.

The data suggest that the sense of coherence can change in response to internal and external events. This change, however, may only be temporary. Measuring SOC scores in this population over the 12- to 18-month time frame in which disease state was measured would have provided greater insight into the role of the SOC in coping with and recovering from cancer. Other implications for future research include increasing sample size and differentiating whether the effects of the intervention are a result of the imagery and relaxation or the support group. Although there is no consistent feasible way identified to standardize immune data, it is important to find a way to reduce the variability observed within and between subjects to ensure that the results of the relationships are real and not secondary to measurement error. Because of the complexity of the study and multiple interactions measured with a small sample, results of this study should be interpreted as a guideline for future study in which the role of the SOC as a mediating variable is replicated and validated. If the sense of coherence is responsive to imagery, disease state, treatment schedule, and symptoms, implications for clinical interventions cut across multiple disciplines. Future research may indeed unravel the mysteries of the role of the sense of coherence in determining and responding to the health state of the individual.

Notes

1. This research was supported by the National Cancer Institute, NIH, NRSA F31 #CA 08430, and the American Cancer Society Doctoral Scholarship in Nursing.

2. NK and LAK cell function are represented as lytic units of activity per 10^6 effector cells, calculated as a linear regression plot from four effector to target ratios ranging from 20:1 to 0.74:1 (Pross, Baines, Rubin, Shragge, & Patterson, 1981). Standardization procedures for additional regression analyses are reported in Post-White (1991). Immune data are reported here in unstandardized form to facilitate comparison with immune results in the literature.

References

Achterberg, J., & Lawlis, F. (1984). *Imagery and disease*. Champaign, IL: Institute for Personality and Ability Testing.

Antonovsky, A. (1979). *Health, stress, and coping*. San Francisco: Jossey-Bass.

Antonovsky, A. (1984). The sense of coherence as a determinant of health. In J. Matarazzo, M. Weiss, J. Herd, & N. Miller (Eds.), *Behavioral health* (pp. 114–129). New York: Wiley.

Antonovsky, A. (1987). *Unraveling the mystery of health: How people manage stress and stay well*. San Francisco: Jossey-Bass.

Benson, H. (1975). *The relaxation response.* New York: William Morrow.
Blalock, J. E., Harbour-McMenamin, P., & Smith, E. M. (1985). Peptide hormones shared by the neuroendocrine and immunologic systems. *Journal of Immunology, 135*(2), 858–861.
Camara, E. G., & Danao, T. C. (1989). The brain and the immune system: A psychosomatic network. *Psychosomatics, 30*(2), 140–146.
Fisher, L. A. (1991). Corticotropin-releasing factor and autonomic-cardiovascular responses to stress. In J. A. McCubbin, P. G. Kaufmann, & C. B. Nemeroff (Eds.), *Stress, neuropeptides, and systemic disease* (pp. 95–118). San Diego: Academic Press.
Judge, G. G., Griffiths, W. E., Hill, R. C., Lutkepohl, H., & Lee, T. C. (1990). *The theory and practice of econometrics* (2nd ed.). New York: Wiley.
Keller, S. E., Schleifer, S. J., & Demetrikopoulos, M. K. (1991). Stress-induced changes in immune function in animals: Hypothalamo-pituitary-adrenal influences. In R. Ader, D. L. Felten, & N. Cohen (Eds.), *Psychoneuroimmunology* (2nd ed., pp. 771–788). San Diego: Academic Press.
Kiecolt-Glaser, J. K., & Glaser, R. (1991). Psychosocial factors, stress, disease, and immunity. In R. Ader, D. L. Felten, & N. Cohen (Eds.), *Psychoneuroimmunology* (2nd ed., pp. 847–868). San Diego: Academic Press.
Levy, S., Herberman, R., Lippman, M., & d'Angelo, T. (1987). Correlation of stress factors with sustained depression of natural killer cell activity and predicted prognosis in patients with breast cancer. *Journal of Clinical Oncology, 5*(3), 348–353.
Locke, S. E., & Kraus, L. (1981). Modulation of natural killer activity by life stress and coping ability. In S. Levy (Ed.), *Biological mediators of behavior and disease: Neoplasia* (pp. 3–28). New York: Elsevier Biomedical.
Locke, S. E., Kraus, L., Leserman, J., Hurst, M. W., Heisel, J. W., & Williams, R. M. (1984). Life change stress, psychiatric symptoms, and natural killer cell activity. *Psychosomatic Medicine, 46*(5), 441–453.
Lynch W. F. (1965). *Images of hope.* Notre Dame: Notre Dame Press.
Mowrer, O. H. (1969). *On learning theory and behavior.* New York: Wiley.
Nowotny, M. L. (1989). Assessment of hope in patients with cancer: Development of an instrument. *Oncology Nursing Forum, 16*(1), 57–61.
Olness, K., & Gardner, G. G. (1988). Psychoneuroimmunology. In *Hypnosis and hypnotherapy with children* (2nd ed., pp. 290–296). Philadelphia: Grune & Stratton.
Padilla, G. V., Presant, C., Grant, M. M., Metter, G., Lipsett, J., & Heide, F. (1983). Quality of life index for patients with cancer. *Research in Nursing and Health, 6,* 117–126.
Plotnikoff, N. P., Miller, G. C., Nimeh, N., Faith, R. E., Murgo, A. J., & Wybran, J. (1987). Enkephalins and T-cell enhancement in normal volunteers and cancer patients. In B. Jankovic, B. Markovic, & N. Spector (Eds.), *Neuroimmune interactions: Proceedings of the second international workshop on neuroimmunomodulation* (Vol. 496, pp. 608–619). New York: New York Academy of Science.
Post-White, J. (1991). The effects of mental imagery on emotions, immune function and cancer outcome. *Dissertation Abstracts International* (University Microfilms No. 9205462).

Post-White, J., & Johnson, M. (1991). Complementary nursing therapies in clinical oncology practice: Relaxation and imagery. *Dimensions in Oncology Nursing, 5*(2), 15–20.

Pross, H. F., Baines, M. G., Rubin, P., Shragge, P., & Patterson, M. S. (1981). Spontaneous human lymphocyte-mediated cytotoxicity against tumor target cells: The quantitation of natural killer cell activity. *Journal of Clinical Immunology, 1*(1), 51–63.

Shavit, Y. (1991). Stress-induced immune modulation in animals: Opiates and endogenous opioid peptides. In R. Ader, D. L. Felten, & N. Cohen (Eds.), *Psychoneuroimmunology* (2nd ed., pp. 789–806). San Diego: Academic Press.

Sims, S. E. R. (1987). Relaxation training as a technique for helping patients cope with the experience of cancer: A selective review of the literature. *Journal of Advanced Nursing, 12,* 583–591.

Spielberger, C. D. (Ed.). (1966). *Anxiety and behavior.* New York: Academic Press.

Stotland, E. (1969). *The psychology of hope.* San Francisco: Jossey-Bass.

Tishelman, C., Taube, A., & Sachs, L. (1991). Self-reported symptom distress in cancer patients: Reflections of disease, illness, or sickness? *Social Science and Medicine, 33*(11), 1229–1240.

Weber, R. J., & Pert, A. (1989). The periaqueductal gray matter mediates opiate-induced immunosuppression. *Science, 245,* 188–190.

Chapter 16

Sense of Coherence, Health, and Immunoglobulin M Among Older Anglo-American and Japanese-American Women

An Exploratory Study[1]

Louis C. Milanesi, Benjamin N. Colby,
Thomas C. Cesario, Shiraz I. Mishra,
Sayuri Kennedy, and Shookooh Yousefi

Antonovsky's sense of coherence (SOC) measure has clearly been a useful tool in behavioral medicine as it is developing in the U.S., Europe, and Israel (Antonovsky, 1987). Coherence and meaningfulness, as constructs relating to adaptivity, should also apply to non-Western societies, for the underlying idea should be universally indicative of well-being. There are two issues that relate to the universality question; the first is theoretical and the second, methodological.

Within Antonovsky's salutogenic orientation, coherence is seen to be positively functional simply for health rather than being a more inclusive, globally desirable, condition. If the general concept of coherence is examined from a cultural and linguistic perspective, however, an argument can be made for the universality of coherence as a globally desirable condition (Colby, 1987a). In examining the question of theoretical universality, investigators may benefit from the work of Clyde Kluckhohn, who developed a value-oriented approach to the study of different cultural groups 35 years ago in a study of societies of the American

Southwest. Kluckhohn's (1958) approach contained elements that were similar to some of the items in the SOC questionnaire. He developed a set of binary value categories, including Good versus Evil for world view, Self versus Other and Individual versus Group for interpersonal relations, and ten additional binary oppositions for other areas of cultural study. Among these pairs of opposites were two world-view pairs that covered conceptual areas also touched upon by items in the SOC measure. These two pairs Kluckhohn labeled Determinate versus Indeterminate and Unitary versus Pluralistic.

Determinate-Indeterminate. This contrast hinges upon the priority given to orderliness (lawfulness) in the universe as opposed to chance or caprice or any factor or factors that make prediction or control impossible in principle. A "mechanistic" emphasis does not necessarily make human effort, including ritual effort, irrelevant. On the contrary, as the cases of Navaho, Zuni, and many other non-literate cultures show, this conception may heighten the amount and detail of ritual behavior, both negative and positive. The Epicurean and Buddhist instances show in other ways how this contrast is not that between theism and atheism. Nor is this exclusively the polarity between "fatalism" or "predetermination" versus "free will" or "accident." Rather, the essential contrast is between a state of affairs conceived as operating in consistent and lawful fashion and one where an indeterminism (of whatever sort) reigns. The former case may eventuate in the outlook of Western science as stated by Karl Pearson or in the attempt to control events by supernatural techniques or in "fatalistic" acceptance. The latter, however, may also have a "fatalistic" toning in a different sense: resignation to "taking things as they come" without rhyme or reason. The indeterminate emphasis may also take the form of extreme voluntarism (either human or divine), since nothing is held to be completely determined or determinable. The outcome in the case of both alternatives will depend upon how this emphasis is juxtaposed with other cultural emphases. Nevertheless, I believe this particular binary opposition to be of absolutely crucial significance.

Unitary-Pluralistic. Is the world, including human life, thought of as a single manifold or as segmented into two or more spheres in which different principles prevail? At first glance this contrast might appear to be a special case of the first. Certainly it would seem logically probable that the unitary emphasis would be likely to be found where the mechanistic emphasis dominates. But there are innumerable instances of "mechanistic" cultures exhibiting the familiar dualisms of "sacred and profane," "mind and body," not merely as categories in a larger whole but as altogether separate realms governed by distinct "laws" and with one construed as more permanent and superior to the other. Conversely, the classical Greeks who believed in ineluctable laws had a profoundly unitary conception of life (Kluckhohn, 1958).

Unlike Antonovsky, Kluckhohn did not attach any evaluational or adaptational significance to either side of these binary value orientations. In contrast, the view that orderliness is functional for health adaptation is built into the SOC scale, resulting in a positive health evaluation of what would be a Unitary and Determinate outlook in the Kluckhohn system, and a negative health evaluation of a Pluralistic and Indeterminate world view. Antonovsky's theory, however, would not amount to a positive evaluation in all cases of well-ordered orientations; as he notes, a Nazi can have a strong SOC (1987).

In this respect, a majority of anthropologists are relativists and one might expect many of them to side with a non-evaluational approach rather than with Antonovsky's salutogenic theory. They would consider any society with a predominantly Indeterminate, Pluralistic (and thus less coherent) world view to be just as positively functional as one with a Determinate, Unitary view. The Navaho studied by Kluckhohn were identified as Determinate and Pluralistic, and, in the relativistic view, theoretically none the worse for their Pluralistic orientation, at least with respect to general functionality.

Rating societies by value orientations is fraught with problems. Different emphases can exist in different areas of the cultural system. Thus Japan's Shinto belief in multiple animal spirits would be classified as pluralistic in the Unitary-Pluralistic pair, but its national ideology and social behavior would be placed on the unitary side of the binary.

This leads to the second issue—methodology and measurement. Kluckhohn did not develop quantitative indices for the value categories, nor did he make studies of variation in the values among individuals within the same society. Finally, he did not consider health indices as possible correlates of value emphases, so there was no outcome or dependent variable that could have been tested, and in the successful testing, lend some validation to what we regard as coherence value categories.

If coherence is universally beneficial for health, one should get the same health-correlated results among Japanese and other non-Western individuals as in the West. While individual scores might be influenced by culturally specific characteristics (discerned in such institutional phenomena as religious beliefs and practices) one would expect individual variation in an SOC measure to correlate with health no matter what the institutionally shaped parameters, or the modal characteristics relating to them, might be in that society.

So far there is one known case of a sense of coherence study done outside Western culture, and the results were inconclusive (as reported by Antonovsky, see Chapter 1). In this study, the SOC questionnaire was translated and used in Africa among a group of Tswana speakers. It is not known whether the problem was a matter of translation or a matter of basic cultural difference. In the case of translation, it may well be that the concepts expressed in the sense of coherence questionnaire are not as readily available in many non-Western societies and would thus require paragraph-long statements along with a liberal use of local metaphors. To determine whether differences are superficially semantic or more realistic in some deeper, embodied semantics would require controlled interviewing approaches such as those used in cognitive anthropology (see Metzger & Williams, 1963).

There is an intermediate step, however, that might be taken first in an exploration of coherence measures across different non-Western peoples. Administering the questionnaire to nationals of non-Western societies who are bicultural with a Western society would ensure that the sample understood the questions and would provide some insight as to the universality of the SOC measure. This is the approach taken in the current study of Japanese-American and Anglo-American women.

Sample

The subjects of this study were Japanese-American and Anglo-American women over 60 years of age living in Southern California, predominantly in Orange County. The Japanese Americans were drawn from a phone directory of Japanese surnames for Orange and Los Angeles counties. The Anglo (non-Hispanic whites) sample was drawn from a list of 4,000 women meeting our age and ethnic eligibility criteria obtained from a private direct mail address company. The list was matched by zip code to communities included in the Japanese sample. The Anglo women were randomly recruited from each area proportional to the distribution in the Japanese sample. Over 7,000 households were contacted in selecting the two samples.

Of the 1,314 respondents who qualified for the study (female, over 60, Japanese or Anglo), 770 or 58.6% agreed to receive a 16-page mail-screen questionnaire. In addition to basic demographic questions, this questionnaire invited participation in either a focused study involving the collection of blood and urine samples and a series of interviews, or a mailed survey. Of the 770 question-naires mailed out, 559 (72.6%) were returned. Of these, 124 (22.2%) of the women agreed to participate in the focused study. Women who were taking medications or had diseases that would interfere with analyses of immune function were excluded. For the focused study, a sample of 60 women (30 from each ethnic group) was selected from the remaining volunteers. Attrition due to illness and family emergency resulted in two replacements and one loss not replaced for a total of 59 subjects who served through the focused (and short-term prospective) part of the research. Subjects were assigned to one of two waves, which alternated each week. Interviewers collected data from two subjects per wave. The mailed survey was sent to a total of 275 women and 169 (61.5%) were returned.

As for the differences between Anglo Americans and Japanese Americans, the Anglo-American women were significantly older (M = 70 years versus M = 67 years), had higher levels of education (M = 6.9 versus M = 6.3), were more likely to have incomes in the $25,000 to $34,000 range versus the $35,000 to $45,000 range for the Japanese, and were more likely to live alone. Among the 30 Japanese, 6 spoke Japanese better than English, 7 had lived in Japan for more than ten years, 15 used chopsticks more often than a knife and fork, 25 had attended Japanese language school, and the parents of all 30 were born in Japan. Many of these Japanese subjects had spent some of their early years in American war camps established shortly after the outbreak of WWII, when Japanese Americans living in California and other western states were forced to leave their homes, possessions, and employment and live in U.S. concentration camps for the duration of the war.

Measures

Urinary Cortisol

Perceptions of distress can be masked by the secretion of endor-phins and other substances (Jamner, Schwartz, & Leigh, 1988). Further, it is not clear to what degree a subject may be reporting actual physiological stress and to what degree the subject relies on the reporting of events and situations as stressors simply because they are conventionally labeled as such in our society. For these reasons, urinary cortisol was chosen as a stress measure closer to actual physiological processes than verbal reports. There are other problems, however, with urinary cortisol as a measure of stress, including diurnal variation, concentration, and experiential influence on receptor structure.

Given the diurnal pulsatile release of ACTH, cortisol reaches maximal levels by the eighth hour of sleep and then decreases through the waking hours. Six to seven samples, each two weeks apart, were collected from each subject at approximately the same time in the late afternoon or early evening. The protocol required all urine samples to be collected within a one-hour interval based on the time the initial sample was collected (+ or − 30 minutes). The subject was reminded to void one hour before the research assistants arrived.

Cortisol was measured using radioimmunoassay techniques. Samples were refrigerated in ice chests if the route traveled to the University of California, Irvine (UCI) was not brief and direct. Once received at UCI, samples were fixed with boric acid. Volumes of the samples were recorded and two 1.5 ml assay samples (one assay and one back-up sample) were pipetted (after mixing) into sterile tubes and frozen at −20° C. When all samples for a given wave of subject interviews were collected, they were transported frozen to the UCI Medical Center (UCIMC) for long-term ultra-cold (−70° C) storage. All assays were performed on the same day to preclude variance due to decay of the (^{125}I) radioisotope tracer. Samples were incubated and decanted following the instructions provided with the GammaCoat™ kits. Samples were immediately counted in an automatic gamma counter with its window adjusted for the (^{125}I) reagent. The determinations were standardized in terms of total creatinine in order to account for differences in urine concentration.

Immunological Measures

Blood Samples. Samples from each subject were collected by a phlebotomist who visited the subjects in their homes early in the study (Time 1) and toward the end of the study (Time 2). The mean interval between the two draws was 40 days. Blood was collected in heparinized tubes. One control was drawn from healthy college student volunteers on each day that samples were collected. Specimens were returned to the laboratory where peripheral blood mononuclear cells (PBMC) were separated by Ficoll Hypaque and stimulated by mitogens, and proliferative response assays were performed as described below. Plasma separated from the cells was stored at −80° C for subsequent quantification of immunoglobulin levels. Plasma from control subjects was drawn along with study subjects and served as normal controls for immunoglobulin levels.

Immunoglobulins. Plasma as obtained above was added to precut wells in commercially prepared plates overlayed with agar and impregnated with specific antihuman immunoglobulins of IgM, IgG and IgA specificities. After approximately 72 hours of incubation at room temperature (to reach the end points), the diameter of the precipitated ring was measured and used to determine immunoglobulin concentrations by extrapolation from graphs prepared using known standards and plotting immunoglobulin concentration against zone diameter. Of all the immunological measures, autocorrelations for the Time 1 and 2 immunoglobulin measures were the highest: IgG r = .77; IgA r = .87; IgM r = .92.[2]

Other immunological measures (natural killer cell activity, total lymphocyte proliferative response, and interferons alpha and gamma) were taken, but correlations were not supported at both times of measurement and thus are not reported here.

Self-Reported Measures

Reactivity Scales and Three Factors. Reactivity was measured by means of a factor that emerged from the Affect Intensity Measure (Larsen, 1984), which, in our study, was shortened to 20 items (Milanesi, 1991). A factor analysis (Milanesi, Colby, Mishra, & Ochoa, 1990) revealed three factors; the first and third were simply the valences of the scale item, the first, positive and the third, negative. However, a second factor was non-valenced (that is, not indexed by positive or negative affect) and was related to strong somatic or bodily responses.

Health Measures. Two variables, HEALTH and HPLNUM, were taken. The first was a single item: "Compared to other people your age, would you say your health is...

1. Much worse than others,
2. Worse than others
3. About the same as others
4. Better than others
5. Much better than others."

The second measure, HPLNUM, was the sum total of an illness inventory of 38 medical problems and signs (such as high blood pressure, cancer, alcoholism, headaches, trouble climbing stairs), which the respondents were asked to check off if any of the conditions had occurred in the past six months (Belloc & Breslow, 1972). Two measures (Time 1 and Time 2) were taken of the illness inventory.

Sense of Coherence. The 29-item scale (Antonovsky, 1987) was administered at two different times with a mean interval similar to that for the 40-day blood sample. Since interviewing extended into the summer with a reduced number of student volunteer interviewers, there were fewer Time 2 SOC measures taken.

Results

General Findings

The mean sense of coherence scores for the two groups were not significantly different from each other by t test. The mean Time 1 score for the Anglo group was 152 (SD = 21.07, n = 24) and for the Japanese group, 146 (SD = 20.78, n = 25). For Time 2 the means were 151 (SD = 24.33, n = 26) and 149 (SD = 26.33, n = 19), respectively, an apparent regression toward the mean. The autocorrelation between the Time 1 SOC and Time 2 SOC measures for the entire sample was .87 (n = 39).

Self-Reported Health

Theoretically (Antonovsky, 1987) and empirically (at least over the short time span of this study, with the high autocorrelation between the two SOC measures) the sense of coherence measure is fairly stable within the same individual. This short-term stability finding was therefore used as a reliability check on the correlations—thus imposing more stringent criteria in the exploratory study of individual SOC items.

The correlations of the SOC and some of its constituent items with self-reported health are shown in Table 1. In the Japanese sample, there was a clear, positive association with health and a negative one with number of health complaints in all six correlations (SOCTOTJ-1 and SOCTOTJ-2 with HEALTH, HPLNUM1, and HPLNUM2). Some of the negative associations were quite strong, ranging from a high −.47 to −.67. For the Anglo sample, only one correlation was significant, though the others were close to significance with correlations in the low −.30s. In the combined sample all six correlations were significant. Significant correlations for individual SOC items are also shown in Table 1.

Table 1
Pearson Correlations of Sense of Coherence (SOC) and SOC Items
with General Health and Two Measures of Health Complaints

Variable	HEALTH	HPLNUM1	HPLNUM2
SOCTOT-1	.48***	− .39**	− .43**
SOCTOT-2	.39**	− .44***	− .39**
SOCTOTA-1	.46**	− .33 n. s.	− .35 n. s.
SOCTOTA-2	.32 n. s.	− .30 n.s.	− .31 n. s.
SOCTOTJ-1	.47**	− .47**	− .57**
SOCTOTJ-2	.48*	− .67***	− .55**
14A-1 (R)	− .41*	.40*	.53**
14A-2 (R)	− .37*	.29 n. s.	.32 n. s.
14J-1 (R)	− .60***	.38*	.53**
14J-2 (R)	− .39*	.64***	.61**
16A-1 (R)	− .45**	.39*	.13 n. s.
16A-2 (R)	− .57***	.56**	.29 n. s.
16J-1 (R)	− .47**	.51**	.43*
16J-2 (R)	− .45*	.67***	.58**
19J-1	.47**	− .52**	− .58**
19J-2	.47**	− .66***	− .58**
21A-1	.40*	− .34*	− .32 n. s.
21A-2	.28 n. s.	− .34*	− .38*
21J-1	.41*	− .47**	− .30 n. s.
21J-2	.57**	− .42*	− .33 n. s.
27A-1 (R)	− .46**	.32*	.41*
27A-2 (R)	− .38*	.33*	.44**
29A-1	.42**	− .19 n. s.	− .43**
29A-2	.32 n. s.	− .32 n. s.	− .39*
29J-1	.23 n. s.	− .13 n. s.	− .32 n. s.
29J-2	.37 n. s.	− .53**	− .52**

Note. SOCTOT = Total SOC score. 1 and 2 = Time. A = Anglo, J = Japanese. R = contrait
item. HPLNUM1 and HPLNUM2 = Health Complaints at Times 1 and 2.
*$p < .05$. **$p < .01$. ***$p < .001$.

Cortisol and Factor 2 of the Reactivity Measure

Contrary to the prediction, no overall negative correlation was found
between the sense of coherence and mean cortisol levels
(CORTMEAN in Table 2). However, there was a negative correlation between total SOC scores and Reactivity Factor 2 ($r = -.43$
and −.41).

In the exploratory analysis of the SOC items, a conservative
criterion required that three out of four possible correlations of

SOC items with both dependent variables be significant in at least one of the two ethnic samples. All these significant correlations were expected to be negative. As seen in Table 2, four SOC questionnaire items correlated significantly with both Factor 2 and cortisol in the Anglo sample but in opposite directions. In none of the Japanese subjects were there at least three out of four possible correlations for any items.

Table 2
Pearson Correlations of SOC, Reactivity Factor 2,
and Mean Cortisol Level

Variable	Factor 2	CORTMEAN
SOCTOT1	− .43***	.08 n. s.
SOCTOT2	− .41**	.00 n. s.
15A-1	− .51**	.38*
15A-2	− .60***	.32 n. s.
18A-1	− .60***	.32 n. s.
18A-2	− .46**	.36**
26A-1	− .69***	.52**
26A-2	− .49**	.16 n. s.
29A-1	− .61***	.47**
29A-2	− .66***	.39*

Note. SOCTOT1 and SOCTOT2 are for the Japanese and Anglo samples combined. Individual items are for the Anglo sample only.
$*p < .05$. $**p < .01$. $***p < .001$.

Immunoglobulin M

The only immunological correlations that appeared to be significant by the defined standards of multiple correlations were for immunoglobulin M (it should be noted, however, that there is a strong autocorrelation between the two IgM measures). For the combined Japanese and Anglo sample the total SOC correlations for the Time 1 SOC measure was .33 ($n = 34, p = .03$) for Time 1 IgM and .46 ($n = 46, p = .001$) for Time 2 IgM. The Time 2 SOC was .25 ($n = 30, p = .10$) and .29 ($n = 43, p = .03$), respectively (Table 3). Separately examined, the Japanese and Anglo samples were slightly weaker but still significant. No patterns emerged from an inspection of the individual items. Items 14 and 24 were significant for all four Anglo measures. No items were significant in all four measures for the Japanese.

Table 3
Pearson Correlations for SOC Variables and Immunoglobulin M

Variable	IgM-1	IgM-2
SOCTOT-1	.33*	.46**
SOCTOT-2	.25 n. s.	.29*
SOCTOTA-1	.39 n. s.	.43*
SOCTOTA-2	.25 n. s.	.25 n. s.
SOCTOTJ-1	.27 n. s.	.56**
SOCTOTJ-2	.23 n. s.	.36 n. s.
14A-1 (R)	− .44*	− .45**
14A-2 (R)	− .47*	− .45**
24A-1	.45*	.35*
24A-2	.44*	.36*

Note. IgM-1 and IgM-2 = Immunoglobulin M measure at Times 1 and 2. SOCTOT-1 and SOCTOT-2 = Total SOC score at Times 1 and 2. A and J indicate Anglo and Japanese. 14A-1 and 14A-2 = Item 14, Times 1 and 2 in the Anglo sample. Similarly for 24A-1 and 24A-2. R = contrait direction.
*$p < .05$. **$p < .01$. ***$p < .001$.

Discussion

The sense of coherence results suggest its underlying constructs to be important for the Japanese Americans and marginally so for the Anglo Americans, at least in matters of general self-reported health. The sense of coherence also correlates with IgM. However, with respect to the IgM correlations, they were the only significant immunological measures found in both Time 1 and Time 2 measures out of all the immunological variables: interferons alpha and gamma, natural killer cell activity, total lymphocyte proliferative response, and immunoglobulins A and G in addition to M.[3]

In looking at the individual item correlations, chance clearly plays a large role, hence the more conservative criteria used in interpreting them. All in all, the immunoglobulin M relationship is suspected to be real, though so little is yet known about the psychosomatic processes that influence the production of immunoglobulin M. High readings on this variable can also be associated with stress (Endresen et al., 1992) and autoimmune reactions. In a sample from the general population (rather than, say, a medically selected sample), levels of immunoglobulins are probably optimal and suboptimal.

If the health-SOC findings are valid, they support the universal theory of coherence as a beneficial cultural value orientation rather than the relativistic theory, which emphasizes the unique effects, categorizations, and clusterings of cultural values. Obviously, different societies have different explicitly expressed values. In terms of overall health and well-being, the universal theory of cultural value orientations would differentiate these expressed values according to their adaptive potential. Those explicit value orientations that provide a sense of coherence ought to be universally functional.[4]

That no significant negative correlations appeared between the summated SOC scores and cortisol raises the possibility that *perceived* coping with *perceived* stress constitutes the major operating factor in the sense of coherence and that these perceived experiences do not cover all the actual stress and stress reduction processes operating at the physiological level (assuming the physiological measures are valid and assuming a causal linkage exists between chronically high levels of cortisol and stress). The production of endorphins, for example, can mask the effects of stress to an individual (Jamner et al., 1988).

Clearly, investigators are on the threshold of a vast and exciting new enterprise that will require extensive interdisciplinary research referencing a wide systemic model, where coherence, meaningfulness, and related variables play an important part. There is already some work toward a systemic approach (Artinian, 1991; Colby, 1987b; Steward & Ware, 1992) and further developments from an anthropological perspective should be useful.

Notes

1. We thank the National Institute on Aging for grant number AG06987 to Benjamin N. Colby, *Stress and Health in Elderly Japanese Americans.*

2. Through an error in the laboratory, the Time 1 immunoglobulin measures for 13 of our subjects, 6 Anglos and 7 Japanese, were lost.

3. It could be argued, however, that if one is testing a causal relationship (which the analysis here does not do) only one of the four correlations on each variable pair is relevant: Time 1 SOC (the independent variable) with Time 2 health conditions, including

immunological responses (the dependent variables). The four-week time span between the two measures, given existing lacunae in our knowledge, was an arbitrary decision. That is, we know that the time gap between these variables is crucial but we have no basis for knowing just how long that gap should be to show the greatest influence from the independent variables.

4. Our special concern has been the study of correlations between psychocultural measures and physiological measures. While we have had higher SOC correlations with measures of depression and adaptive potential (AP), we have not included those results in this chapter inasmuch as these correlations are something of a validity indicator for the SOC rather than an indication of causality. Also, the adaptive potential measures are still under exploratory development, and not all sectors were used in the study, so that any use of AP as validation may be premature at this point. Finally, we consider the manageability component of the SOC scale not to be a coherence component as outlined by Colby (1987a) but rather a variable in its own right that might be described better as a sense of control or self-efficacy in a general theory of adaptive potential (Colby, 1987b).

References

Antonovsky, A. (1987). *Unraveling the mystery of health*. San Francisco: Jossey-Bass.

Antonovsky, A. (See Chapter 1). *The sense of coherence: An historical and future perspective*.

Artinian, B. M. (1991). The development of the intersystem model. *Journal of Advanced Nursing, 16,* 194–205.

Belloc, N. B., & Breslow, L. (1972). Relationship of physical health status and health practices. *Preventive Medicine, 1,* 409–421.

Colby, B. N. (1987a). Coherence in language and culture. In R. Steele & T. Threadgold (Eds.), *Language topics: Essays in honour of Michael Halliday, Vol II* (pp. 451–460). Amsterdam/Philadelphia: John Benjamins.

Colby, B. N. (1987b). Well-being: A theoretical program. *American Anthropologist, 89*(4), 879–895.

Endresen, I. M., Relling, G. B., Tonder, O., Myking, O., Walther, B. T., & Ursin, H. (1992). Brief uncontrollable stress and psychological parameters influence human plasma concentrations of IgM and complement component C3. *Behavioral Medicine, 17*(4), 167–176.

Jamner, L. D., Schwartz, G. E., & Leigh, H. (1988). The relationship between repressive and defensive coping styles and monocyte, eosinophile, and serum glucose levels: Support for the opioid peptide hypothesis of repression. *Psychosomatic Medicine, 50,* 567–575.

Kluckhohn, C. K. M. (1958). Toward a comparison of value emphases in different cultures. In L. D. White (Ed.), *The state of the social sciences*. Chicago: University of Chicago Press.

Larsen, R. J. (1984). Theory and measurement of affect intensity as an individual difference characteristic. *Dissertation Abstracts International, 5,* 2297B.

Metzger, D., & Williams, G. E. (1963). A formal ethnographic analysis of Tenejapa ladino weddings. *American Anthropologist, 65,* 1076–1101.

Milanesi, L. (1991). *Differential vulnerability to negative social exchange.* Doctoral thesis, University of California, Irvine.

Milanesi, L. C., Colby, B. N., Mishra, S. I., & Ochoa, G. (1990). *Emotional reactivity, social exchange, and well-being among older women.* Conference presentation, 70th annual convention of the Western Psychological Association, South Dakota.

Steward, A. L., & Ware, J. E. (Eds.). (1992). *Measuring functioning and well-being: The medical outcomes study approach.* Durham, NC: Duke University Press.

Index

C

S

About the Editors

Hamilton I. McCubbin is Dean of the School of Human Ecology; Professor of Child and Family Studies and Social Work; and Director of the Center for Excellence in Family Studies, the Institute for the Study of Resiliency in Families, and the Family Stress, Coping and Health Project at the University of Wisconsin—Madison. He holds academic degrees from the University of Wisconsin–Madison (BS, MS, PhD). He undertook postdoctoral studies at Yale University, University of Minnesota, and Stanford University. He has authored, edited, and coedited 18 books and maintains scholarly research on families over the life cycle and families under stress, with particular emphasis on family postcrisis responses and resiliency.

Elizabeth A. Thompson is Research Associate and Postdoctoral Scholar at the Center for Excellence in Family Studies and the Institute for the Study of Resiliency in Families at the University of Wisconsin—Madison. She holds academic degrees from St. Olaf College (BA) and the University of Wisconsin—Madison (MA, PhD). She is the author or coeditor of six books and maintains scholarly research in the advancement of qualitative methods with families faced with stigmatized hardships and adversities.

Anne I. Thompson is Assistant Dean at the School of Human Ecology and Associate Director of the Center for Excellence in Family Studies, the Institute for the Study of Resiliency in Families, and the Family Stress, Coping and Health Project, University of Wisconsin—Madison. She holds academic degrees from the University of Wisconsin—Madison (BS, MS, PhD) and undertook postdoctoral studies at Bryn Mawr College. She is the author, editor, and coeditor of eight books and maintains scholarly research on families, the workplace, and health.

Julie E. Fromer is Editor at the Center for Excellence in Family Studies and the Institute for the Study of Resiliency in Families at the University of Wisconsin—Madison. She holds academic degrees (BA) from Dartmouth College, New Hampshire, and (MA, PhD dissertator) from the University of Wisconsin—Madison.